Portrait Photography

THE ART OF SEEING LIGHT

Don Blair
with Peter Skinner

AMHERST MEDIA, INC. ■ BUFFALO, NY

Dedication

In loving memory of my sweet wife Donna, and to the legacy of our three beautiful children, our ten "grandchickens," and nine great "grandchicks." You are the inspiration behind every photograph I make. —Don Blair

About the Cover Image

Careful balancing of ambient, early morning light with bare-bulb electronic flash was critical to the success of this image, made in Chicago at a national convention of the Professional Photographers of America (PPA). A group of Japanese photographers who watched Don Blair create the image described the setting with its subtle hues as a "true Japanese watercolor"—an apt description indeed. Exposure was determined by the ambient light in the f11–f16 range and the output of the bare bulb adjusted accordingly. To create a high-key effect, the model was dressed in white. The background light outlined the model's graceful pose. A touch-of-warmth reflector was used to feather light into the front plane of the image. The photograph was made on Kodak Portra 160 film; exposure was f11–f16 at 1/125 second. Don used a Hasselblad camera with an 80mm lens.

Published by:
Amherst Media, Inc.
P.O. Box 586
Buffalo, N.Y. 14226
Fax: 716-874-4508
www.AmherstMedia.com

Publisher: Craig Alesse
Senior Editor/Production Manager: Michelle Perkins
Assistant Editor: Barbara A. Lynch-Johnt

ISBN: 1-58428-131-6
Library of Congress Card Catalog Number: 2003112487

Printed in Korea.
10 9 8 7 6 5 4 3 2 1

Table of Contents

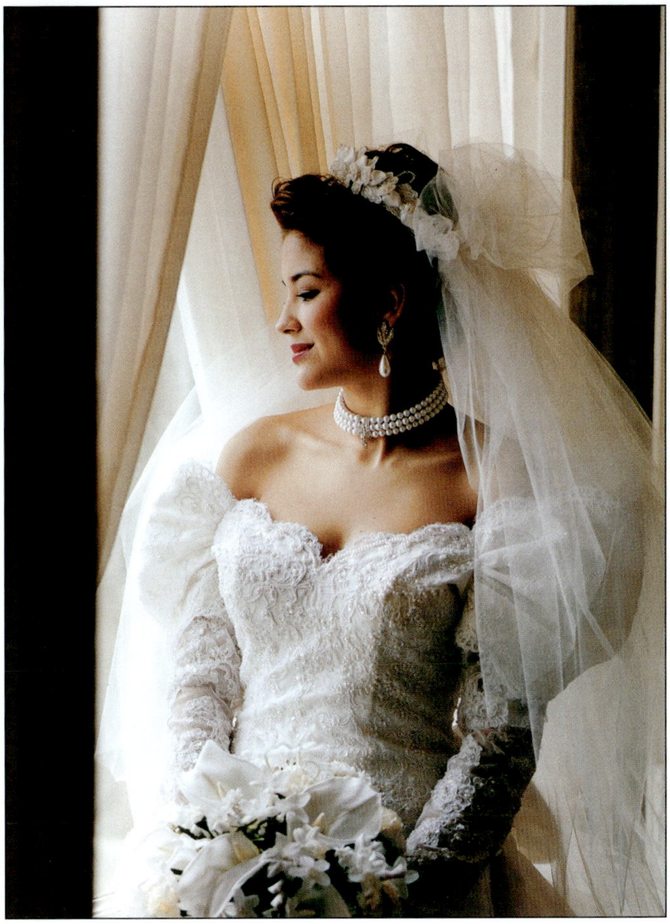

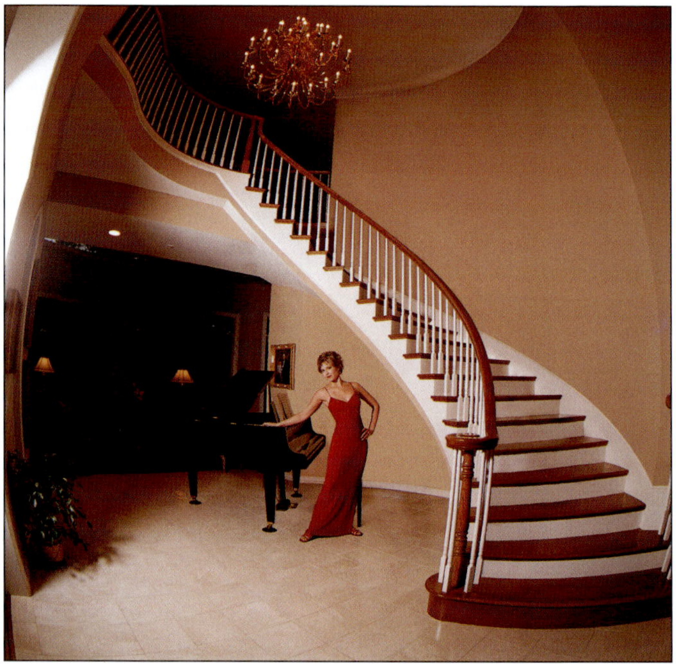

Introduction

by Peter Skinner

For about fifty years, the name Don Blair has been synonymous with fine portraiture, craftsmanship, and extraordinary contributions to the industry. This master of the genre has carved an indelible niche in the annals of his profession, in both the U.S. and abroad.

Here is a photographer who can truly look back on some of the most significant developments in the technology and techniques of photography, not simply as an observer but as a practitioner—one who has been hands-on throughout. Honing skills and harnessing advancements in technology have gone hand in hand in Don Blair's career.

Technology, however, is merely a tool—how it is applied rests in the hands of its user. In that regard, Don Blair is a master craftsman. Beyond that, he is a gifted and caring educator—hailed as one of the leaders in this field—who has been unstinting in sharing his knowledge with photographers throughout the United States and in numerous other countries.

Quite simply, Don Blair is the epitome of the veteran professional photographer. His technical skills and overall approach to his craft are steeped in the traditions of portrait photography, but by no means is he bound to or bogged down by that tradition. Just as he has been willing to share his knowledge, so is he enthusiastic about adding continually to his own vast bank of knowledge. From the day Don entered photography, he eagerly capitalized on advancements in emulsions and equipment. Today, even though a veteran, he remains a keen student of new techniques and ideas espoused by other luminaries. As digital technology emerged, he did not shy away from electronic imaging but appreciated and grasped its potential. Innovative marketing and promotional ideas were embraced to make his studio more efficient and profitable. The learning process, he points out, never ends. Where Don Blair is concerned, the cliché about "old dogs and new tricks" simply does not apply.

Where Don Blair is concerned, the cliché about "old dogs and new tricks" simply does not apply.

As with any accomplished professional, Don Blair has built his success on a solid foundation of the basics. And if professional photography is a combination of art, science, and business, then he is proficient in all three areas. His images testify to his mastery of the first two; his thriving business in Murray, Utah, is solid proof of the third.

Given that better film—and now digital imaging—cameras, optics, lighting aids, and a host of other advancements in photographic equipment have contributed to technical proficiency, there is one constant, undeniable and vital facet that every photographer must master to be able to truly create memorable images: the art of seeing light—the theme of this book. Seeing light is something that Don has preached and promoted in his lectures, seminars, written works, and videos for many years. Whether you are using film or electronic capture, lighting is the key.

1. The Essence of Seeing Light

The importance of correct lighting cannot be overemphasized, because it is the foundation for our photography. Whether the light source is natural or artificial, the competent photographer must know how to work with it.

Light is referred to and measured in many terms—its brightness and contrast, whether it is specular or diffuse, direct or indirect, ratios of light, etc. As photographers, it should become second nature to us to be able to recognize and use—or avoid, if it's not right—these various types of light. While "seeing light" sounds simple enough, I have found that one of the hardest things to teach is how to really see light: not just to look, but to *see* and evaluate the effect the light is having on the subject and how it will react with film.

Above all, train your eyes to look for the subtleties of light, whether in the studio or in a natural setting, and your photography will improve dramatically. And here's a tip: to get an idea of how the film will "see" the shadow detail, squint as you look at the subject. Immediately you will get a pretty good impression of how the camera (either film or digital), which is not as sensitive as the human eye and cannot record as wide a range of light and shadow, will capture the image. Make a habit of experimenting with this method when out and about—whether in the shopping mall or in a forest—and you'll see that it does work. Once you have mastered seeing light, you are on your way to being able to control or harness it, and thus create the images you want.

Technology has taken much of the guesswork out of photography, especially in areas such as measuring the quantity of light, but I maintain that our best tool is one that has been used by photographers for ages—our eyes. Train your eyes to see light, and you are well on your way to being a good photographer. It's that simple. Of course, you have to know how that light will interact with film or digital capture, because those materials cannot accommodate the range of light that the human eye can. That comes with experience and practice.

I maintain that our best tool is one that has been used by photographers for ages—our eyes.

PRACTICE AND A BASIC RULE

And how do you practice? There are many ways, I think, to train yourself to look for and evaluate light. The simplest is one of the most effective. Go for a walk through a park in either the early morning or late afternoon and study the effect of light on trees and leaves. Look for where the shadows fall, because that will determine the direction of light. Change the angle at which you look at the subject and watch the changing effect of the light.

One of the most important things in successful outdoor environmental portraiture is being aware of how changing the camera angle can improve the photograph. Even though the light remains the same, by simply changing the camera position, the photograph can go from being "nice but ordinary" to "dynamic and great." I will refer to changing the camera position throughout this book, so be aware of how much difference—and improvement—this simple technique can make in an image.

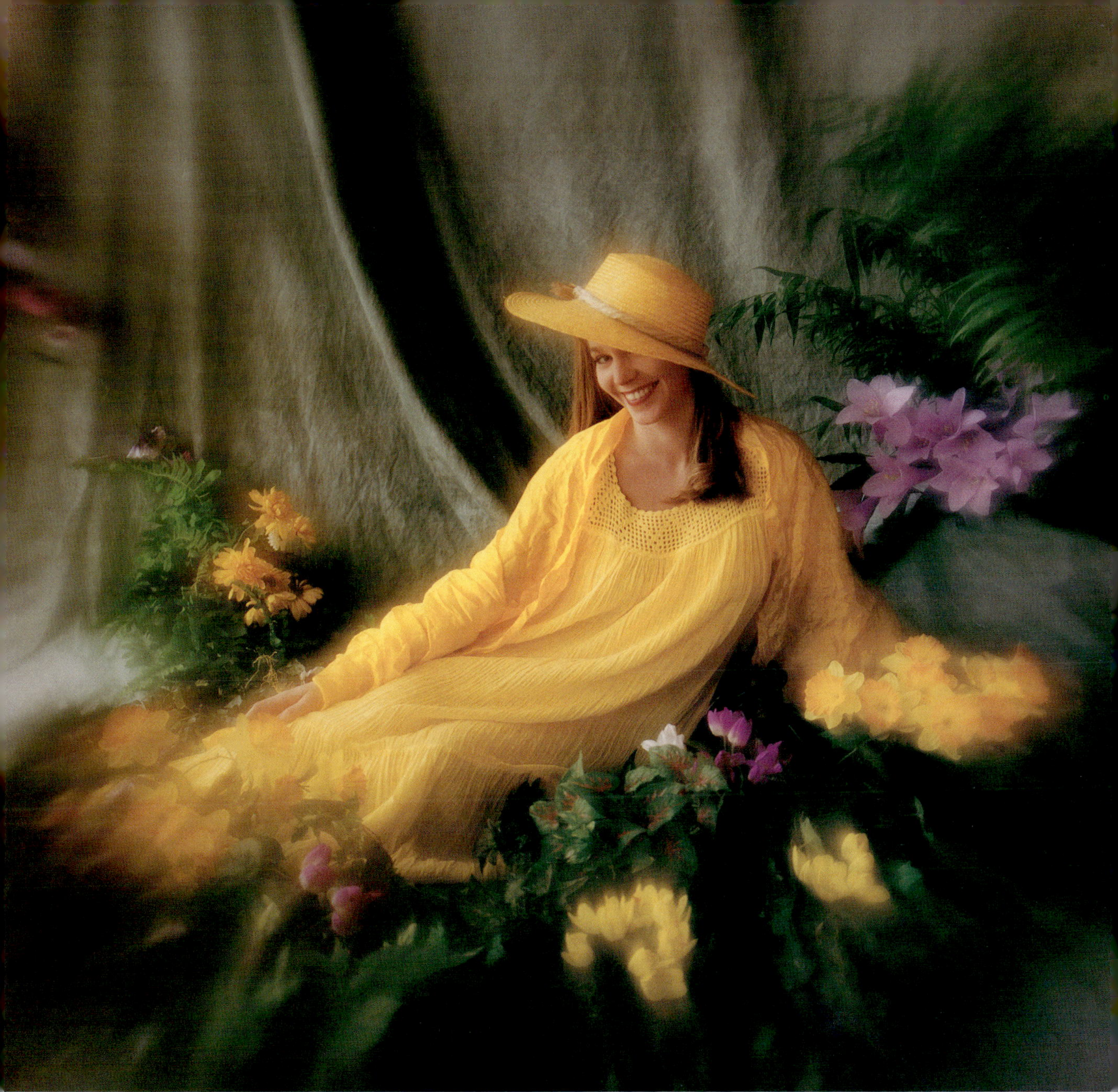

Don stood on a ladder to create this image. The principal illumination was window light, and the background was positioned at an angle to reflect skimmed light onto the subject. The subject was far enough away from the background so the window light skimming off it also worked as a secondary or accent light. A touch-of-warmth reflector, placed to the side of the camera, helped wrap ligh

Whenever I am teaching a group of photographers, I emphasize this important rule: The angle of incidence equals the angle of reflection. This simply means that light bounces off a subject at the same angle at which it hits it. If you understand and apply this rule when you light a subject, either with natural or artificial light, your portrait photography will improve by leaps and bounds. Keep this rule in mind at all times when you are setting up a portrait session, regardless of whether it's in your studio or on location. Repeat it to yourself, especially when you are planning a shoot: The angle of incidence equals the angle of reflection.

WHAT TO AVOID

One of the lighting mistakes that I see most often when photographers are using artificial light sources is overlighting, where photographers literally blast their subjects with light.

Another common error is placing lights so they create more than one shadow on the subject's face—this results in an unnatural portrait, a real no-no. As we know, in nature there is only one main source of light—the sun—and as a result, there should only be one direction in which shadows fall. To have any more than one shadow direction immediately makes the photograph look unnatural. In my opinion, a successful photograph is one where the average viewer is not even aware of the lighting that was used to create it. I say "average" because photographers, whose vision is trained, will be able to (or should be able to) determine the lighting by scrutinizing the photograph.

While there are quite a few light sources that should be avoided; two really stand out, and I urge you to avoid them if excellent portraiture is your goal (and it should be). The first is harsh, overhead light, typically found at midday in bright sunlight, which creates deep, ugly shadows. That is a fairly obvious form of light to avoid.

The other, and perhaps not so obvious, is the light that is directly behind the camera and straight onto the subject. This is a flat, even light and, while it is not ugly like overhead sunlight, it produces a flat, uninteresting result. Even if it is diffused daylight that does not make your subject squint or create deep, distracting shadows, the straight-on light is boring and uninteresting. The solution is simple, and you will see images that illustrate this remedy in this book—move the camera angle until it is about 15 or 20 degrees to the side of the subject and see what happens. Right before your eyes there will be a new interplay of light and shadow, a ratio of light. Same light, different photograph. To put those statements to the test, place someone in the lighting situations that are described and see the effects for yourself.

SWEET LIGHT

So much has been said and written about light and its properties that often we lose sight of how powerful and effective daylight, light in its simplest form, can be. Daylight is one of the most beautiful and reliable sources of light available for creating memorable images. Please note that I said *daylight*—not *sunlight*. (True, daylight comes from sunlight, but whenever I refer to daylight in this book, please be aware that I am not referring to the direct light from the sun which, as you know, can be harsh and unflattering.) Daylight is the softer, more pleasing light that we find along the edges of forests, under trees, filtered through windows, and under balconies or other structures that create open shade. Even though diffused, it is still directional and wraps around the subject, creating the form and shape—the modeling effect—that we want.

The best time to photograph people outdoors is early morning or late afternoon, when the light is softer and does not have the harshness of midday light. These are the times when you get what is commonly known as "sweet light," and the best portraits are invariably made during those periods. It's no

Often we lose sight of how powerful and effective daylight, light in its simplest form, can be.

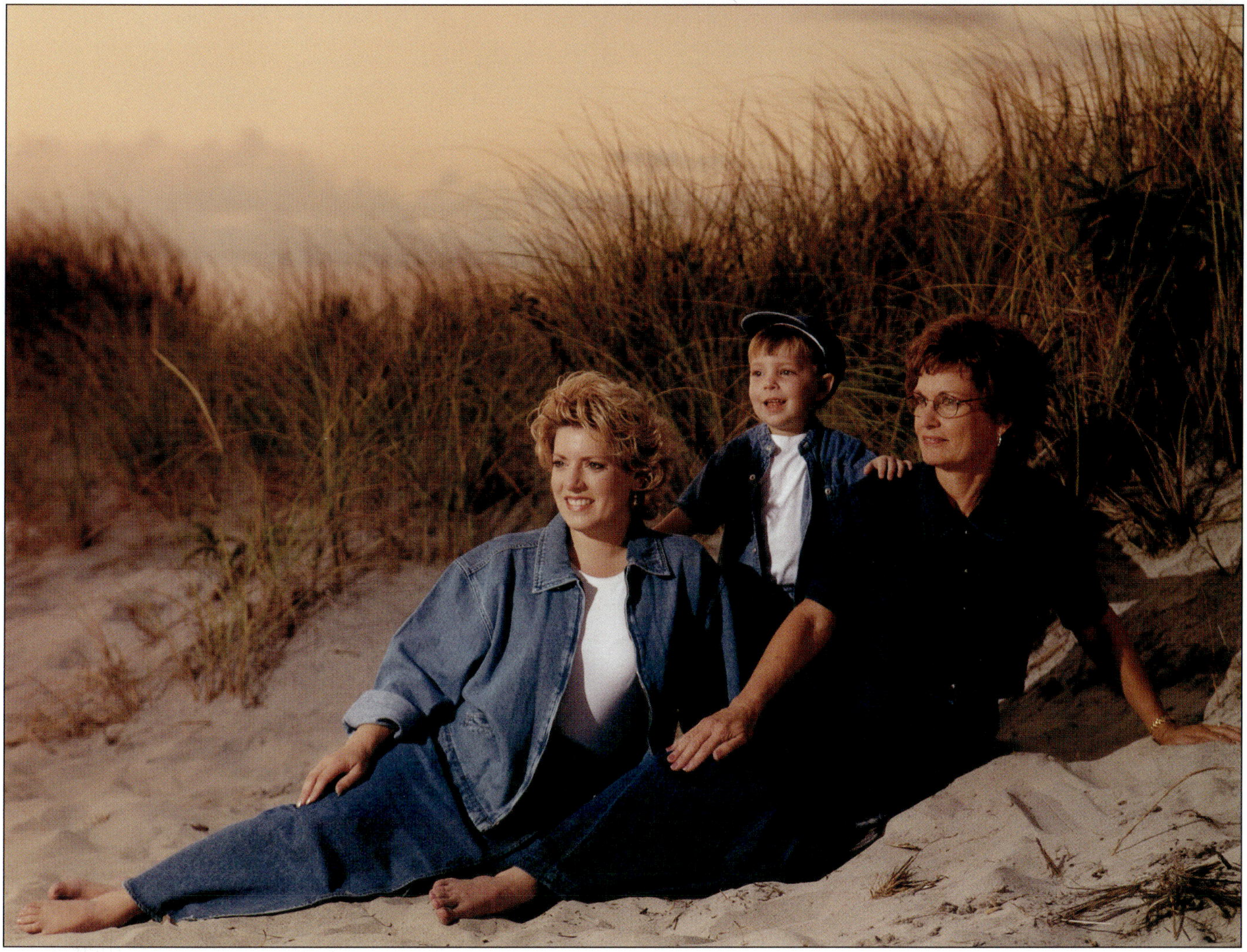

Late afternoon light and the magic of bare-bulb illumination were used for this environmental portrait of a grandmother, daughter, and grandson on the beach at Long Island, New York. The warm, sunset effect at the top of the image was enhanced with a rose-colored Lindahl filter, while a touch-of-warmth reflector picked up the edge of light from the bare bulb and wrapped light around the subjects. The portrait was made with a Hasselblad camera using an 80mm lens and Kodak Portra film. The exposure was f5.6 at 1/60 second.

coincidence that the truly great environmental portrait photographers consistently create memorable photographs—it's because they make their photographs in the best lighting conditions.

Lighting sets the whole mood of an image. Photographers in other fields, such as editorial and photojournalism, might light their subjects for effect to illustrate magazine or newspaper stories. In portrait photography, I feel our responsibility is to make the subject look as good as possible while capturing and portraying the character and personality of that person.

Of course, there might be occasions when, for various reasons, you are unable to photograph people at these optimum times, and there are ways to modify or enhance the existing natural light to achieve the results you want. In some cases we might have to add light using reflectors to bounce in natural light, or employ artificial light, or subtract light by blocking the light overhead.

In my opinion, the best place for an environmental portrait is on the edge of a tree line, in that area where the daylight yields the ratio of light (the difference in exposure between the highlight and shadow side of the face) that is needed to show shape and form. Our eyes can see a much wider range of contrast than film, so photographers must be aware of the ratio of light that film or digital capture can record while maintaining a well-exposed highlight side and detail in the shadows. On the edge of a tree line we will often find just such an ideal situation.

OBSERVATIONS ON LIGHTING

Throughout this book, I will be doing all I can to help you learn about how to control light and make it work for you. A lot has been written about lighting, and I would advise any photographer to read as much as they can on the subject, attend workshops, and practice, practice, practice. One of the best photo schools, the Brooks Institute of Photography in Santa Barbara, was founded in 1945 by Ernest H. Brooks on the basic idea of "learning by doing" which is not only good advice, it's the underlying principle of that school today. No matter how much you read and study theory—and these are very important aspects of our craft—to create consistently good portraits, you must have complete control of the tools of the trade.

Many photographers feel they need complex setups to make good portraits. That's not the case. Our job as portrait photographers is to create good portraits—not to draw attention to the lights used. If the lighting makes more impact than the essence of the subject, then I feel we have failed. I believe a good rule of thumb is to use the minimum number of lights to make a pleasing portrait. Often, something as simple as light coming through a window and a simple reflector is all that you need. Keep it simple and it will be easier to control.

Make no mistake about it; lighting control is the key to successful portrait photography. Whether you are outdoors and harnessing natural ambient light (and invariably using some supplementary light to give Mother Nature a helping hand), or in the studio, you have to control the light to make the photographs. In the studio, the photographer has complete control of light quantity, quality, and placement. However, once you have learned how to set lights in a studio, you can apply the same techniques on location. So, if you want to test yourself (and as photographers we should always be testing ourselves, our equipment, our materials, etc.), the studio is the ideal place to do so.

Make no mistake about it; lighting control is the key to successful portrait photography.

UNIVERSAL PRINCIPLES

Good Lighting Is for All Media. The principles of good lighting can be applied to any image capturing-medium, whether it is negative or transparency film or digital. Once you have learned to use light effectively, you can apply it to any capture material or format of camera. We are fortunate today that technology has given us so much to work with. My advice is not to become a slave to one type of source but to understand and use the capabilities of each depending on the subject and effect desired. Of course, having so much choice of equipment can also be confusing, but eventually most successful photographers learn to use what works for them and develop their own techniques based on the foundations of the craft. You will too, if you apply yourself diligently and practice until the basics become second nature.

Previewing Your Lighting Results. Modeling lights are a huge advantage in portraiture. While experienced photographers often have a feel for how the final image will look and may not have to rely on modeling lights, few would argue that having these lights is

FACING PAGE—This is a classic, traditional portrait lit with a parabolic reflector with barndoors, and a 45-degree (or Rembrandt) lighting pattern. Other lights incorporated were a fill light at the lens axis, an accent light, and a subdued background light. Note the slight tilt of the model toward the camera.

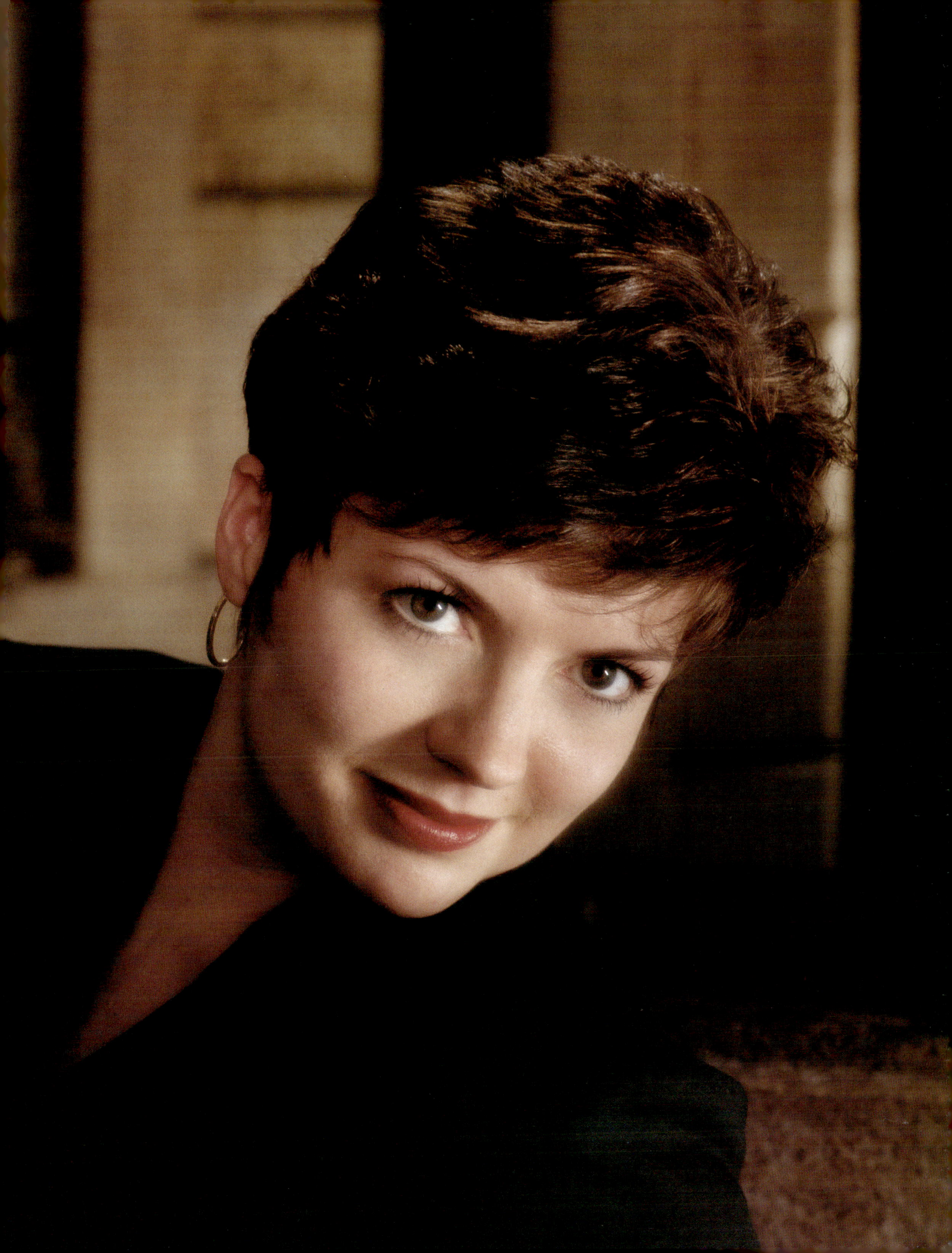

usually essential. In the past, Polaroid film was a great way to see the initial effect of lighting patterns before the final image was made, but today digital technology has made it even simpler. With digital equipment, you can see the result immediately. These are tools that photographers can, and should, use.

The Look of a Single Light. The goal of good lighting is to give dimension to the portrait, to achieve roundness and form and bring out features (or downplay them) on the subject's face, and skilful lighting can do this. It is important to remember that while several lights may be used, the final image should appear as if lit with a single light. Therefore, one light source must be predominant, just as the sun is in an outdoor setting. This main light determines where shadows fall and what highlights are emphasized. The other lights supplement that main light and modify it, filling in shadows to add detail, or providing separation from the background. These modifiers play a secondary or supplementary role but are no less important to the final result.

While several lights may be used, the final image should appear as if lit with a single light.

TECHNIQUES AND TERMINOLOGY

Throughout this book you will see references to things such as light ratios, dragging the shutter, lighting patterns, main light, fill light, accent or "garlic" light, and other terms that are part of the photographer's vocabulary. Let's outline some of these terms.

Light Positions and Functions. In portraiture, we use different lights for specific purposes. Generally, the lights I will or might use are as follows.

Main Light. The main or key light is the predominant light source, which determines the feel of the photograph and dictates the direction of the light and where shadows fall.

Fill Light. The fill light is always positioned very close to the camera lens and usually on the opposite side of the camera to the main light. It is used to fill in the shadows created by the direction of the main light.

Hair Light. The hair light is set high and behind the subject to provide separation and highlights on the hair. It should not spill over onto the subject.

Accent Light (or "Garlic Light"). An accent light, or what I call a garlic light, helps add roundness and depth and also contribute to separation from the background. Now, why do I call it a garlic light? Simple. A good chef knows that when you add garlic to a recipe, and too little has no effect, too much is overpowering. Think of your accent light in the same way. Every time you want to use it, think garlic—not too little, and definitely not too much.

Kicker Light. Another light that may be used is a kicker, a light behind the subject that highlights a certain area of the subject, such as the hair.

As you become more comfortable with using these different lights you will learn what works best for a given subject to produce the best result. But, and I will keep stressing this, be careful of overlighting. Don't blast too much light—from any direction—onto your subject and be careful that the hair lights don't overpower the highlights. Invariably, less is better. Essentially, you're looking for separation from the background.

Lighting Ratio. This is the difference between the amount of light on the highlight side and the amount of light on the shadow side, expressed as a ratio.

Lighting ratios get a bit confusing because it's easy to overlook the fact that the main light illuminates only the highlight side of the subject while the fill light, which is usually placed very close to the camera, throws light on the whole subject. Thus the fill light adds illumination to the highlight side as well as the shadow side.

For example, if the main light were set at f11 and the fill light were set at f8, the ratio would be 3:1. To see how this works, let's say

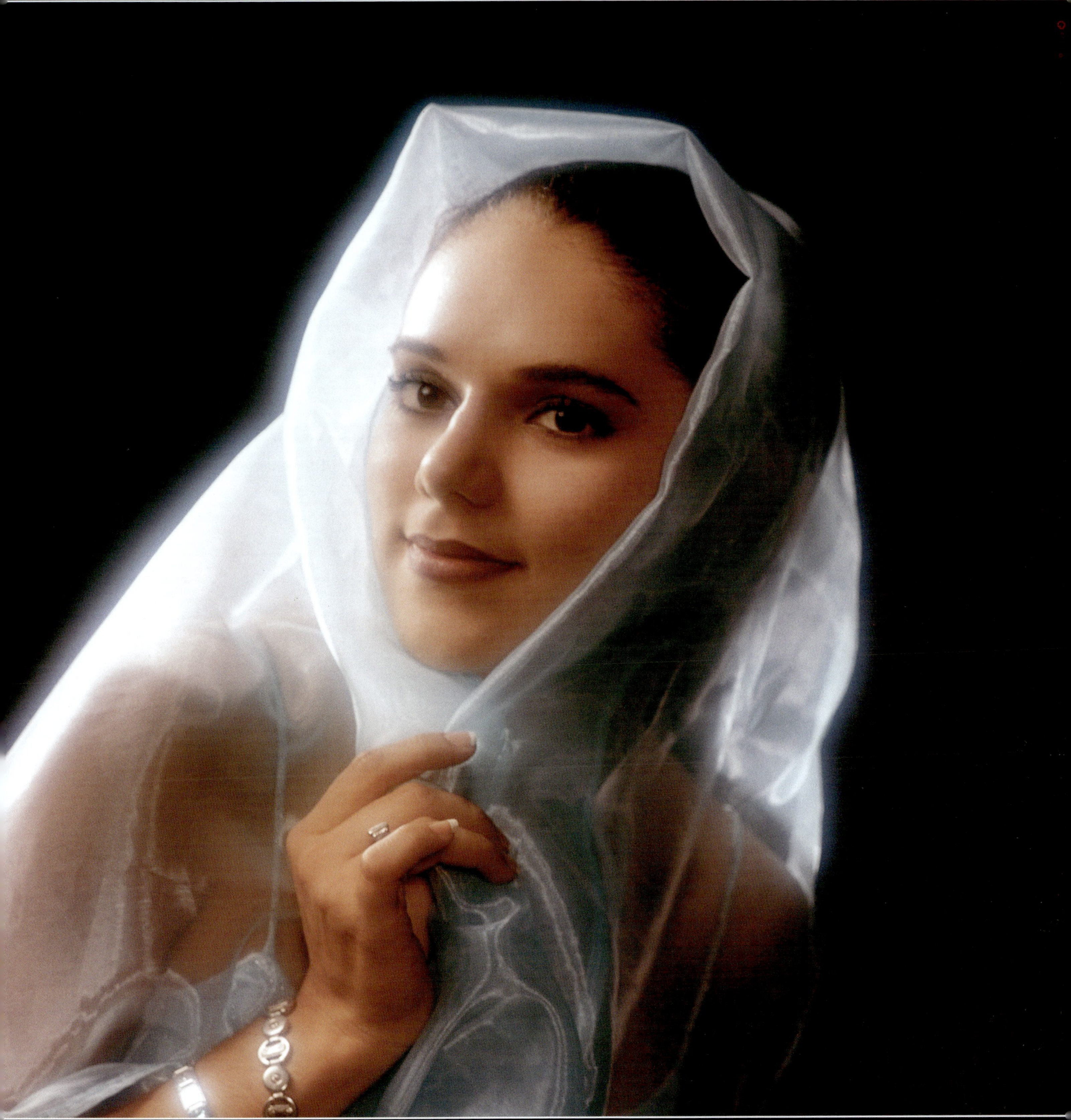

This portrait was lit in a modified-loop pattern with a parabolic reflector fitted with barndoors. An accent light provided the wrap-around effect that gives shape and form. A No. 2 soft-focus filter added the touch of light blue around the edges. The image was made on Kodak Portra 160 film with a Hasselblad camera and a 180mm lens.

f8 is equivalent to one unit of light; f11 would then be two units. The light on the highlight side is three units (two units main light plus one unit fill light), while the light on the shadow side is one unit (one unit fill light). The ratio is, therefore, 3:1.

I prefer to photograph at a 4:1 ratio, which is a difference of 1½ f-stops between the highlight side and shadow side. Here's the math again: the fill light at f8 equals one unit of light; the main light at f11.5 equals three units. The light on the highlight side is four units (three units main light plus one unit fill light), while the light on the shadow side is one unit (one unit fill light). Thus, the ratio of highlight to shadow is 4:1. Similarly, to increase the ratio to 5:1, you need two stops difference, such as f16 for the main and f8 for the fill.

I always regard the fill light as the one that gives us the base density in the shadow area. It is a nondirectional light, and it provides us with detail in the shadow area. Most film manufacturers love the 3:1 ratio as it is the easiest to control and is a very safe ratio to work with. Personally, I like to use a 4:1 ratio. It is more dramatic and dynamic but still gives us rich detail in the shadow area. You can add more punch to a photograph with a 4:1 ratio. Throughout this book, you will see exactly what I mean, since we have included many examples of photographs created with a 4:1 ratio of lighting.

Be aware, however, that to make a 4:1 ratio work well, you need to ensure the light is feathered so it wraps around the subject. Feathering is one way to avoid overlighting a subject, and I will explain the various techniques and terminologies a little later.

Lighting Patterns. The terms for portrait lighting patterns include broad and short lighting, Paramount lighting, butterfly lighting, loop lighting, modified loop lighting, 45-degree or Rembrandt lighting, split lighting, and rim lighting. These patterns are differentiated principally by the placement of the main light.

Broad and Short Lighting. Essentially, there are two main types of portrait lighting, broad and short. In broad lighting, the main light illuminates the side of the subject's face closest to the camera; in other words, the camera and main light are on the same side. It covers the broad scope of the subject's face and can be advantageous when photographing someone with a long, narrow face. Generally, a broad light illuminates the person's face from the ear to the point of the nose. It's not really a precise form of lighting, but it's safe, what I would call a "never miss" type of light. Broad lighting has a tendency to flatten out shadows and facial features, so more dramatic and powerful portraiture is the domain of short lighting.

In short lighting, the main light illuminates the side of the face turned away from the camera; the camera is on one side of the subject, the main light on the other. Short lighting is a bold, dramatic way of lighting a subject—what I would call a "gutsy" light that brings out personality and character—and is favored by many great portrait photographers.

Butterfly or Paramount Lighting. The first thing you will notice is that the shadow, which is directly under the subject's nose, has a butterfly shape. To achieve this, the main or key light is placed above the subject and in line with the subject's nose. This is a classic 1950s Hollywood-era light and also became known as a glamour light. It is used primarily on women with high cheekbones and needs to be done well, otherwise it can be unflattering.

I always regard the fill light as the one that gives us the base density in the shadow area.

Loop Lighting. To create the characteristic loop-like shadow on the subject's face, the main light is placed slightly lower and to one side of the subject. A variation of this is the modified loop light, which can be used with either short or broad lighting. This can be a very flattering light as long as the shadow doesn't cross over and get into the subject's eye.

Rembrandt or 45-degree Lighting. This, as the name implies, is a classic lighting pattern. Its principal feature is a triangle of light on the shadow side of the face. It is what I call a "depth light," and it can be very dramatic, producing an effect similar to short lighting.

Split Lighting. As the name suggests, in this pattern, the lighting evenly divides the shadow side from the highlight side. In essence, the light cuts the face in half—one side is in shadow, the other is in light. To achieve the classic split lighting, you must be careful not to let light spill over from the highlight side onto the shadow side.

Rim Lighting. The main light is placed behind the subject, thus outlining the person with a rim light. You will notice the same effect outdoors when someone stands with their back to the setting sun and is silhouetted by it.

These are traditional patterns and have their place. I recommend that you keep your lighting as simple as possible while learning to master each pattern and, above all, strive to avoid overlighting your subjects. Often, less is more—and this is a great rule of thumb to follow. In fact, great portraits can be made with one light, and you are encouraged to master this simple, effective technique, perhaps with a single umbrella or soft box. Once you are comfortable with the fundamentals of portrait lighting, you can modify the lighting to suit the subject and your visual goals. There are guidelines for portrait lighting, but no hard and fast or rigid rules.

There are guidelines for portrait lighting, but no hard and fast or rigid rules.

INSPIRATION

My advice, and I know it's something that many other veteran photographers will recommend, is that photographers will be well served by studying the lighting in the works created by the master painters. If you can't visit galleries such as the National Art Gallery in Washington, DC, or New York's Museum of Modern Art, or any of the other great collections of art in this country, go to your local library and borrow a few books on the subject.

My greatest inspiration has come from the old Dutch Masters. These artists of the Renaissance period strived to capture the most alluring light through their own talent and the inspiration that they received from natural light. We owe a great deal to those masters, people like Rembrandt, after whom one of the classic lighting patterns has been named, and their study of light has taught us a great deal about how important light is in creating beautiful portraits.

Just as those talented painters were able to "guide light" onto their canvas so it seemed to glow, so should we try to do the same with the light that comes through our lens onto film or electronic capture media, which is our canvas. So, please study the work of the old masters and I am sure that, like me, you will be inspired in your own photography.

2. *Portraiture—My Way*

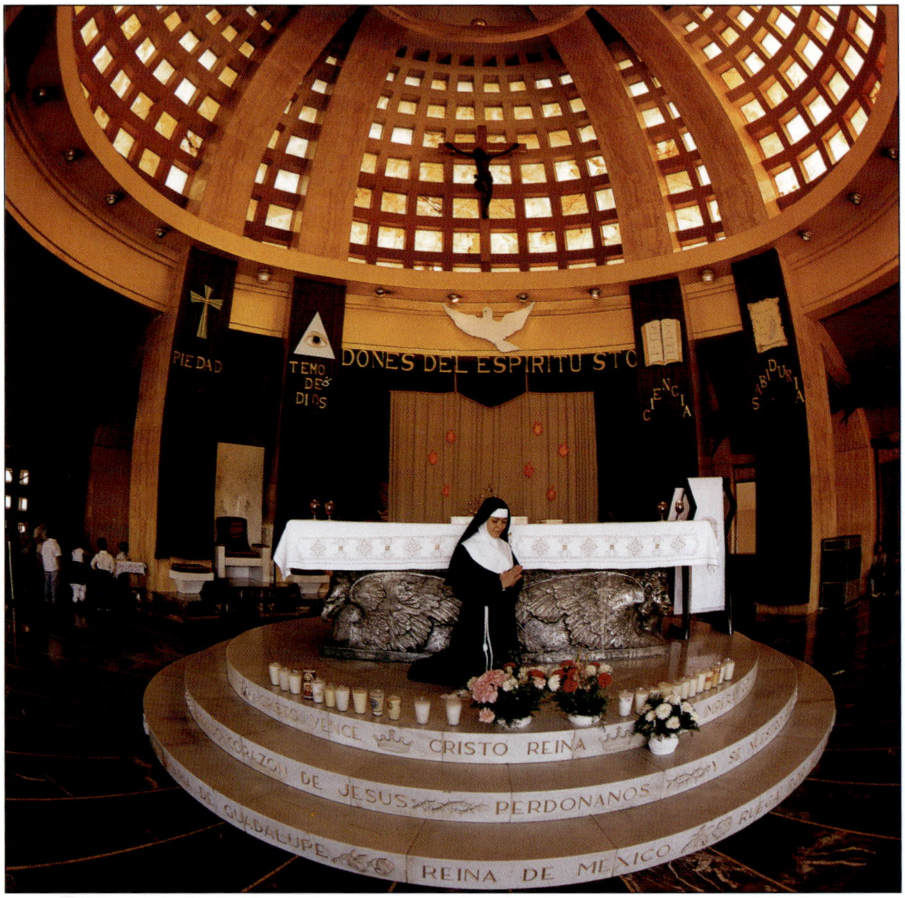

This evocative image of a nun praying in a church in Mexico was lit with ambient light—daylight and a spotlight—inside the building. To ensure a depth of field that was sufficient to maintain focus on the principal subject in the foreground and the essential detail in the background, Don used a wide-angle 30mm lens on his Hasselblad. Due to the long exposure, a sturdy tripod was imperative.

As a portrait photographer, I have always taken the approach that everyone is beautiful, and it is my job to bring out that beauty and capture it on film. It's become my obsession to make the subject look as good as possible, and I would encourage you to make that your goal too—especially if you want your images to stand out and be memorable.

In portraiture, lighting and posing work together to bring out the essence of the person's character in a pleasing manner. Our responsibility is to communicate the personality of the subject, and to do that we must be able to make the subject feel comfortable and relaxed throughout the whole process. Keep in mind that most people don't really feel comfortable in front of a camera.

The term "portraiture" covers the photography of individuals of all ages, families, and other groups. This range of subjects in itself poses a lot of challenges. Because we must photograph people of all different ages and backgrounds, we photographers must have the right personality and temperament for the job. Not all photographers are comfortable with all age groups and this has led many of us to specialize in specific areas, such as babies, weddings, or executives.

Regardless of the subject, however, lighting and posing are key ingredients in successful portraiture. But there is much more than just technical sophistication behind the creation of truly great portraits. While those factors—lighting and posing—are essential, you should not forget the importance of the location and the objects surrounding the subjects. I have always felt that this type of environmental con-

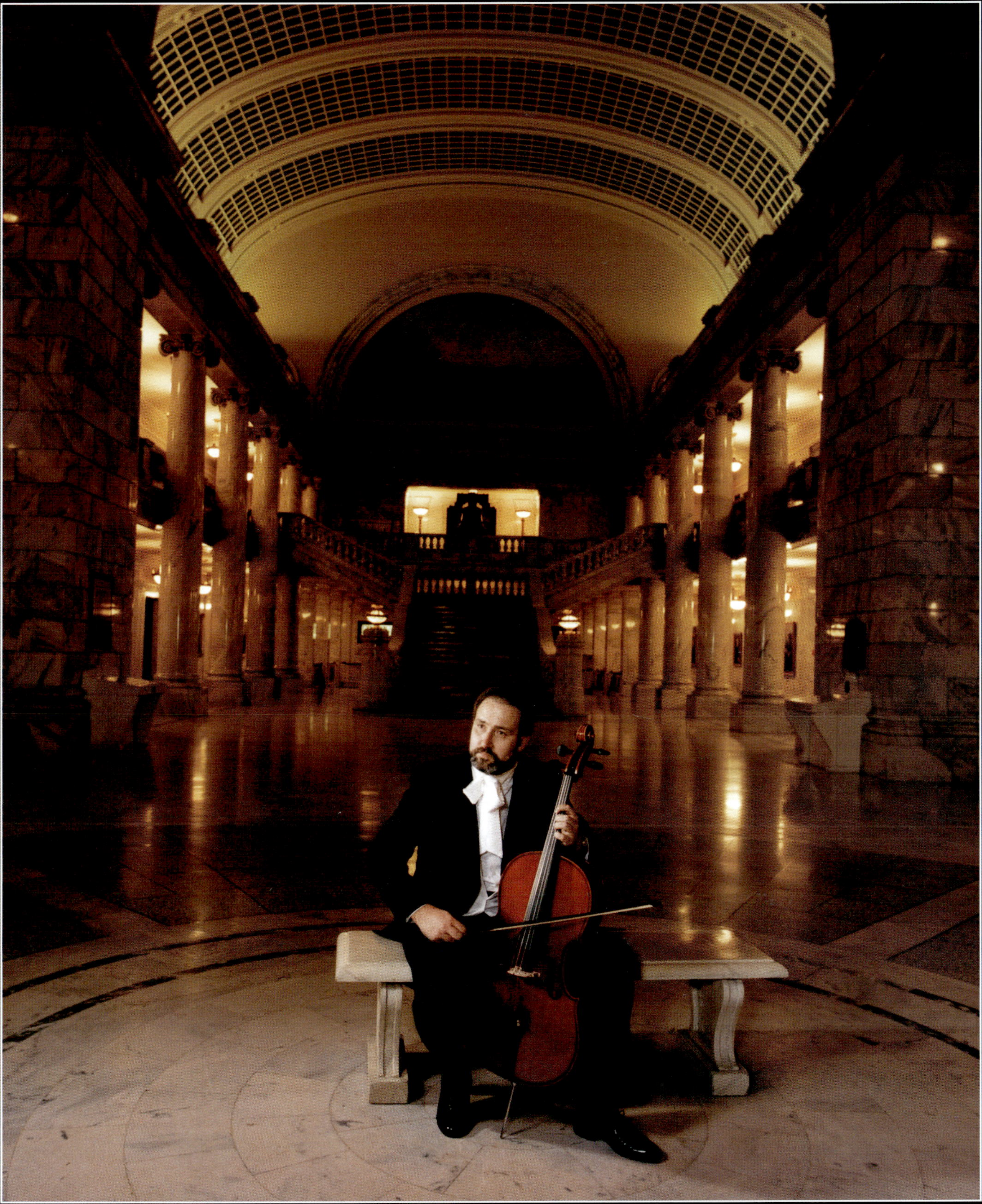

Because of the size and depth of the state capitol rotunda in Salt Lake City, Don was able to use an 80mm lens for this portrait of a musician and still have adequate depth of field. A parabolic light with the barndoors pinched down was placed on the left and used for the main light, while a accent light close by but higher outlined the subject's shoulder to give separation. A broad umbrella light acted as fill. Metering the background in situations like this is a judgment call. After several readings were made and then averaged, a long exposure was used to give a full exposure without burning out the highlights.

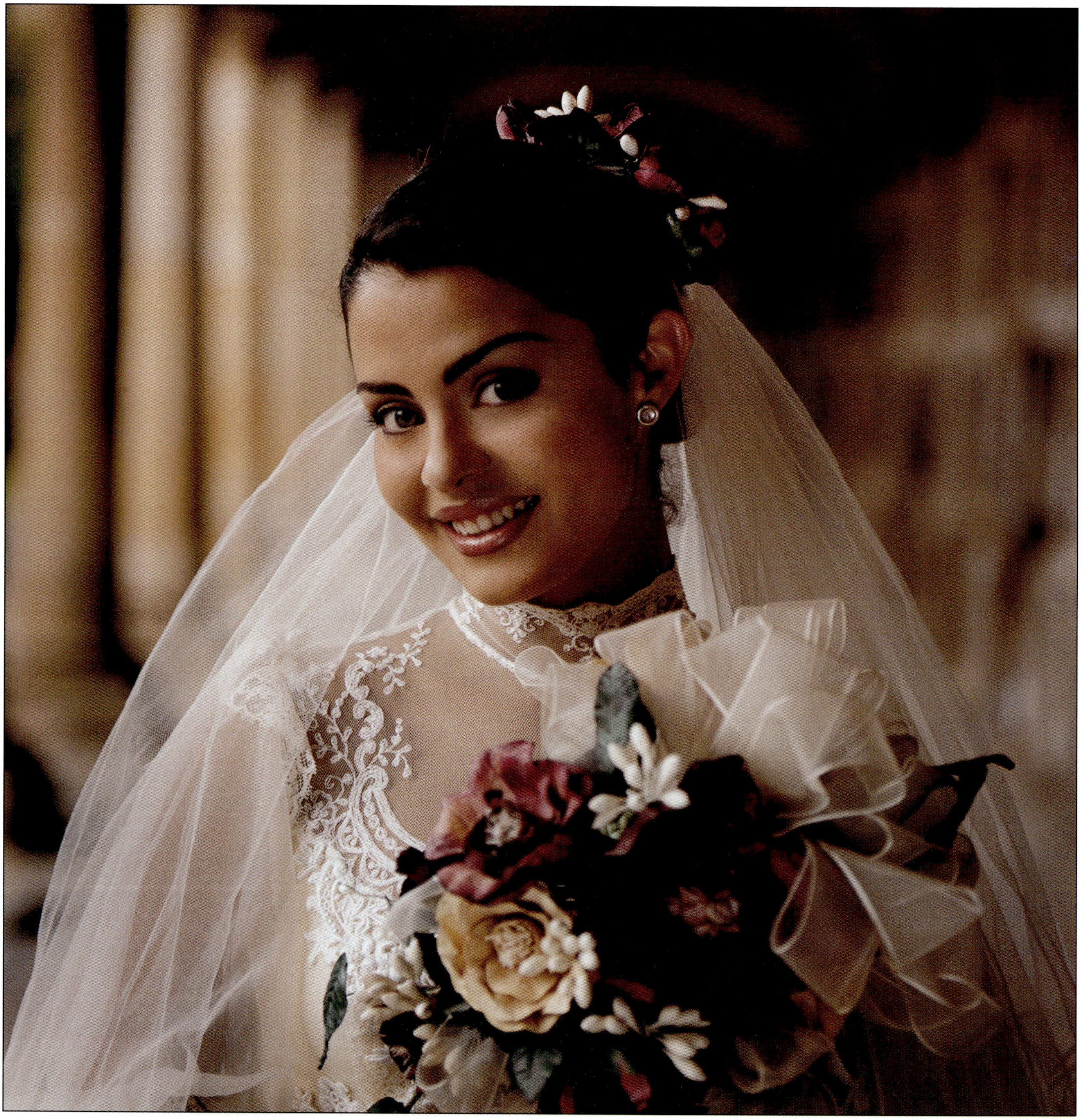

This stunning portrait of a bride was created by harnessing the natural beauty of window light, filling in the shadows, and wrapping light around the bride's face with a touch-of-warmth reflector. Note how the light along the edge of the veil separates the subject from the background, and also the graceful tilt of the bride's head and her natural smile.

cern is essential to capturing the true essence of the person or people I photograph. In fact, the environment, whether in the family home or outdoors in a park, plays a major complementary role in portrait photography.

I have always taken the approach that our studio could complete any assignment in the time that the subject has available. But I always tried, also, to get in those few extra shots or poses that could be converted into additional sales. After all, while we enjoy what we

The forgiving nature and versatility of the bare bulb make it a wonderful all-round light source. Just don't become a slave to it; otherwise all your photographs will look the same. This bridal couple was lit with late-afternoon daylight and a bare bulb to the left that added specular highlights to the bride's dress. Seagulls flying overhead complemented the setting.

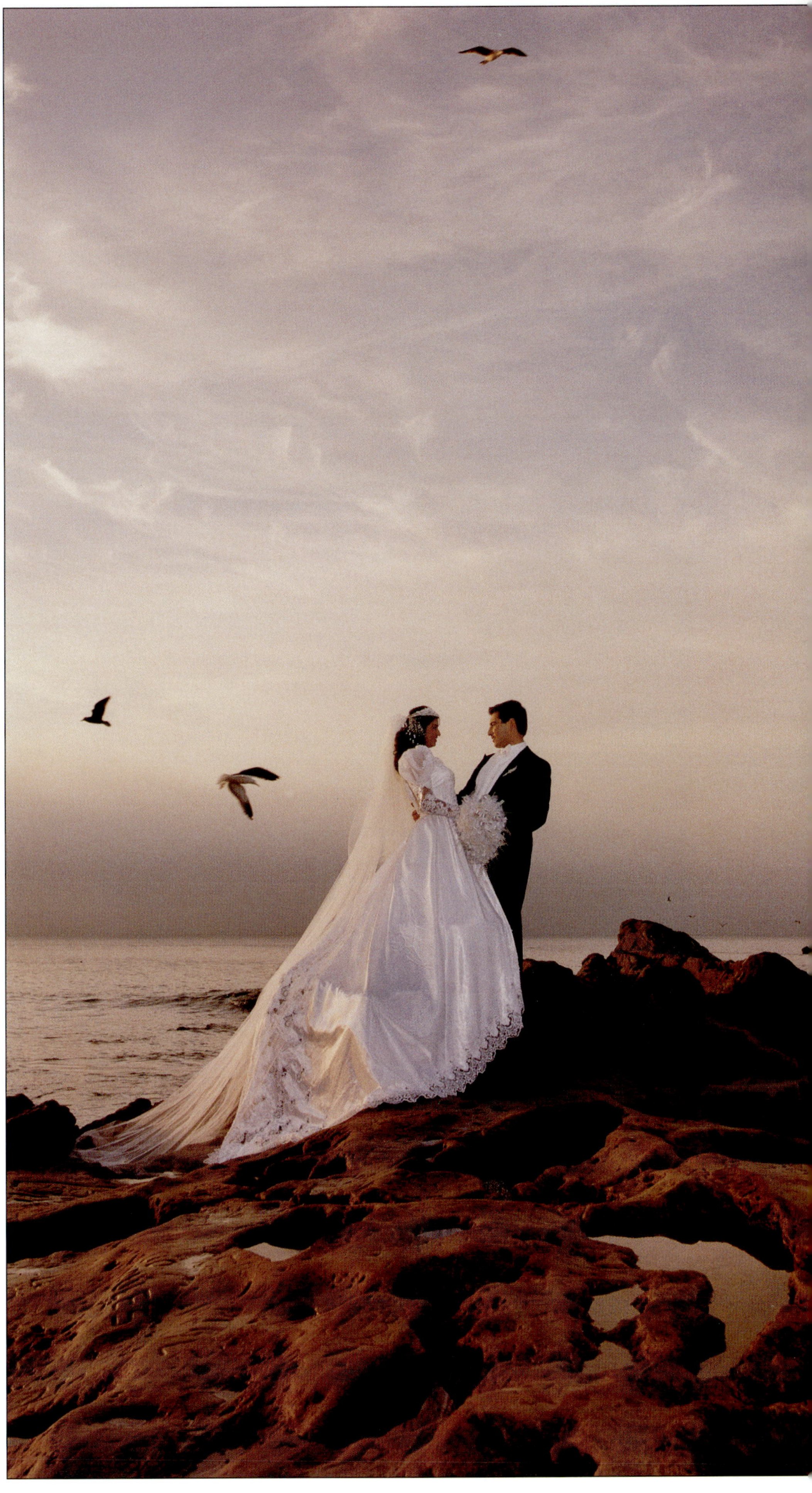

do, we're also professionals and should never overlook any chance to generate greater revenues. If you want to be a successful professional portrait photographer, your marketing and salesmanship—or that of someone else working with you—should be as important as your creative skills.

PREPARING FOR PORTRAITURE

Let's stop a moment to discuss the preparation for the photograph. I have broken down the process into four categories so that it is easy to remember the sequence.

First, you must establish the overall pose, or it may be referred to as the overall setting. This is where we establish the background and how we will place our subjects. (Choosing the living room and the part of the room, for instance.)

The second step is to generalize the light. By this, I mean establishing the direction and the type of light, whether you will use natural light, studio or portable strobe light, or a combination of the two. You also must determine the general placement or location of the light in relation to the subject's pose.

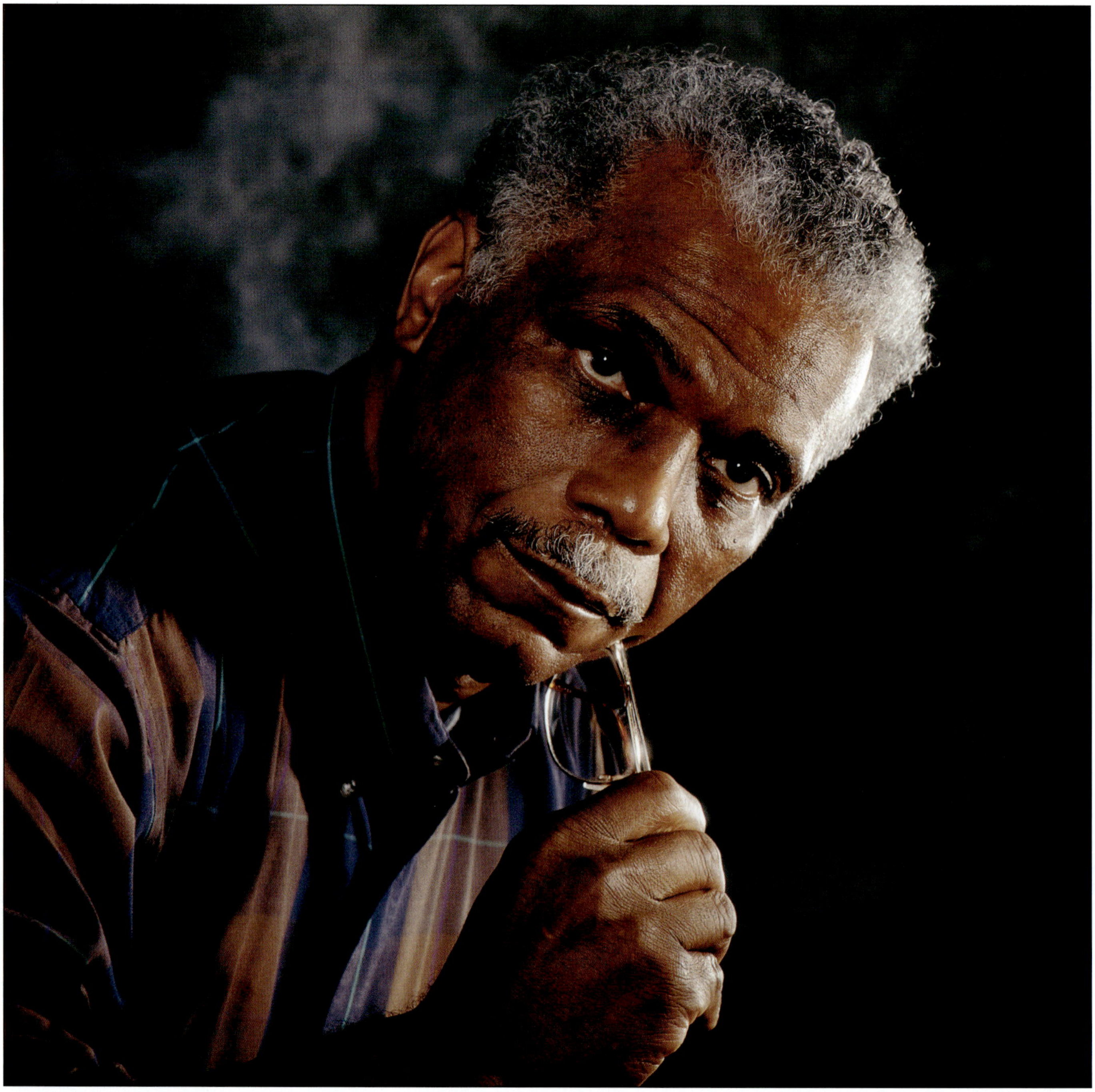

Note the strong hands and masculine pose in this split-light portrait. Barndoors on the main and fill light facilitated precise control over the illumination on the man's face and hand, while an accent light from behind highlighted the edges of the face and hand.

After that is done, it is on to step three, which is to finalize the pose. In doing so, you are preparing the subjects for the final places they will take, the direction of their faces and bodies, and the placement of their hands and legs.

Once the pose is satisfactory, you must finalize the lighting. You may need to move the lights slightly to best conform to the final pose you have selected and to give you the quality of light that you need to accomplish an exquisite image. Now you are ready to make the exposure.

Throughout this book, I will cover many aspects of portrait photography that will, I hope, help you with your photography, but before going any further, I would like to give a broad overview of some of the situations and subjects portrait photographers are most likely to encounter.

THE EXECUTIVE PORTRAIT

Businesspeople are also busy people, and time is usually of the essence. This can pose logistical problems for photographers, especially if you don't plan ahead. If you rush through a sitting with an executive, the chances are good that you will come away with a technically good but superficial photograph. We want to go well beyond the superficial.

Get to Know the Subject. I make it part of my job to know about the person before the sitting. Make it part of your modus operandi too. Find out what has made the person successful by asking the subject or others in the office. Is there a memento in the office that is special to the person that could be included in the photograph? What is the essence of this person? Knowing information like this will give you better insight before the shoot.

Select the Location. Plan ahead and scout the location. I try to visit a day or two beforehand, at the very least an hour or two ahead. Knowing the location and getting there ahead of time to set up can be the difference between a so-so photograph and a great portrait.

Place the subject in a location that puts him at the center of attention. That doesn't mean that he is in the center of the frame, but it does mean that he is the focal point of everything in the scene. There should be no other prominent elements. If there are large foreground or background elements, they should not be lighted more brightly than the main subject, since the viewer's eye is naturally attracted to the brightest object in the frame. These tips apply to both indoor and outdoor locations.

Keep an open mind when selecting locations for executive portraiture. Consider, for example, an executive who is in charge of a large manufacturing plant. That plant may be the perfect location to place the subject. Why? Because the setting is an integral part of what that person is and does. The setting also lends itself to a dramatic image because of the foreground and background possibilities inherent in a large plant. By placing the subject prominently in the middle ground of the composition, you have the flexibility to look deeply into a dramatically lit background that will frame and define the main subject. A carefully placed foreground object can also serve to draw the viewer's eye into the image and guide it toward the main subject.

When setting up for the executive portrait, don't hesitate (with the subject's permission) to tidy up a desk, remove any superfluous items, and make the setting look as professional as the subject you're photographing. I have replaced art on office walls and made many other adjustments to the environment to get the look and feel that is going to work best. Be diplomatic when doing this—no executive will want his or her office completely rearranged but a few polite suggestions (for example, "This will make it look great!") will usually be appreciated.

Lighting. Once I have seen the setting and I know where I will place the subject, my only concern becomes the lighting. I want to be prepared completely when the subject arrives, so that all I have to do is fine-tune the lights. This is absolutely critical with a busy executive. When he or she walks in the door, I can focus on interacting with the subject because I have already dealt with the technical details.

For an effective executive portrait, the first thing to consider is the fill light. While the main light is often looked upon as playing the key role, and it *is* an important part in the foundation for the lighting, I now start my lighting setup with the fill light and work from there.

I like to use a high ratio of lighting in a portrait, especially in an executive portrait. It helps to add depth and presence to the

Getting there ahead of time to set up can be the difference between a so-so photograph and a great portrait.

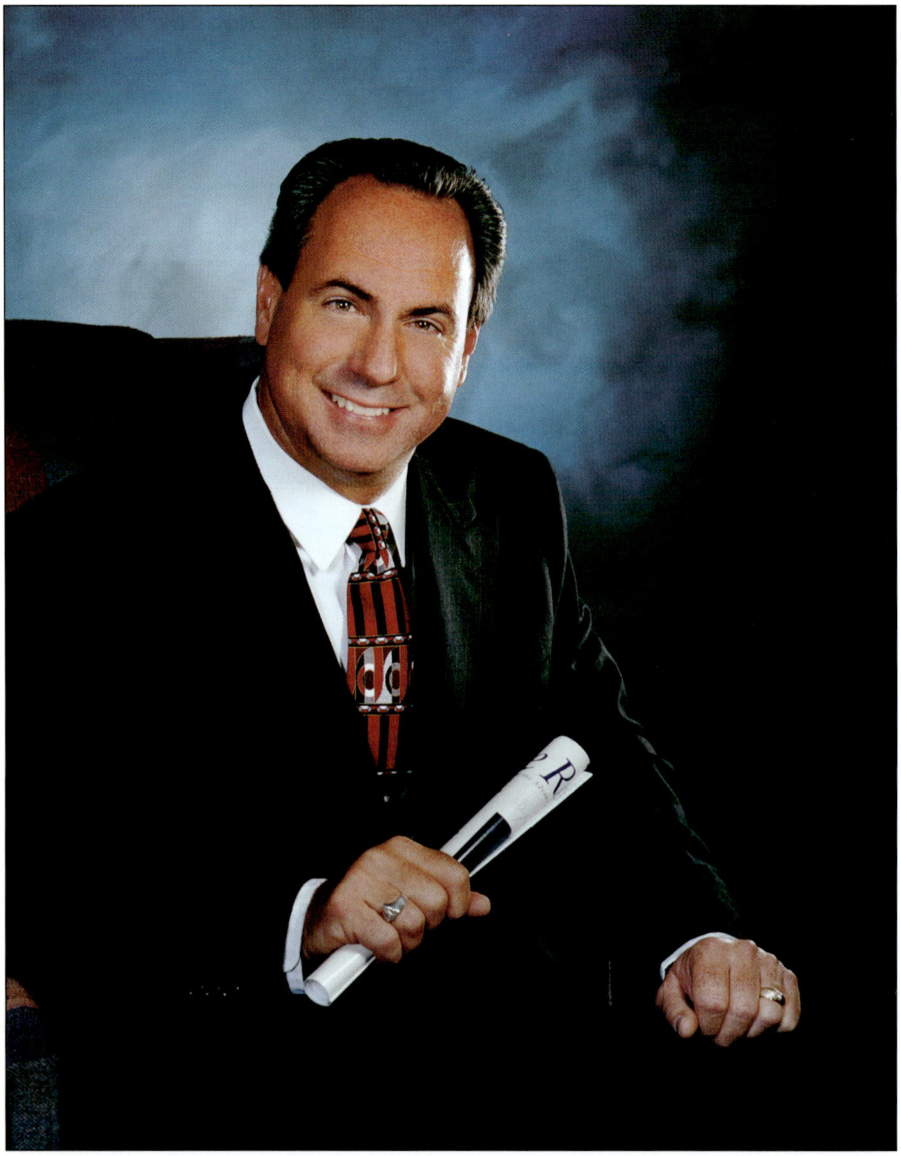

A punch panel provides wonderful light for executive portraits such as this. The setup was standard, with the main light and an accent light placed on the right. A hair light behind and to the right of the subject illuminated his hair and provided some separation, while the background was lit with a fairly narrow beam of light. Umbrella fill was also used to give the 4:1 ratio that Don prefers.

image, and it also lends a psychological strength that people like to see in a portrait of a high-powered businessperson. Use the modeling lights to check your lighting.

You will also want the light to wrap around the subject. In order to create this wraparound lighting, it is essential to add an accent light that "rakes" across the front plane of the subject. Place this light near and behind the main light and adjust it with a barndoor or snoot to create a very small beam. A barndoor works best because it is flexible, and you can adjust the beam of light so that it adds what I call just a "kiss" of light. This "kiss" of light should be at half the power of the main light, so that it does not overpower the main light or burn out the highlights on the subject.

What we are really aiming for is added detail in the face and a gentle falloff on the shadow side of the image. In many cases, I utilize a bare bulb strobe to create a greater roundness and separation between the subject and the background. This also helps in creating the rich wraparound effect that I seek whenever possible.

When using strobes, it is important to turn off the modeling lights during the exposure. This is essential, because in settings with important foreground and background elements, you'll often need to "drag" the shutter. Dragging the shutter means making long exposures that allow the natural light to be recorded in the background, separately from the exposure of the main subject. This provides a full view of the environment and allows the viewer's eye to see into the picture, creating a feeling of depth in the final photograph. Keeping the modeling lights turned off ensures that the main subject is not part of the background exposure and that there is not a "ghostly" image of the subject in the final photograph. Bear in mind that these are not multiple exposures, but one long exposure.

While I adjust the lights, I talk with the executive to put him or her at ease. This is when it helps to know a bit about them. From my experience, it is quite likely that the first exposure will be the best. And in many cases, you only have time to grab a few quick exposures before the subject leaves.

Lens Selection. When using medium-format equipment, in my case the Hasselblad, I often use a 40mm lens for environmental portraiture and place the subject in the center of the negative, which is the sharpest area of the film. Also, this lens gives me the depth of field and perspective I need. Additionally, because the subject is in the center of the negative, if the composition needs to be improved, I can always crop the image for final printing. Just remember, when using the wide-angle lens for portraiture, that you must keep the camera perfectly level and the subject right in the center to avoid creating distortion.

Using a wide-angle lens and getting in close allows for full attention right where you want it—on the subject. If your subject is in an office, place him or her so that you are shooting into the corner of the room. This gives the feeling of converging lines, adds drama, and emphasizes the main subject.

Also, you can add a little action to the executive's photograph by getting the subject to do something with their hands, such as holding a book, an annual report, or something related to their job. This will make the portrait look very natural.

FAMILY PORTRAITS

Environmental portraiture is challenging and fun. It also offers great potential to expand your business, since it will bring you into contact with business leaders and other prominent people in your community. You can capitalize on these contacts to build your business.

In making a family portrait, I choose a location that is appropriate

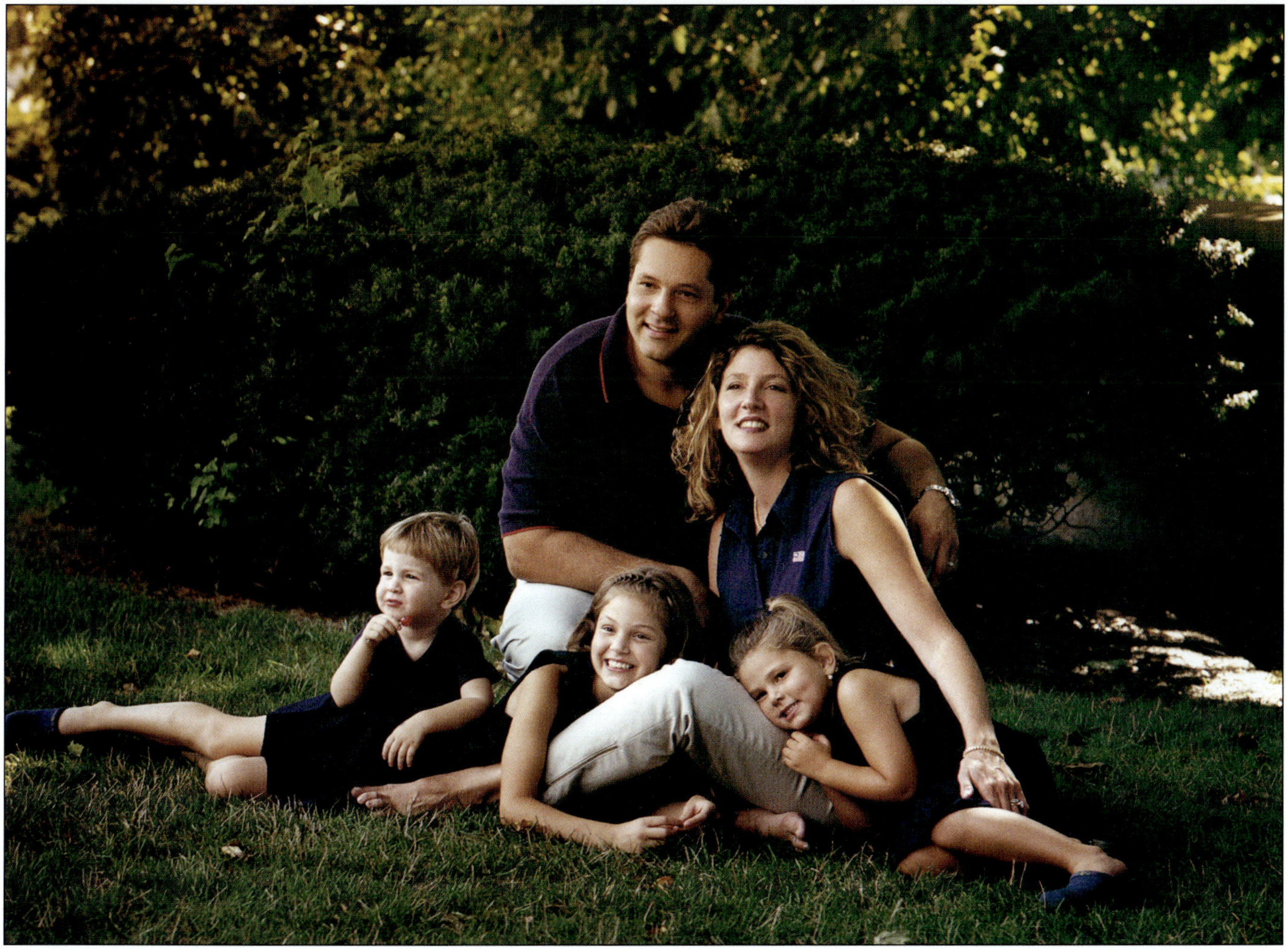

Natural, warm afternoon light is ideal for family portraits such as this. A touch-of-warmth reflector enhanced the ambient light on the subjects without affecting other parts of the image. Note the effectiveness of the triangle composition. Don describes this as a simple, fun shot.

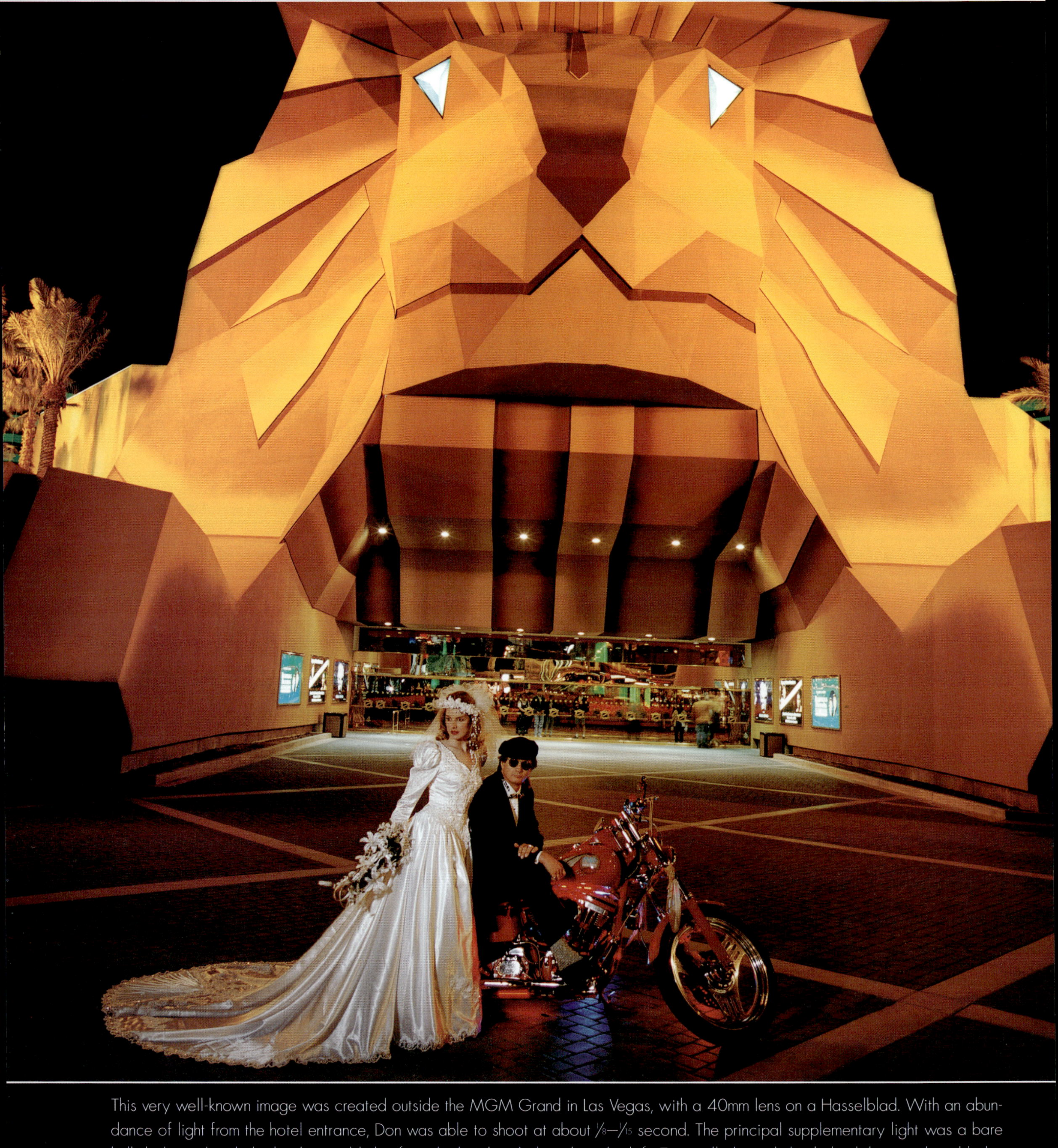

This very well-known image was created outside the MGM Grand in Las Vegas, with a 40mm lens on a Hasselblad. With an abundance of light from the hotel entrance, Don was able to shoot at about $\frac{1}{8}$–$\frac{1}{15}$ second. The principal supplementary light was a bare bulb balanced with the background lights from the hotel and placed on the left. Two gelled mini lights behind the couple added a touch of red under the motorcycle and to the edge of the dress. Note the detail and shape to the bride's dress and its "molten silver" look. This is a classic Don Blair image.

for the entire family. This may be an elegant living room or a sweeping staircase for an indoor situation. Also, remember that when working indoors we want to shoot into the corner of the room to create a pleasing setting for the family to fill. Photographing into the corner also adds structure and depth, which helps draw us into the photograph and makes for a more interesting photograph than having the family placed against a one-dimensional background, such as a wall.

Creating a Classic. Remember, if you do your job correctly here, you are actually creating an image that the family will cherish for quite some time to come. You must always bear in mind just how important this image is to the family who has asked you to create it. Because of this, you should plan for the longevity of the portrait. Try to steer clear of trendy clothing and accessories that could quickly date your portrait. Pose the group in a more classic or what some might call conservative manner. While this conservative approach may not allow you to try the latest rage in portraits, the family will not have to put the image in storage because it becomes outdated.

Timelessness is also an important factor from a sales point of view. Perhaps your client wants to build a wall of portraits that shows the family's change over the years. If the portraits have a classic look, the family is more likely to come back year after year for another portrait to add to the growing collection on display.

Setting. In preparing the setting, I try to put myself in the shoes of the family members. I find out their passions and what they share in common. My family, for example, loves basketball. If the family is very musical, the centerpiece of their living room could be a grand piano, or there could be other valued instruments that they would like included in the picture. These are all things that I keep in mind when I first talk with the family about their sitting, and I work to integrate each family's special interests into their final picture.

Once I have set the stage for the location of the image, it is time to bring in one of the main subjects. Often this is the mother. I will use her as the base to establish the location of the others in the photograph. This way I do not tire the children, who are often prone to distraction when sitting still too long.

You must always bear in mind just how important this image is to the family who has asked you to create it.

Using Props. With the main person in the scene, I add any final props to the setting. Perhaps I will replace a large plant with a smaller one, or decide to bring in a cherished heirloom like a rocking chair or a piece of sculpture. Don't be afraid of rearranging the setting to make it look good—anything that defines the family and contributes to the warmth and love that the family feels for one another is a good choice.

Lighting. Some of the techniques that I use for environmental portraiture apply to other categories of portraits. For example, the bare-bulb technique of adding roundness and texture to the subject works well in many other situations. Keep this in mind as you read the following sections.

Many photographers use broad bank or umbrella lighting. While this type of lighting is successful in giving a good negative with a full range of tones in the subject, it falls far short of the kind of carefully-lit image that can win awards and the gratitude of valued customers. The broad "blast of light" approach does not satisfy the need for roundness in the features, and it does not flatter the face or body in the way that selectively-modeled and higher-ratio lighting does.

Let's assume that you are creating a family portrait in a living room, and the family will be gathered around the piano. To the right of the subjects is a large window. How should you go about lighting this scene?

To start, use the beautiful natural light that is coming into the room through the window. This will be your main light. Also, try to balance the light outside with that

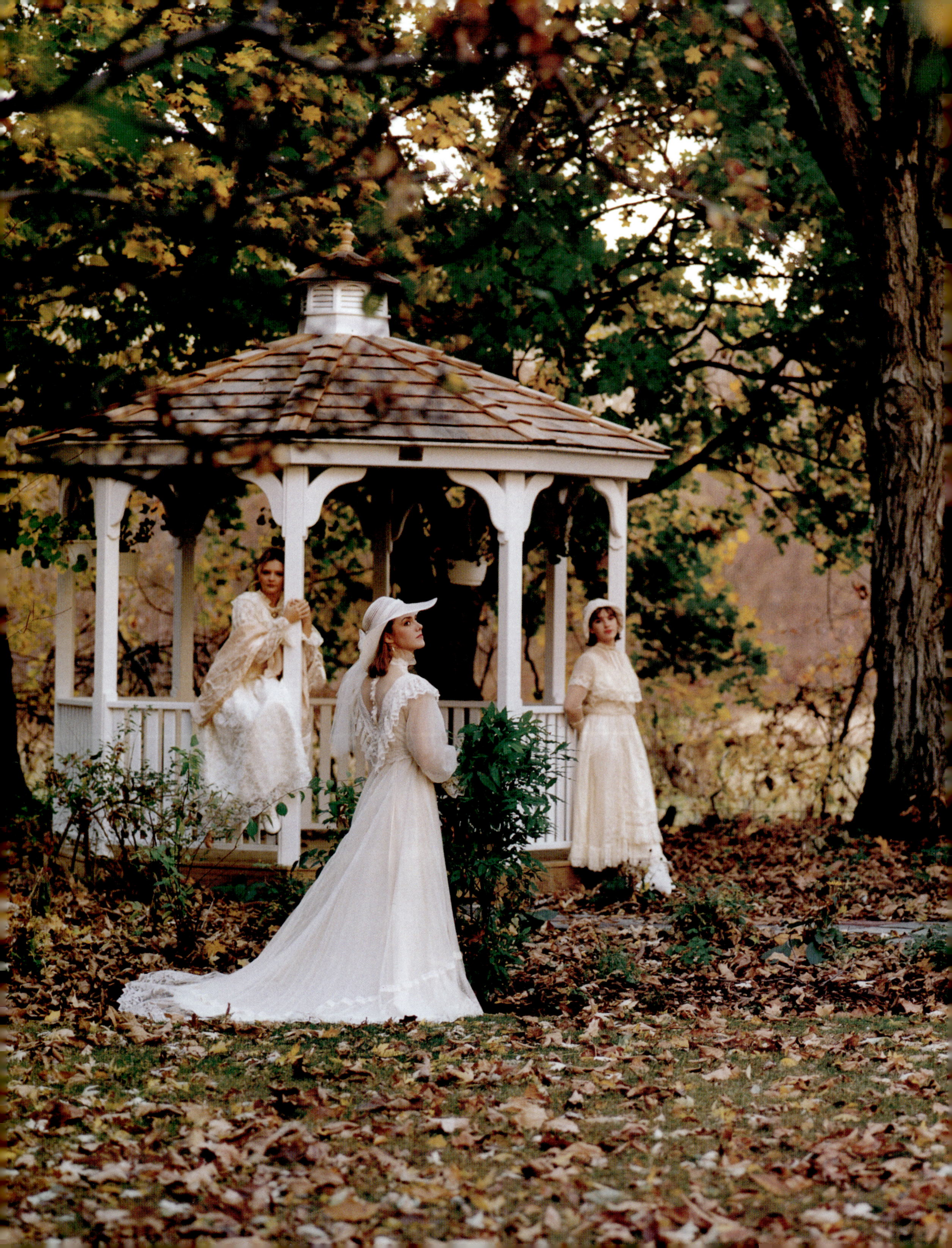

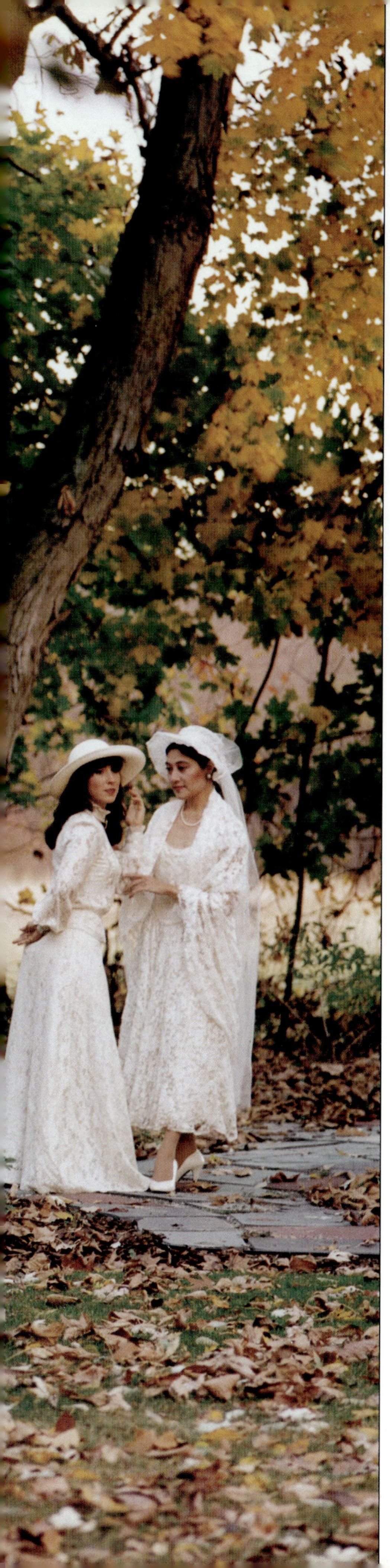

There are magic moments at day's end when "sweet light" makes for great outdoor portraiture. The setting around this gazebo was ideal for a romantic image with a nostalgic flavor. Careful positioning and posing of the five models ensured that the beautiful, diffused daylight would not be wasted.

inside the home. This will give a more natural and pleasing look.

To further enhance the details in the room and the facial features of the subjects, add a bare-bulb flash close to the camera. The bare bulb will help to bring additional light to the shadow side of the scene and will provide the roundness that I like in my portraits.

Also, it is good to warm up the scene a bit. So far, we have a cool balance because of the window light and the bare bulb. You can warm up the scene by adding a backlight to help separate the family from the background. Try placing a table lamp from the living room behind and to the left of the subjects. This incandescent bulb will provide the hint of warm backlight that you will need to establish a golden glow behind the family.

Finally, add a strobe light with the barndoors closed down so that just a pinch of light will rake across the family members. Warm this light with a color gel so that it matches the backlight and serves to additionally warm up the entire scene.

Posing. With the lighting complete and the children in place—let's say one is on the carpet in front of the piano, one is leaning against the piano to the left of the mother, and the last child is sitting to the right of the mother on the piano bench—you are ready to fine-tune the pose.

Looking carefully at the way the light is falling on the subjects, move them into the light so that the splash of light from the barndoored strobe is raking across the front of their faces. Turn their faces into the main light and their bodies into the shadow.

Remember that placement of hands is very important and can be a key to an effective image. Flat hands are unattractive. Equally, fingers turned in on a flat hand can look like claws. Be sure to have the subjects extend their fingers so that they are long and graceful looking, with the edge of the hands turned toward the camera. Also remember to assure the sitter that what may seem or feel awkward to them comes across as quite natural from the camera's view.

Lens Selection. As with my executive portraiture, I invariably use a wide-angle lens that lets me work quite close to the subjects (and thus be able to communicate with them easily). I also favor a triangular composition, because it helps avoid the common mistake of having heads on top of each other, or a line of heads in the same plane.

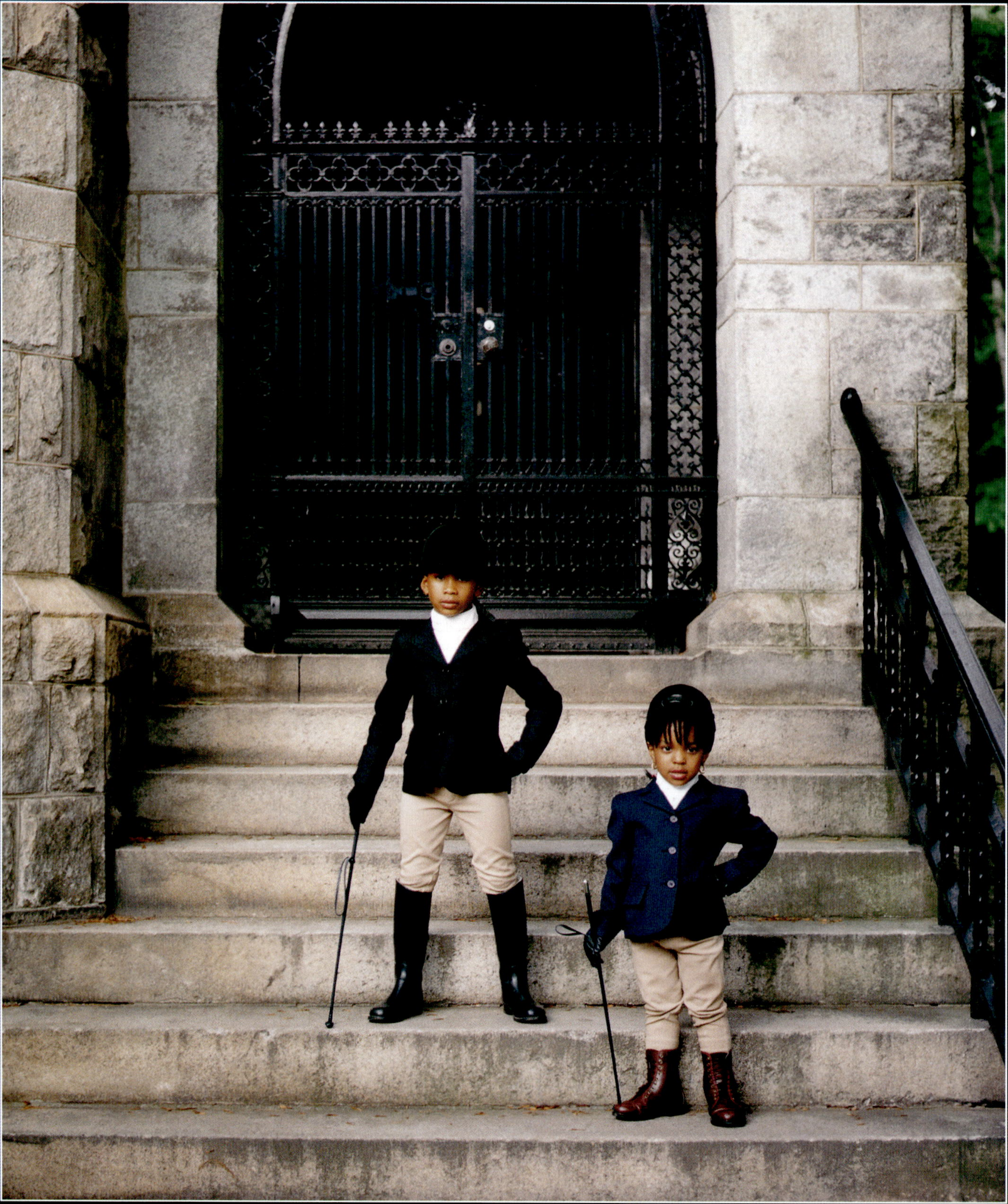

All this delightful duo needed to make their day were some horses—they're certainly decked out for a day's riding. Soft natural light, good posing, and cooperative, cute models make this picture.

CHILDREN'S PORTRAITS

There are some special concerns when photographing babies, children, and other young people, such as teens and high school seniors. While the fundamentals of lighting and posing discussed earlier are generally the same for all specialty portraits, it is important to remember some special techniques that can make dealing with these young portrait subjects the most fun it can be.

Infants and Small Children. These smallest of subjects can be temperamental and difficult. But with a little patience and understanding, it is quite simple to take advantage of their inquisitiveness and wonder at everything new in the world.

Often, parents are wary about having to bring their child at a preappointed time, because a baby's mood is so unpredictable. My solution for this is to set up an appointment with the understanding that it must be flexible. You really have no choice. The parents will appreciate your sensitivity. Ask the mother to call on the day of the sitting and let you know if all is well with the baby. If all is not well, you can reschedule for another time.

Also, try to determine the best time of day for the child based upon eating and sleeping habits. This will make the appointed sitting time more likely to be a success.

Types of Portraits. Babies are especially good candidates for high-key portraiture because this method brings out the warmth and color of an infant. High key lighting is a soft, open kind of light that invites the viewers to close in on the tiny subject's round and smooth features. Mother-and-child photographs are also appealing. They are often alluring to the viewer because they emphasize the love and affection that exists between the subjects. You can create these photos in a more dramatic setting with a longer lens to emphasize the closeness of the mother and child.

Clothing Selection. Be aware of the child's clothing. Discuss the clothing in a presitting meeting. Coordinate the clothing so that items like blankets and props have colors that complement one another. When photographing children (or any subject) outdoors, it is important to dress them in clothing that is appropriate to the setting. It would not make sense to photograph a child wearing a suit next to a babbling brook. Also, in today's more casual world, it is appropriate for children to wear comfortable and sporty clothes in such rustic settings.

As the photographer, you should dress casually to put the subjects at ease. It is also important to limit the number of people at the location so that the children are not confused or distracted. Other than you and your assistant, only the parents (one or both) should be present.

An Assistant and Props. In photographing small children and babies, it is essential to have an assistant and some props handy to attract their attention. Your assistant should be behind the camera and create as much fuss as possible to gain the attention of the child. Soft toys, small rocking chairs, and carriages are all good props, both to keep the attention of the child and to set an appropriate mood. While your assistant is distracting the child, you can concentrate on other elements of the photograph, the lights, the pose, and the setting.

Basic Pose and Camera Height. Babies should be at floor level on pillows or perhaps in a cradle. It is important for the camera to be at the same level as the child. In doing so, you can relate to the youngster at his or her own level. Also, by bringing your camera down to their level, you are gaining an understanding of how they see the world.

While your assistant is distracting the child, you can concentrate on other elements of the photograph.

Studio Lighting. I suggest using a broad parabolic fill light supported by a bare-bulb strobe. The bare bulb adds the softness that you cannot get from an umbrella or a bank light. It also wraps the child in soft, open light.

Outdoor Images. Let's assume that you are photographing two children in a wooded setting out-

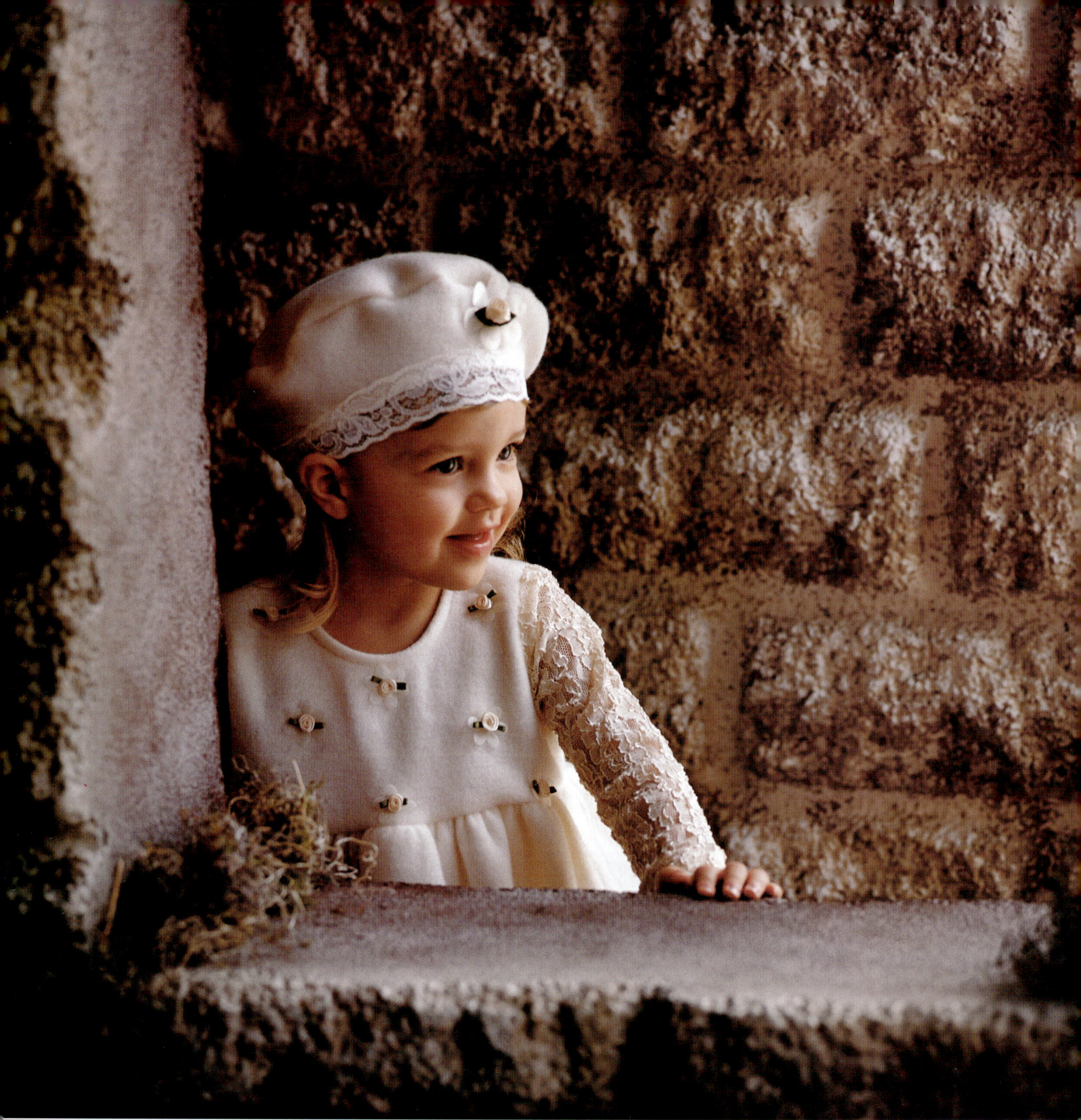

This cute little girl with the happy smile and sparkling eyes was leaning on props made by Off the Wall with window light coming from the right. A touch-of-warmth reflector helped pick up shadow detail (note the detail in the girl's dress).

doors on an overcast day. You can turn this to your advantage with a minimum of effort.

First, establish the direction of the light and place the children so that the light falls on them in a lateral direction. This means placing the subjects so that they are protected from the light on one side by a barrier of foliage. This barrier provides the necessary shadow for a well-modeled portrait. If possible, place children so that foliage is also overhead. This will serve to block harsh overhead light and reduce the possibility of "raccoon eyes." If this natural foliage barrier is not available, use a black gobo or umbrella to create the same effect.

With the children in position, the general lighting is also somewhat ready. You simply need a fill light to supplement the main light from the sun. Again, I suggest a bare-bulb strobe (portable) that you can use to provide a wraparound effect and create a pleasing, specular highlight on the more defined facial features. Often, I add a warming gel to the bare bulb to create the warm feeling of a sunset photograph.

Now you must finalize the pose. With children, it is important to let them do what comes naturally, with a minimum of direction. Children can become uncooperative if they feel they are being overly manipulated. Try to make a game out of this part of the sitting so that the children are at ease and appear as natural as possible in the portraits. It is not necessary to demand a smile. If their smile is not there, you will only increase the child's resolve not to smile by insisting upon it.

Once you are satisfied with the final pose, fine-tune the light. You may want to add an accent light. This is a controlled light with a barndoor that adds just a pinch of light to the fine features of the subjects. This is the final ingredient required to turn a dull, flat image into a stunning, exciting one.

Teenagers and High-School Seniors. Be sensitive to the particular concerns that teens have for acceptance among their peers. They want to feel that they fit within the mainstream of others their own age. This may mean that they are nonconformists in the adult world, but that they are part of the "scene" in their own world. Be aware of the latest trends in both clothing and hairstyles, and try to be sensitive to their requests for particular settings and poses. For teens, it is necessary to let them feel that they have control. Your job is to suggest possibilities and give them reinforcement and reassurance that they look great.

It is also important to recognize the two types of "senior" portraits. The first type of portrait is created for use in a school yearbook, which must conform to certain dimensions and feature a lower lighting ratio so that they will reproduce well in print. The second type of portrait is the one for friends, family, and displays, which can be more daring and feature a higher lighting ratio for dramatic appeal.

Seniors like activity and bright colors in their portraits, so consider using unusual backgrounds and props.

Teens may not feel comfortable when they have a parent around them. A friend usually makes a better companion in this instance. As difficult as it may be, you must assure the parents that you have their interests in mind and that you desire to provide them with a photograph of which they will be proud. Keep in mind that, if you provide the seniors with several poses that they think will impress their friends, they are likely to be cooperative when you ask them to pose in a more traditional setting to satisfy their parents.

Seniors like activity and bright colors in their portraits, so consider using unusual backgrounds and props like brightly-colored geometric shapes or large numbers that spell out their class year. Teens also like the latest music blaring in the background as they pose. While it may not be your favorite music, remember who it is you are trying to please. Make the sitting as much fun as possible. You might even ask your subject to bring along a friend or two. Then, you can photograph

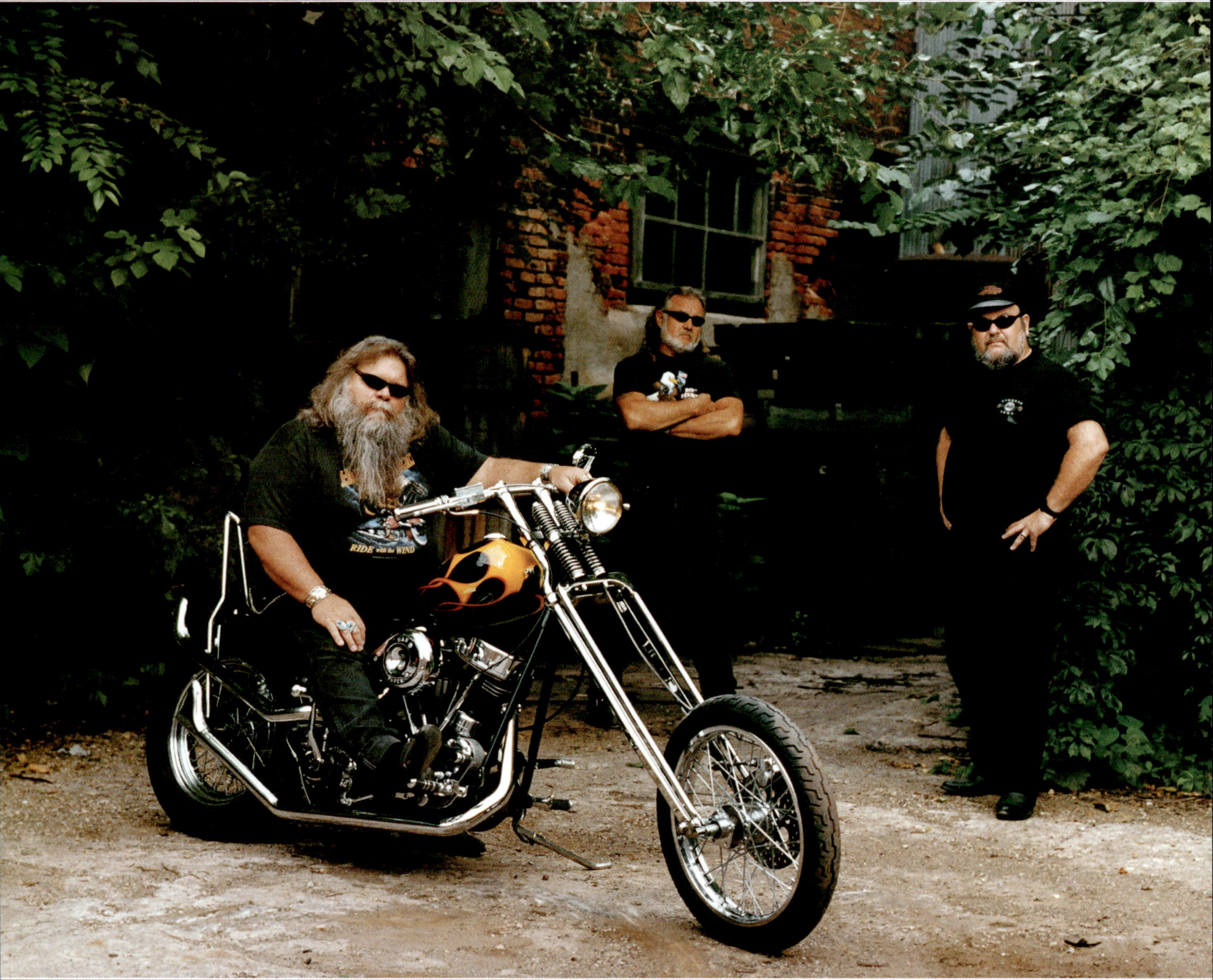

This strong portrait of three bikers was made using ambient light. Its strength lies in the "attitude" of the subjects, the power of the motorcycle, and the triangle composition. The bike's headlight, turned on for the shot, added to the effect.

them together and work quickly to keep the energy level high.

Try to photograph several different settings with, perhaps, a clothing change as well. To stay on schedule, you can also book several students at once, and while one is changing, you can photograph another.

GROUP PORTRAITS

Photographing several people for a group portrait is always a daunting experience. Where do you start? How do you set the pose so that everyone is visible? How do you light them so that the light is still attractive and effective? Somewhere along the way, we are all faced with such a challenge.

Remember the Fundamentals. First and foremost, it is important to remember the fundamentals of lighting and posing. These basics are really not much different for large groups than for individuals or couples. What may be a little more challenging, however, is to capture the relationship that these people have to one another. Whether they are a large family, a club, a group of coworkers, or an orchestra, they are still individuals who must be captured collectively on one frame of film.

Planning and Organization. Preplanning for any sitting is important, but it is absolutely essential with large groups. Preplanning provides you with a wealth of knowledge about what to bring, what is already there, and how you can begin when the people start coming in the door.

When the fateful moment begins, it is extremely important to remember one special aspect—you have to stay in charge! You must be in control of the group at all times because, given a free moment, the subjects will fall into chaotic disorder from which you will not be able to recover.

Groups and Subgroups. One of the first things to consider is the makeup of the group. Are they family members, perhaps posing for a family-reunion photograph? If that is the case, how does the group break into subgroups? Determine this and place them together. Consider the size of each person and how they will come together to create a pleasing composition. Perhaps all the grandchildren should be grouped together rather than with their respective parents.

Establish Planes. Establish one or several "planes" on which to place individuals in the group. These planes will make it simpler for you to finalize your lighting and allow you to include everyone within the camera's range of focus. Sometimes a setting, such as a staircase or a gently sloping hillside, can provide you with a natural organization of planes.

Lighting. In terms of lighting, the same rules apply as to those of conventional portraiture, only on a grand scale. Be aware that your main light must be sufficient to light all of the subjects. I also like to supplement the main light with my bare-bulb strobe, which in some cases may require several strobes to meet the requirements of the entire group. Finally, placement of the accent lights is critical in highlighting the individuals in the group. With the planes of subgroups established, you can use accent lights to add depth and perspective more easily.

There is no question that there are as many ways to make a portrait as there are professional photographers. What I have provided here is designed to give you insight into some of the ways in which I make my most pleasing portraits. You can use these ideas and blend them with those you already know to come up with a distinctive style all your own.

Use these ideas and blend them with those you already know to come up with a distinctive style all your own.

As you read other chapters and sections in this book and study the photographs, I am sure you will be able to use some of my ideas and techniques in your own portrait photography. I am proud of "portrait photography my way," and you should be proud of the way you make portraits too.

3. Dragging the Shutter

Photographers in my classes often ask how I get such well-balanced exposures when using artificial lights (such as electronic flash units) in conjunction with existing or ambient light. The answer is quite simple: I drag the shutter during the exposure. This simply means that when I press the shutter, the flash fires to light the main subject—that is the person or the group I am photographing—and then the shutter stays open for a few seconds longer to let ambient light do its thing for the background or in other areas not lighted by the flash.

THE CONCEPT

Here's the basic concept: the electronic flash is used to light the main subject and draw the viewer's attention to that point; the ambient light, which you record by using the slower shutter speed (longer exposure), sets the mood of the photograph. In effect, the shutter speed governs the tonal qualities of the photograph.

CAMERA AND FLASH SETTINGS

To get the correct exposure when dragging the shutter, all you have to do is make sure the f-stop you select for the shot is balanced with the reading for the background. This means that if the ambient light reading is f11 for three seconds, set the strobes for f11. So, when you press the shutter the aperture will close down to f11, the shutter will stay open for three seconds, and the ambient light will fill in the background and other areas of the setting. However, the ambient light will not be bright enough to detract from the main light by overpowering it. It will act in a supporting role by providing shadow detail and creating the mood. The result is a very natural-looking image.

ADDITIONAL CONSIDERATIONS

Now, while all that *sounds* simple, there are a few things to take into consideration. If you use the following guidelines, you'll soon master dragging the shutter and create the images that have the stamp of professionalism. It's a very useful technique and one that I have used for many years with excellent results.

Even some professionals, who should know better, will sometimes try to get away without using a tripod.

First—and this sounds obvious but it's something beginners often don't do—use a tripod. Even some

FACING PAGE—If you've ever photographed people in a dark room using only a single flash, you know how the image looks: the subjects are illuminated and the background is pitch black. A simple way to combat the dark background is by using a long exposure—dragging the shutter. In this lounge bar scene, the three people were lit with a punch-panel soft box placed high and to the right, while an umbrella at the lens axis was used as a fill light. Four low-wattage (about 150 watts) gelled hot lights were used to illuminate the model's red hair (it matches her dress nicely), the bottles on display, and other areas of the background. A small amount of smoke from a smoke machine was wafted into the set. When the exposure was made (on Kodak Portra 400 negative film, using a Hasselblad camera with a 40mm lens) the aperture was set at f11. After the flash fired, the shutter was held open for about ten to twelve seconds, so the background was illuminated. Obviously, for long exposures like this a tripod is a must, and the models have to remain still.

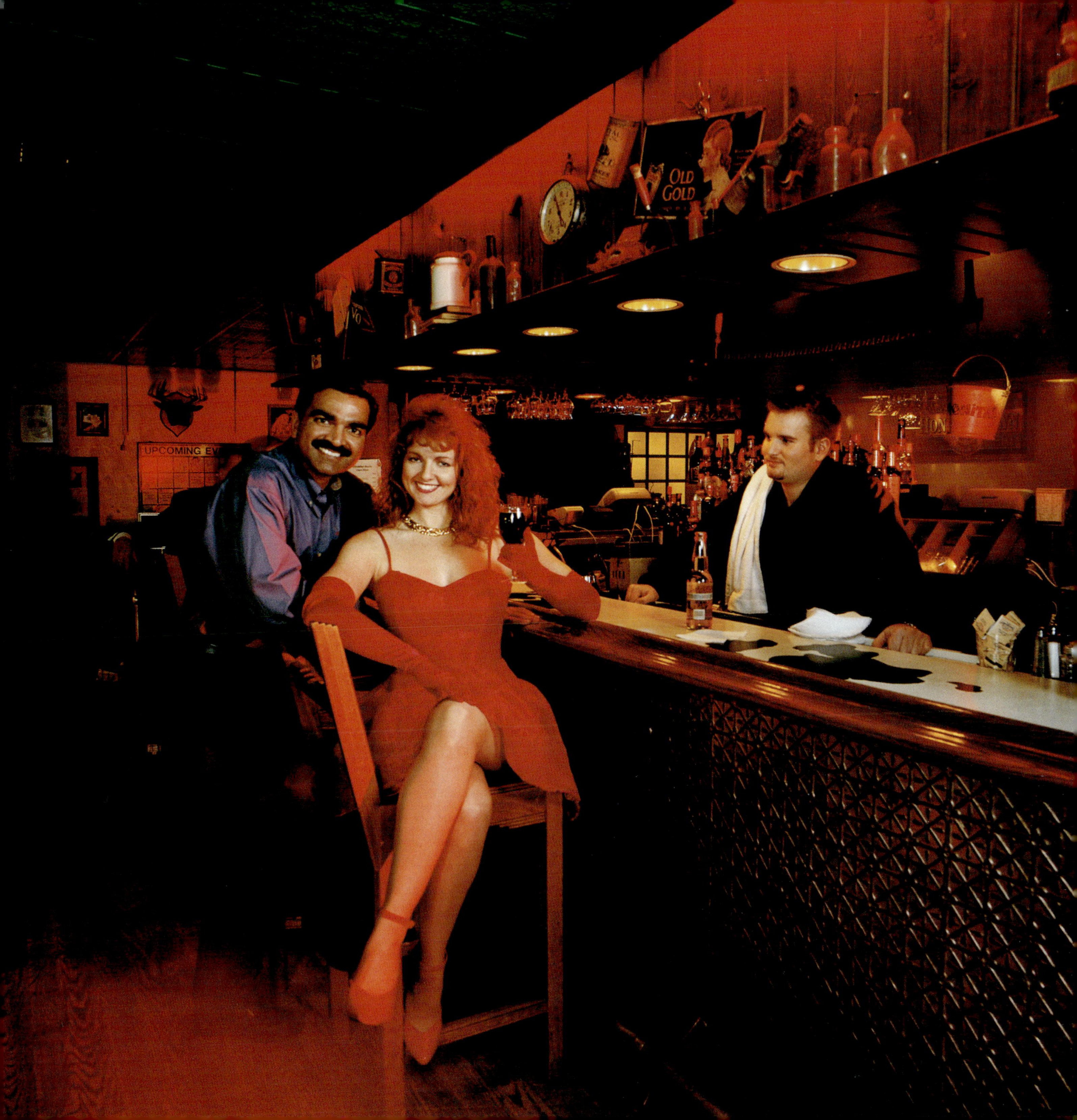
OLD GOLD
UPCOMING

professionals, who should know better, will sometimes try to get away without using a tripod. Of all the tools we have at our disposal, a sturdy tripod is at the top of the list. Invest in a good tripod; you'll never regret it. Also, use a cable release. Here's the sequence I recommend:

- Determine your lighting patterns with the modeling lights on your flash units.
- Meter the background ambient light in several areas and then average the reading. This is a judgment call. One area might be f11 another f8. If you can increase the illumination in the darker area (with a brighter lamp or similar) it can be worth the effort.
- Balance the flash with the background light to make sure the f-stop is the same.
- Turn the modeling lights off. This is very important, because during a long exposure those lights will affect the amount of light on the subject.
- Raise the mirror in your camera. This prevents or minimizes camera movement during the exposure, especially if it's fairly long.

Tell the folks you are photographing that the exposure is going to take a few seconds and they should remain still throughout. Often, people will want to move immediately after the flash fires. There might be times when the exposure is for ten seconds or longer, in which case making sure your subjects stay very still is even more important. This works better for adults; it's pretty hard to keep children or pets still for that long.

Tell the folks you are photographing that the exposure is going to take a few seconds and they should remain still throughout.

BALANCING FLASH WITH AMBIENT DAYLIGHT

The same technique can be used when balancing your flash with daylight. For example, if you are photographing somebody inside a room and want to record detail in the outside scene, the shutter speed will determine the correct exposure for the exterior. Once you have selected an f-stop for the photograph and set your flash accordingly, say f11, select the shutter speed that will give you the desired exposure for the scene outside—it might be in the vicinity of f11 at $^{1}/_{125}$ second. You can vary the exposure for the outside scene (you might want it brighter or darker) by varying the shutter speed. And please, use that tripod.

4. Add a Touch of Warmth

As photographers, we often have to use supplementary lights to enhance the available or ambient light. In an outdoor setting, the light is influenced by numerous factors, like an abundance of ultraviolet light reflecting off the surrounding foliage or green grass. You should always be aware that the color of the surrounds *does* influence what happens on film. While our eyes adjust so that everything appears normal and without color shifts, film is not as discerning.

FILTRATION

One of the most common things we have to do is warm up the light, and that usually means putting on filters or gels (depending on what lighting aids we are using). For years, when I was faced with that situation, I used color correcting filters—often the CR3, a warming filter that saved the day for me on hundreds of occasions. It is an excellent filter and proved an invaluable tool for me during my career.

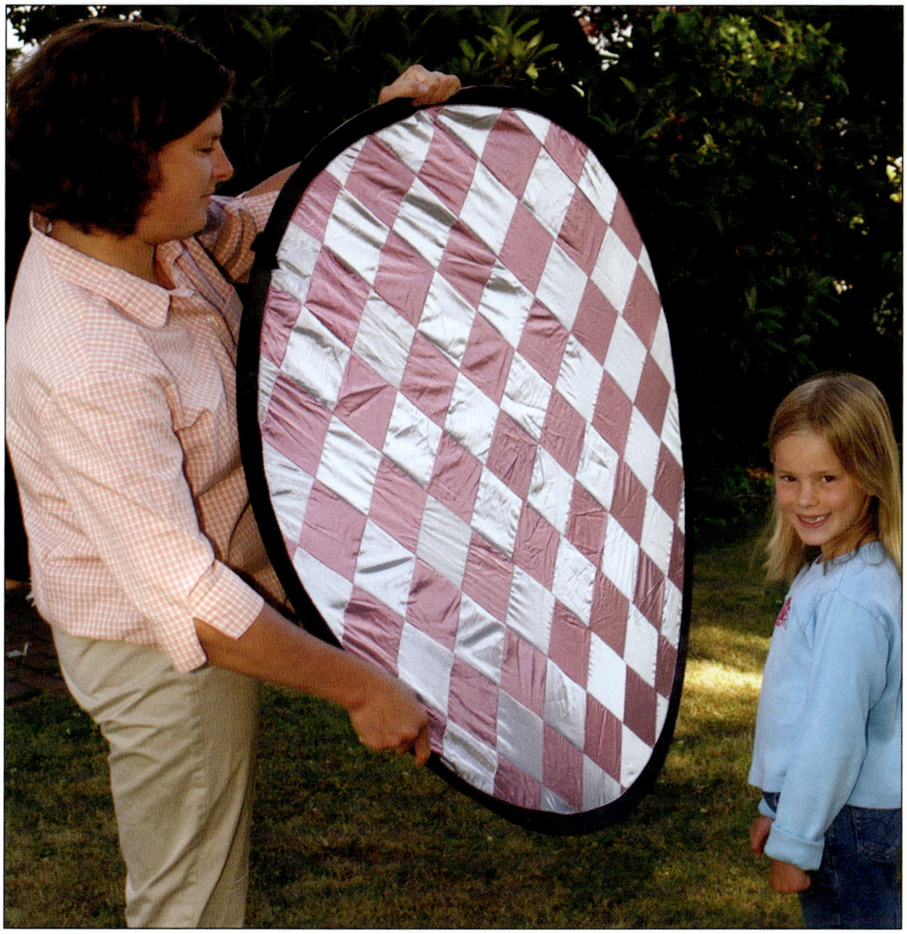

The touch-of-warmth reflector adds a slight bit of warming to your image. Photograph by Peter Skinner.

TOUCH-OF-WARMTH REFLECTORS

I have found something, however, that works even better in most situations than the good old CR3 filter. It is the touch-of-warmth reflector. Now, like filters, reflectors have been around for many years and most photographers have one or more in their kits. White, silver, and gold are very popular and I have used them all. However—and I know choice of reflectors is a personal thing and depends on the effect you want—I have found that the silver reflector tends to be a bit hard or harsh for my liking. And, similarly, the gold reflector tends to give a yellowish look that I don't really like.

I have found the ideal solution is the touch-of-warmth reflector, a reflector that has a grid pattern of magenta and silver squares. It's ideal outdoors, in the studio, and when using window lighting. It warms up the subject nicely but almost unnoticeably. Of course, the CR3 filter did the same thing, but it also affected the whole portrait scene, not just the subject. Used correctly, the touch-of-warmth reflector provides a delicate warm light on the subject but does not influence the look of the natural light that falls on the rest of the scene.

The touch-of-warmth reflector provides a delicate warm light on the subject but not the rest of the scene.

ANGLE OF REFLECTOR

When using a reflector, angle it (or feather it) so the light skims the subject and is not simply directed straight back onto the subject. It should do more than simply fill in shadows; it should enhance and supplement the existing light. Tip the reflector so the light wraps around the subject.

5. *Metering with Confidence*

The light meter for measuring flash or ambient light is a vital tool, and it's one that absolutely every professional photographer should master and have complete confidence in using. The following pointers will help you develop your expertise in metering technique so you will get the most consistent results.

The bright background, with a reading of about f16, outlines the form of this model on a bench (an Off the Wall product). Light from a bare-bulb flash was balanced with the background ambience. A touch-of-warmth reflector provided an added highlight that completed the delightful image. The simplicity of the background, the delicate posing of the model's hands, and the way she leans to the right are also key elements.

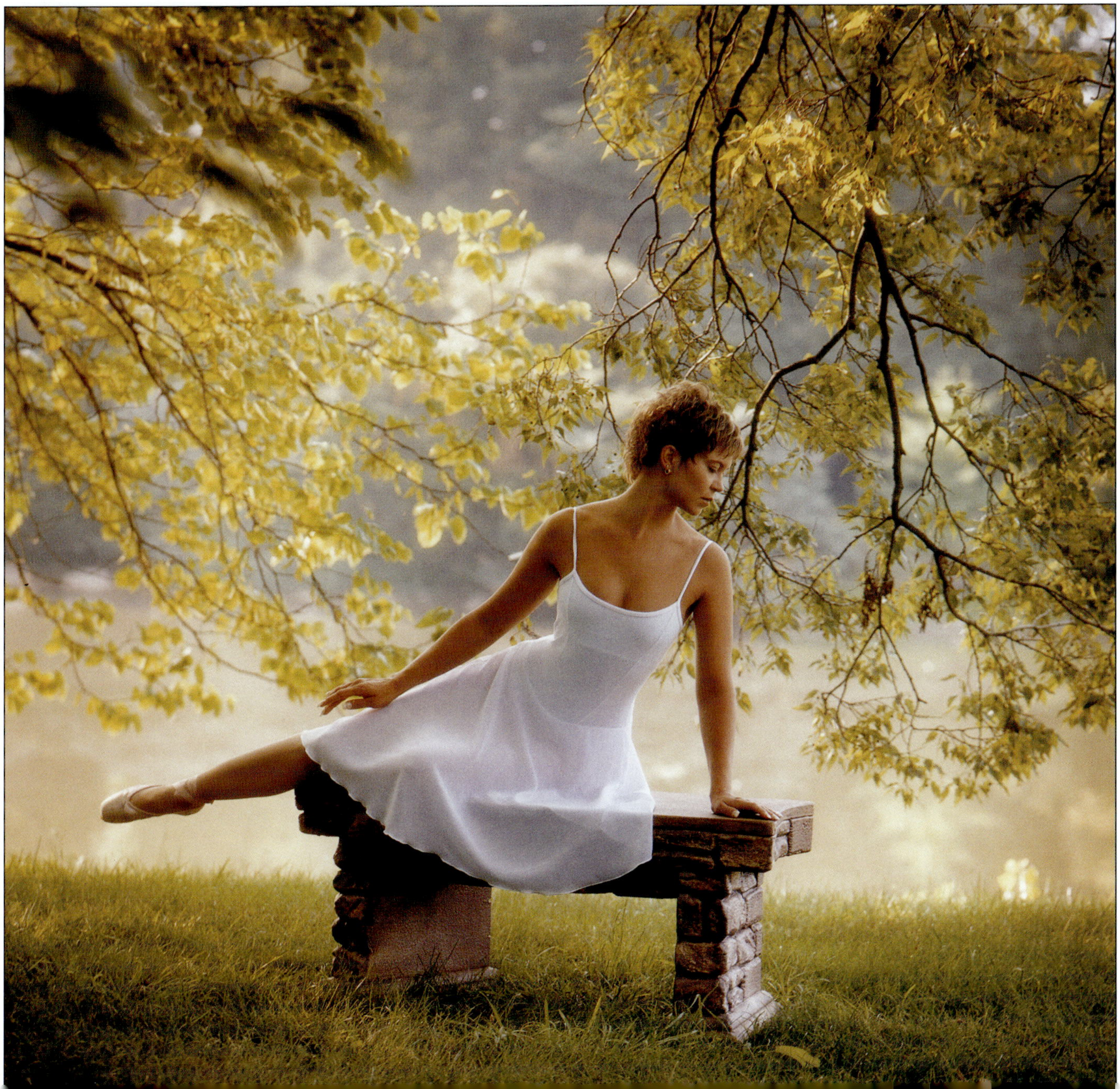

SETUP SEQUENCE

Typically, you will be using several lights. I start building my lighting set with the fill light because I like to see what effect it is having and what detail I can see in the shadow side. My lighting sequence goes like this: Fill light, main light, accent light, hair light, background light.

METERING IN THE STUDIO

I measure each light individually by placing the flash meter at the subject's face and directing the meter at the light itself. (Usually, this will be done before your subject arrives, so everything will be in place beforehand.) The typical exposure for the main light will be around f11½, and from that you can set the power of the other lights to get the ratio you want.

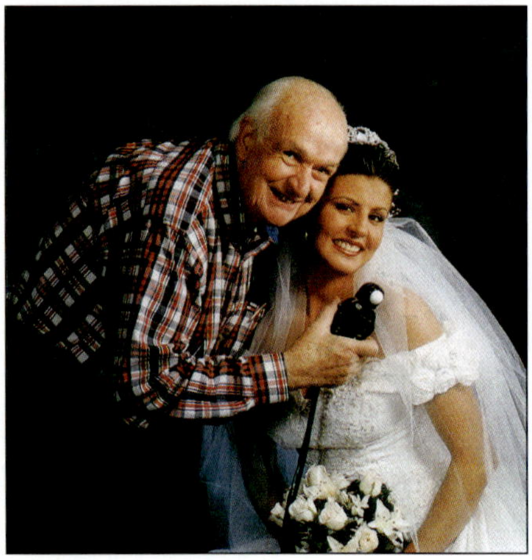

The meter is placed at the subject's face and pointed at the camera.

Eventually you will become very familiar with the power from your lighting sources so you will know instinctively what exposure you will be getting, but always use the meter to make sure. In a typical setup, the main light might read f11½; the fill light f8; the hair light f8; the accent light, f8½; and the background light f8. The hair light and background light should be the same f-stop as the fill light so they provide separation from the background. Be careful not to make the hair lights so powerful that you lose detail in the highlights.

Once you have metered each light separately, pointing the meter at the light, then meter with all the lights on, pointing the meter at the lens.

These guidelines will give you an idea of what you will be looking for. Above all, remember to feather the light so you are working with the edge of the light and not simply blasting your subject with light.

OUTDOORS

When working outdoors, I spot meter right from the camera and have found this to be the most reliable and accurate method. If your camera has a built-in spot meter, that should work.

First, I meter the background area to make sure I am in the ballpark with a reading of, say, f11. I then meter the shadow side of the subject—let's say it's f5.6. Since I am usually trying to work with a 4:1 ratio, this means I will want the highlight side of the subject's face to read 1½ f-stops brighter, about f8.5. (A ratio of 3:1, which would be 1-stop difference between the highlight side and shadow side, will work just fine too. In fact, the 3:1 ratio is one that film manufacturers really love because they know that is the ideal ratio to give rich detail on both highlight and shadow side. The 4:1 and higher ratios do, however, give a more dramatic look.)

6. Harnessing the Versatility of the Bare Bulb

Often overlooked by photographers is the simple, effective lighting that we can create with the bare bulb on the electronic flash unit. Over the years I have made the bare bulb one of the most important tools in my lighting arsenal. It can be used on location as a main light, an accent light, a fill light, or simply as an overall supple-

The zoom effect of the Lindahl filter draws the viewer to the vivid yellow dress and hat of this model in a field of yellow flowers. The image was made near a highway in Texas, where Don climbed a ladder to achieve this elevated view. Ambient light was supplemented with the scattered light of a bare bulb that opened up the shadows under the model's hat without being obvious.

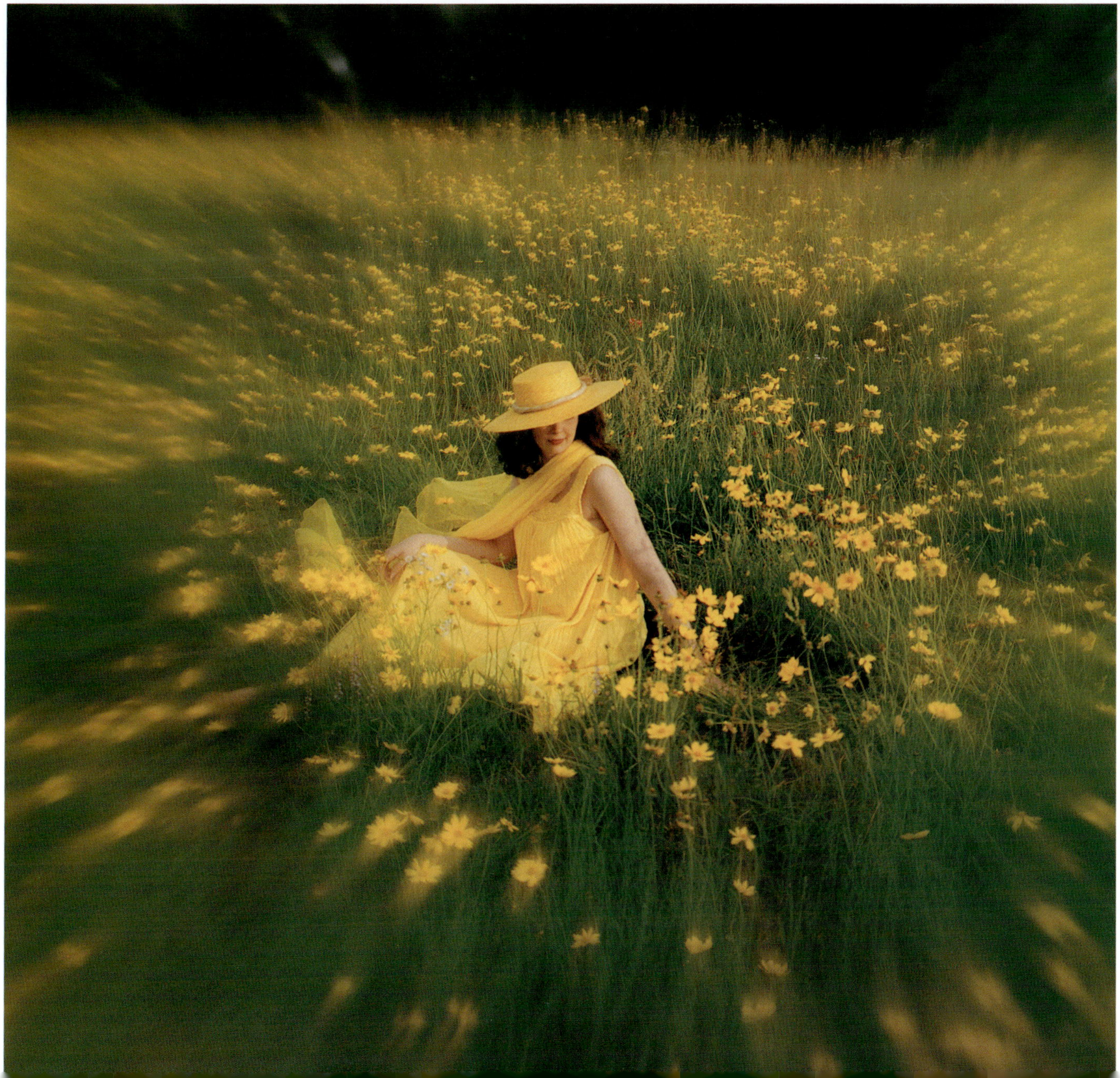

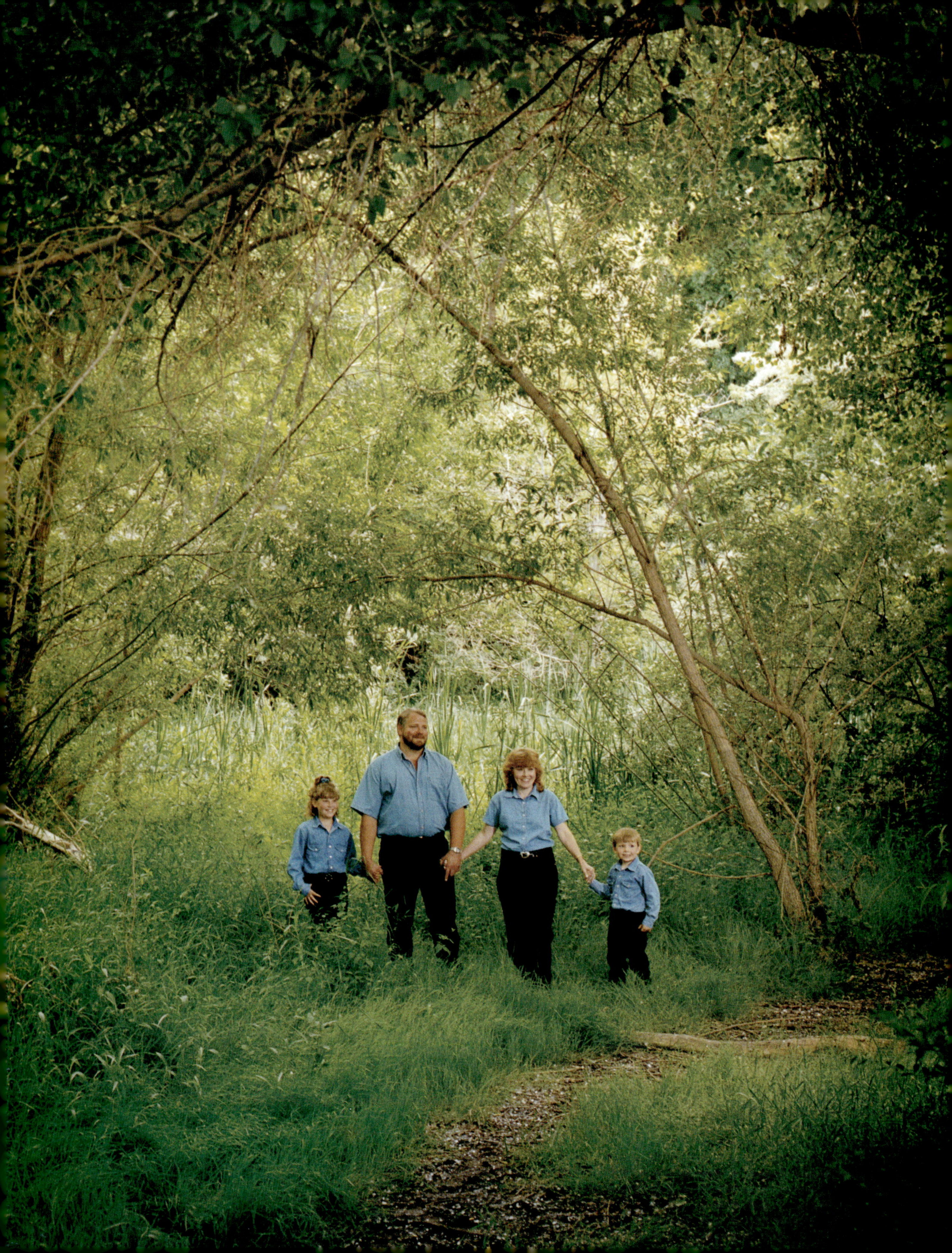

FACING PAGE—This family portrait was lit with a combination of natural light sources, which served as the background and separation light, and a bare-bulb flash. The key to using bare bulb is to have the flash tube vertical for one or two people, but turn it horizontally for larger groups to take advantage of the wider angle of light coverage.

mentary light to brighten the entire scene. Used correctly, the bare bulb gives a very natural look to the photograph, adding specularity and punch—an extra burst of light that can turn a nice picture into a beautiful portrait.

AVOIDING RACCOON EYES

Among the advantages of using the bare bulb is that it helps us avoid those dark shadows under the eyes—what I refer to as raccoon eyes. This is something to be avoided, and the touch of light from a well-placed bare bulb will solve the problem easily. The key is not to place the light too high, just high enough to add light under the subject's eyes. If you use modeling lights, you can see the effect. As a test, raise and lower the light and watch the shadow effect under the subject's nose and eyes. You will soon see the pitfalls of raising the light too high.

OUTDOORS

The bare bulb can also be used in conjunction with different focal length lenses and, thus, is useful for both environmental portraits with a pictorial approach, where the location sets the mood, as well as for traditional portraits.

Battery Pack. On location I usually use a battery pack to power the lighting unit, and this adds to its versatility. Obviously, if you don't have an electronic flash that can run off a battery pack, you will need to be near a source of electricity. That can be a bit limiting, but not impossible. Just make sure you take long power cords with you when going on location. But if you plan on using your electronic flash units outdoors a lot—and the chances are you will—the battery pack is a good investment. (If you are on location and using a battery-powered light, be careful of draining the battery; modeling lights drain power quickly.)

Bare Bulb as the Main Light. In an outdoor situation where the

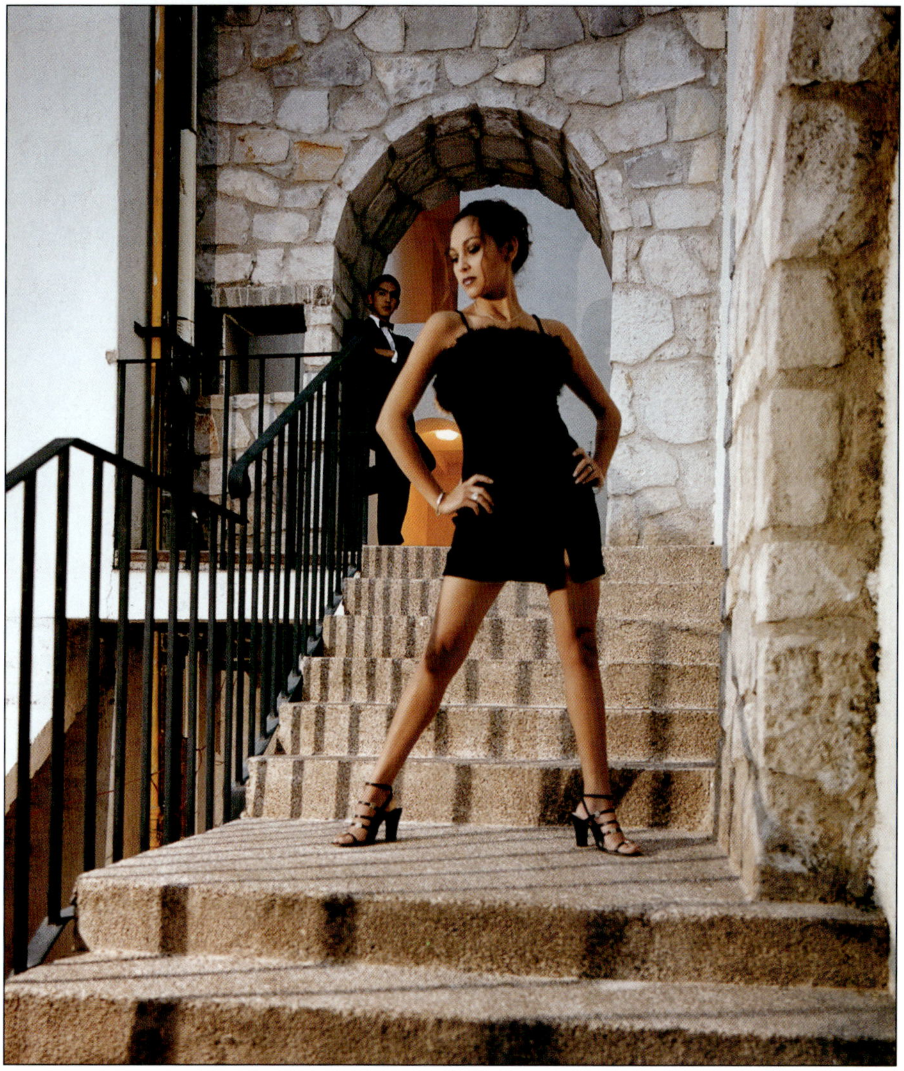

A bare-bulb flash, elevated on a pole to the left, highlighted the model's right side and supplemented the natural, ambient light that swept across the setting, adding shape and texture to this portrait made on location in Mexico. The man in the background was lit by ambient light only. Note how the woman is dynamically framed against the archway.

bare bulb will be the main light, it must be placed so the light it throws will come from the same direction as existing daylight—and please note that I said *daylight*, not *sunlight*. Direct sunlight, unless it's late in the day when it becomes softer, tends to be too harsh and unflattering for portraiture. If direct, harsh sunlight is influencing the photograph, move to a new location or wait until the light is less intense.

After placing the bare bulb (usually about ten feet from the subject) and making sure it's tucked away out of sight, spot meter the shadow side of the subject's face. This will determine the exposure we want. For example, the reading might be f5.6 at $^1/_{15}$ second. With a flash meter, set the power on the bare bulb for f5.6. This will be the key light, and its purpose is to add punch to the existing daylight. Trust me, it will do just that. As mentioned previously, I would also suggest you turn the modeling light on so you can see the effect created by the bare bulb—but be sure to turn it off before making the exposure. With the relatively slow shutter speed, the modeling lights could affect the exposure.

After you have checked all the above, finalize the subject's pose and make the photograph.

The exposure mentioned above is just an example. In some cases, when you're in a brighter location, the ambient reading might be something like f8 at $^1/_{125}$ second, so you would have to adjust exposure accordingly. The bare bulb is very effective in brighter light, so don't feel you have to limit it just to low-light situations.

Balancing Flash with Daylight. There will be times when you will want to balance the ambient light outdoors with a subject under a canopy or something similar. The goal will be to make a portrait and also show the surrounding environment as it appears. Therefore, you will want to balance the light on the subject under the canopy with the surrounding ambient light. The bare bulb is an ideal light source in this situation.

To balance the flash with daylight, take a meter reading of the ambient light, which might be f11 at $^1/_{25}$ second. With a flash meter, read the amount of light that is being thrown from the bare bulb source onto the subject's face and balance it with the ambient f-stop (here, f11). In this situation, where the subject is under a canopy, make sure the bare bulb is positioned low enough to throw light onto the subject. You can use the modeling light to check that this is the case, as

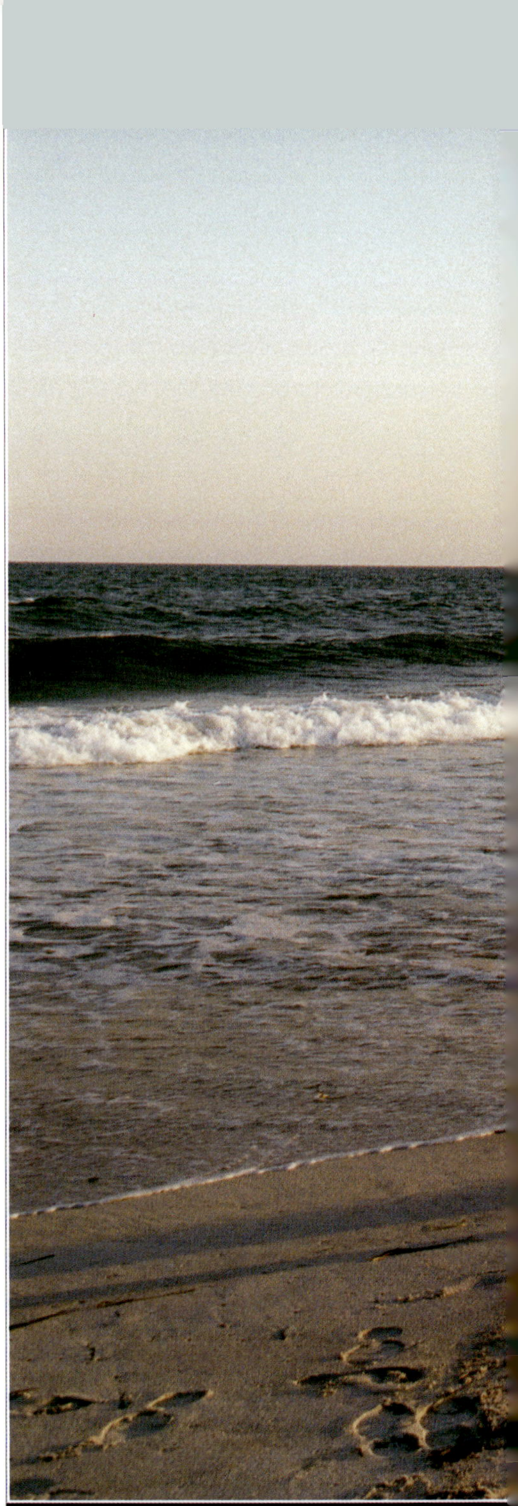

A gentle ocean breeze on Long Island, New York, and late afternoon light enhance this image. A bare-bulb flash with the tube in a vertical position and placed about ten feet from the model added a specular highlight to her arms and shoulders. Don balanced the flash output with the ambient light for an aperture of around f5.6.

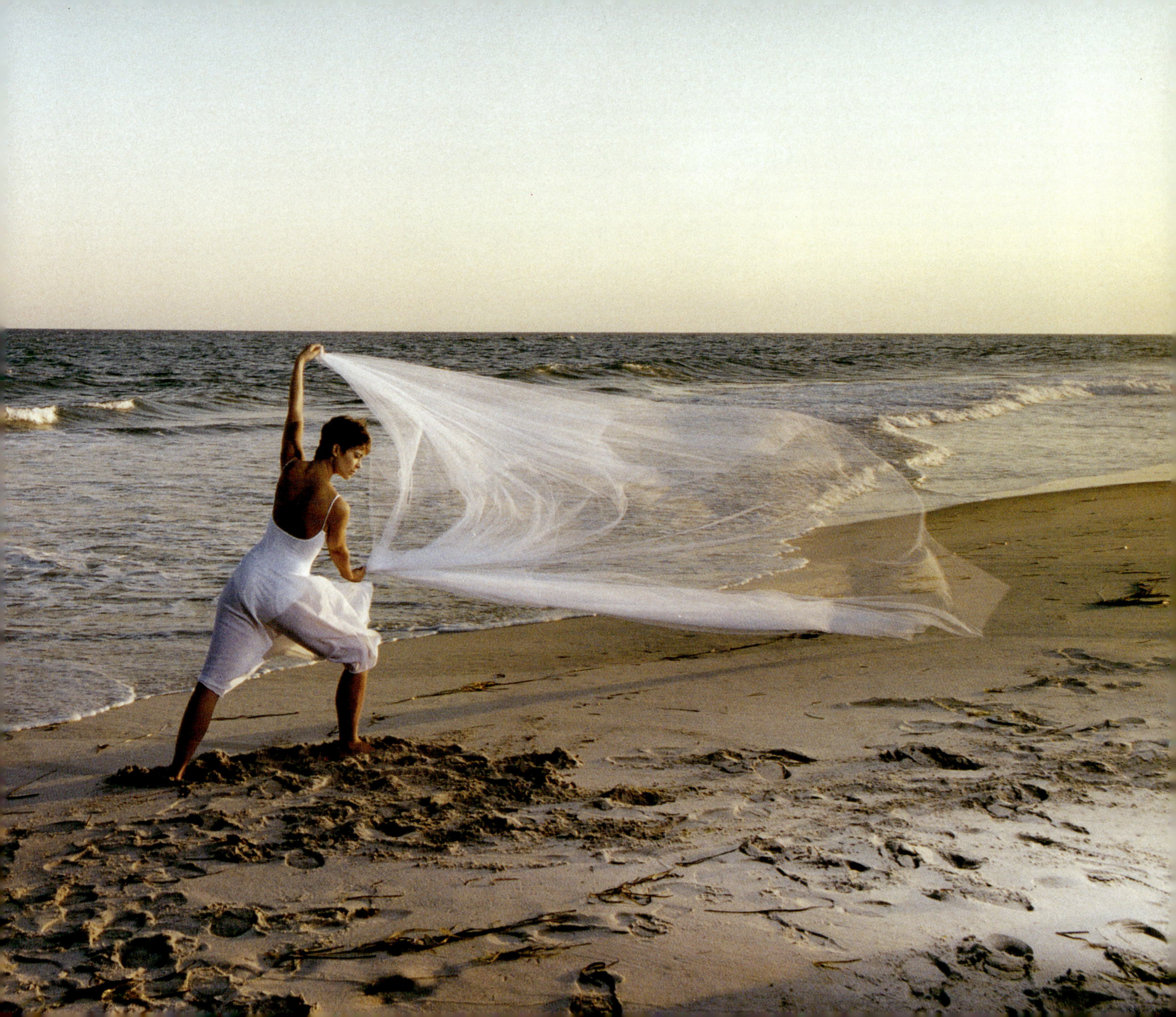

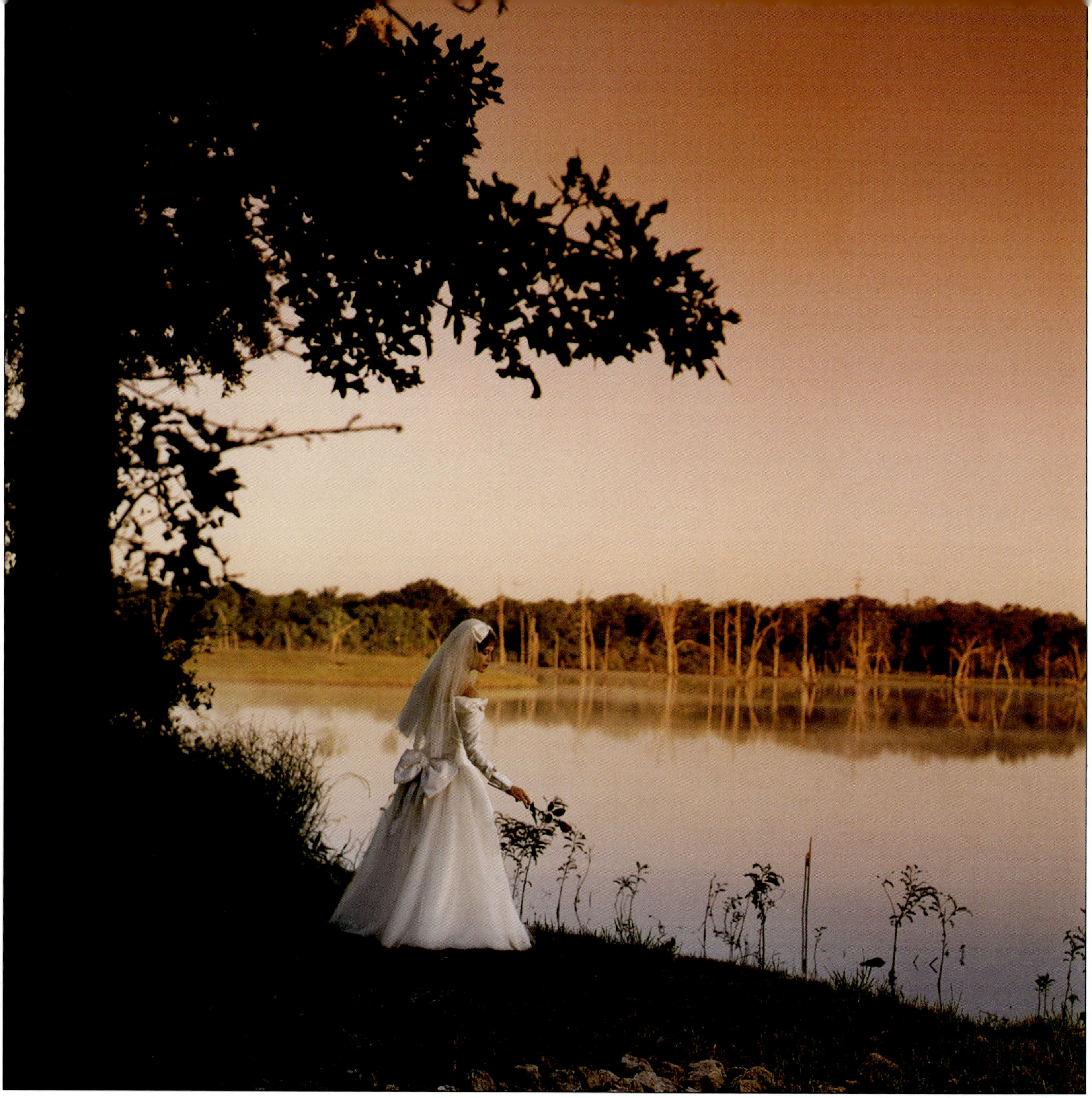

Note the delicate detail and texture in the bride's dress in this early-morning lakeside shoot at Texas A & M College. A touch of light from a bare bulb on the right, near the edge of the lake, was all that was needed to turn what would've been a nice environmental portrait into a beautiful image.

well as to study the lighting pattern that is created on the subject's face. Again, you must be sure that you turn the modeling light off during the exposure.

This technique is quite easy to implement and very effective for a variety of situations. Keep in mind that it's important that the light from the flash look natural and not be overpowering.

INDOORS

One of the great attractions of the bare bulb is its wraparound effect. This makes it a very useful light for portraiture indoors, such as when photographing an executive on location. For such assignments, additional lighting, such as an accent light, will also generally be used. Often, I will drag the shutter to let ambient light set the mood.

Setting up to use the bare bulb indoors is not too different from using it outdoors in an environmental setting. It can be even more convenient, since handy power sources mean that you can use the modeling lights as much as you like, previewing the effect on the subject and then metering the light. If you are using a slower shutter speed, or are dragging the shutter, turn the modeling lights off when making your exposure.

There are many other advantages to using a bare bulb, and I encourage you to master the technique of using it. It really is a versatile light, and once you understand how to use it effectively, it's also one of the simplest. There's a lot to be said for keeping things simple, and if you can make great portraits simply, so much the better. While I caution against making it your principal lighting source for all occasions (if you become a one-light-source photographer, all your photographs will look the same), don't hesitate to use these bare-bulb techniques to brighten up a scene or add punch to ambient lighting.

While teaching at the Winona School in Atlanta, Georgia, Don took a group of photographers to this delightful setting in the swimming pool area of a hotel. A single bare bulb balanced beautifully with ambient light to illuminate the model framed within the poolside gazebo. Bare bulb is a very forgiving light source and can be used either as fill or accent or as the main light depending on the amount of ambient light.

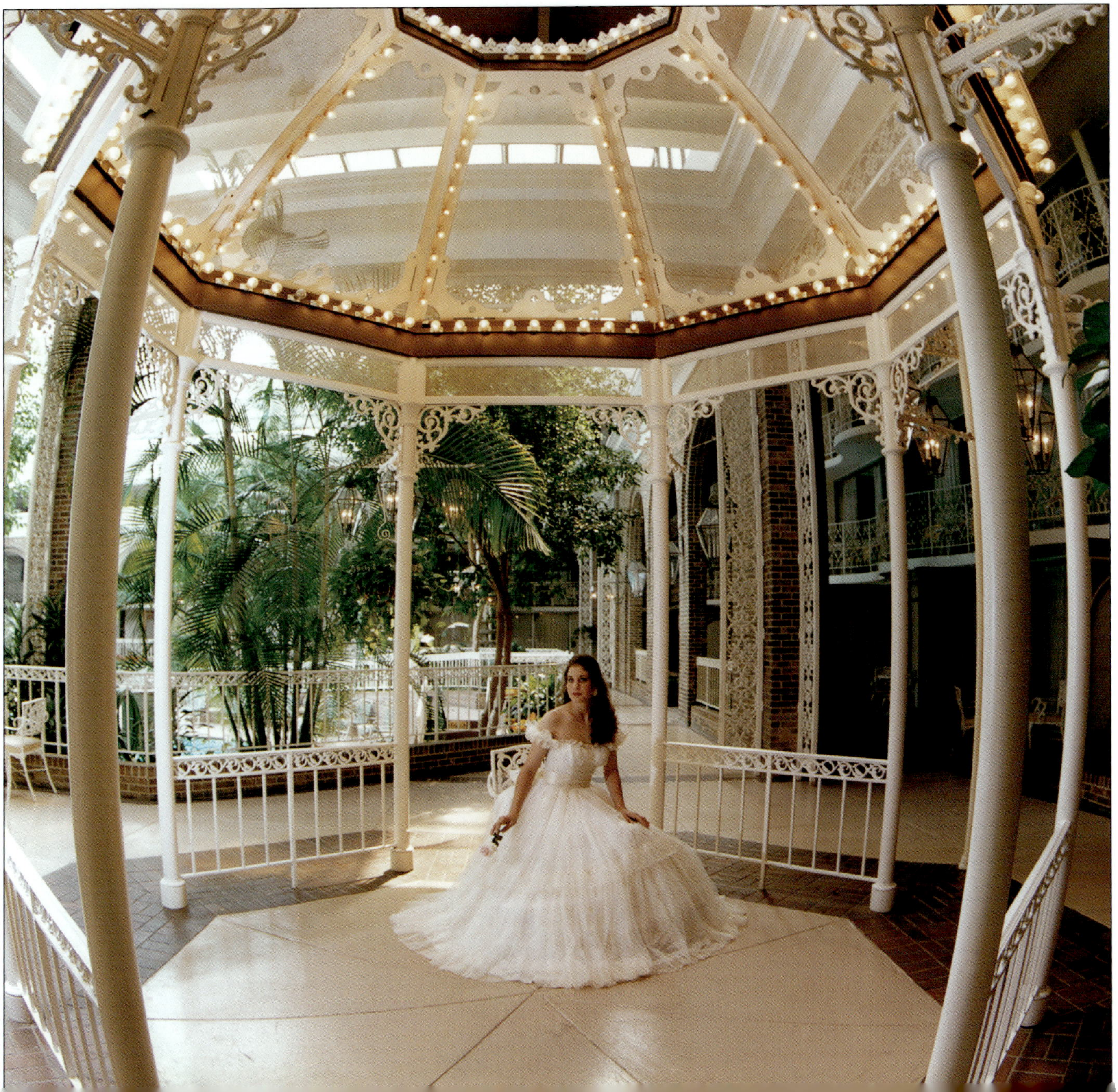

7. Punch-Panel Light

One of the most useful lighting tools for location portraits, and one that I really like when the location or setting is a strong supporting element of the image, is the punch-panel light. This is simply a 17-inch soft box with an interior panel of material that has a 7½-inch oval cut out of the center.

This means that the light on the edges is diffused through two layers of material (the interior panel and the front panel of the soft box), while the center of the light passes through only one diffuser and thus is one f-stop brighter than the edges. This gives us a beautiful, very natural-looking feathering, or falloff, of light.

I refer to this unit as a punch panel, because as the light is directed through that oval cutout section, it is basically "punching" light onto the central subject. As a result, the viewer's attention is immediately drawn to the brightest—and most important—element of the photograph: the main subject.

SHADOW DETAIL

After being drawn initially to the subject, the viewers' eyes should wander around the image, taking in other details. Our goal is to create images that highlight the main subject and also provide sufficient detail or information in the supplementary elements to command the viewer's attention. This means that shadow detail is a vital aspect of portrait photography, whether the shadow falls on part of a person's face or in the environment of the setting itself. That's one of the reasons that I warn photographers to be careful of overlighting. Blasting too much light into a picture is something to be avoided.

EXPOSURE

When determining the exposure with the punch panel, I spot meter the center section of the image and then read the edges to make sure there is about a 1-stop difference.

I also meter the ambient light, that is, the light from room lights or other sources, and then set the shutter speed on the camera to ensure correct exposure. Usually, this will be a fairly long exposure—often in the vicinity of two or three seconds—and requires dragging the shutter. The result is a balance between the ambient and artificial light.

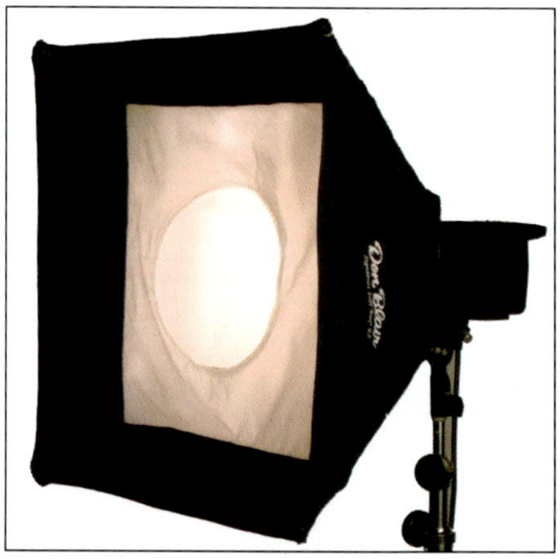

Punch panel.

One big advantage of dragging the shutter, allowing ambient light to illuminate the background and fill in the shadows, is that it eliminates having to use too many lights. When on location, I often use just one punch-panel light source in combination with ambient light, and the results are beautiful. When in a studio setting, I usually employ other units for fill, background, hair, and accent lights.

I encourage you to incorporate a punch-panel light into your standard location lighting kit. It's a beautiful, very controllable and consistent form of lighting—and the natural-looking falloff from the center to the edges ensures that the viewer's attention goes to the main subject first.

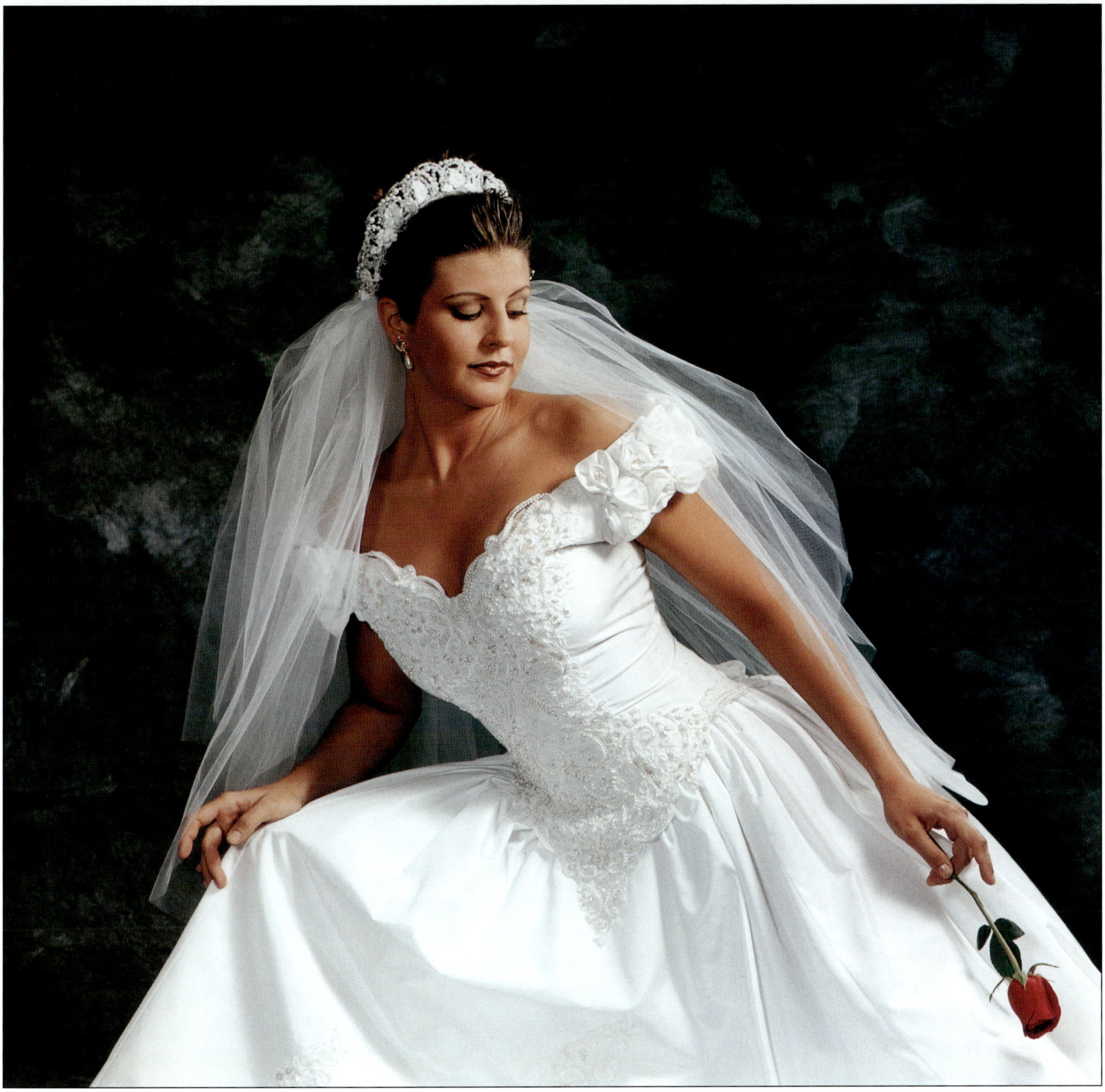

The beautiful light from the punch panel enhanced this delicately posed bridal portrait. Note the detail in the bride's gown and veil, captured by the direction of the light. A feeling of motion was created by having the bride lean to the left, while her outstretched left arm followed the line of her body. The gently held rose is an ideal complementary element.

ABOUT THE PHOTOS IN THIS CHAPTER

While the main light for all the portraits in this chapter was a punch panel, it was used in conjunction with other supplementary lights. In the studio, I always use an umbrella fill at the lens axis to provide shadow detail, and usually incorporate additional lights, such as an accent or garlic, a hair light, and, on occasion, a background light.

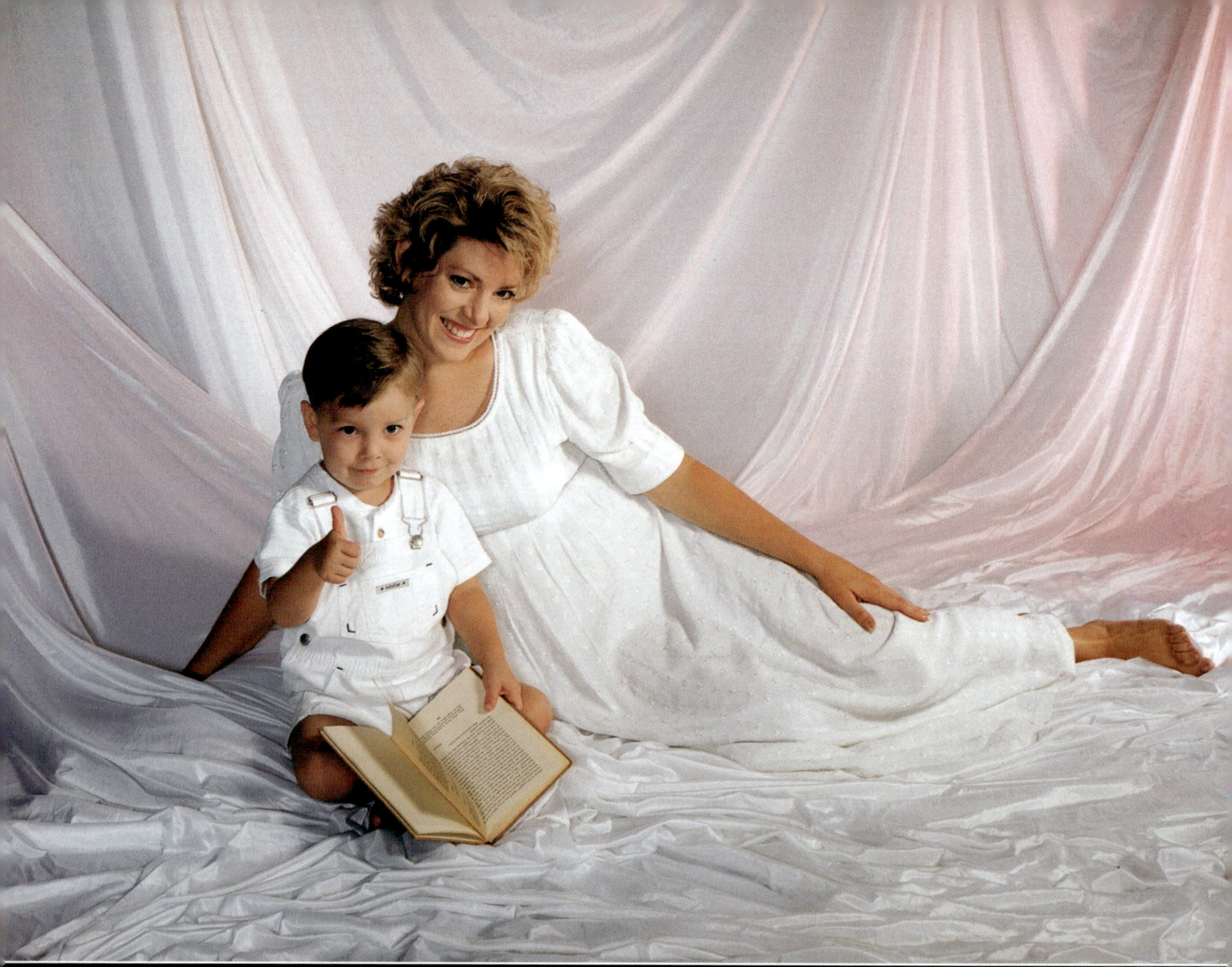

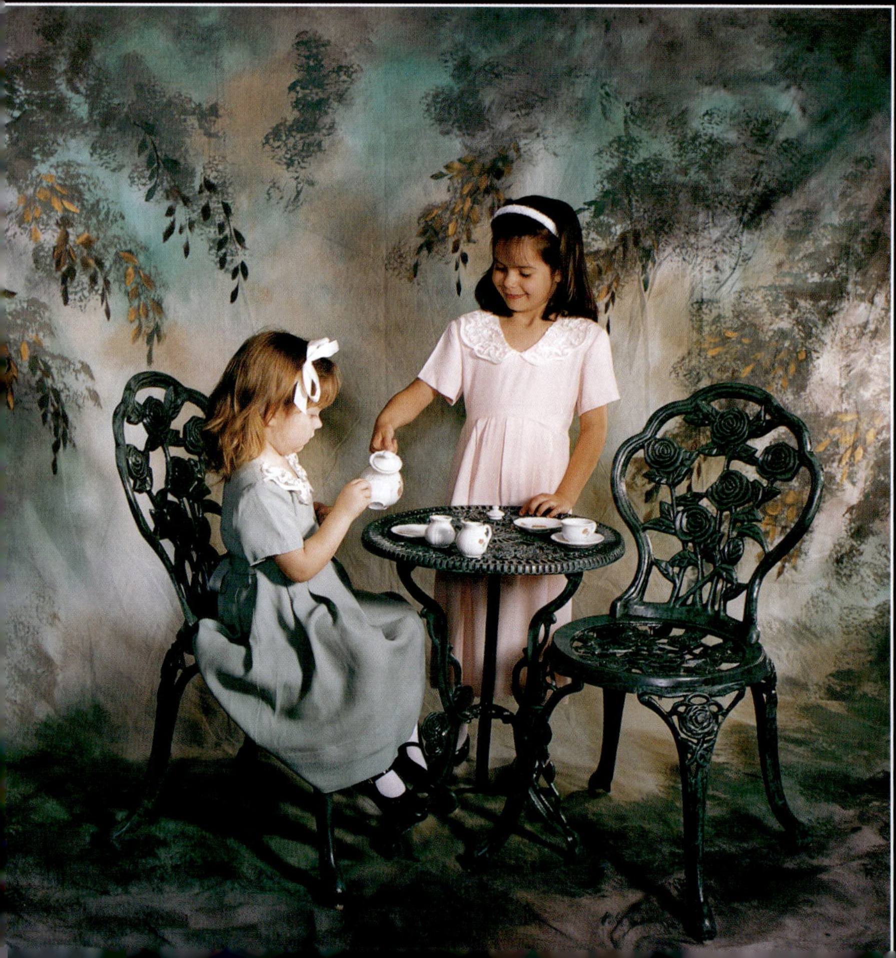

ABOVE—Thumbs up! Four lights were usec in this studio image of mother and son. A punch panel, set at f11½, provided the main illumination, while a fill light at f8 ensured shadow detail was held. A warming gel was used on the backgrounc light, and the set was completed with ar accent light that highlighted the duo's hai and gave separation. The rappor between the young boy and the photographer is evidenced by the "thumbs up."

LEFT—This outdoor setting in the studic was lit with the punch panel, and the falloff light effectively draws us to the center of the image, where the young gir is pouring tea for her companion. A background light separated the pair from the painted backdrop, while an accent light on the same side as the main light, highlighted their hair. The delightful setting has more than a little humor—the seated girl's little legs are not quite long enough tc reach the floor! And it's obvious the girls were suitably attired for the occasion.

Punch panel lighting and soft focus combined to give an ethereal feel to this appealing portrait of a bride. The delicate pose of the hands, the tilt of the shoulders, and the bride's demure expression contributed to the success of this image. The base density was determined by the fill light, while an accent light, placed on the same side as the main light, added sparkle to the bride's beaded headpiece.

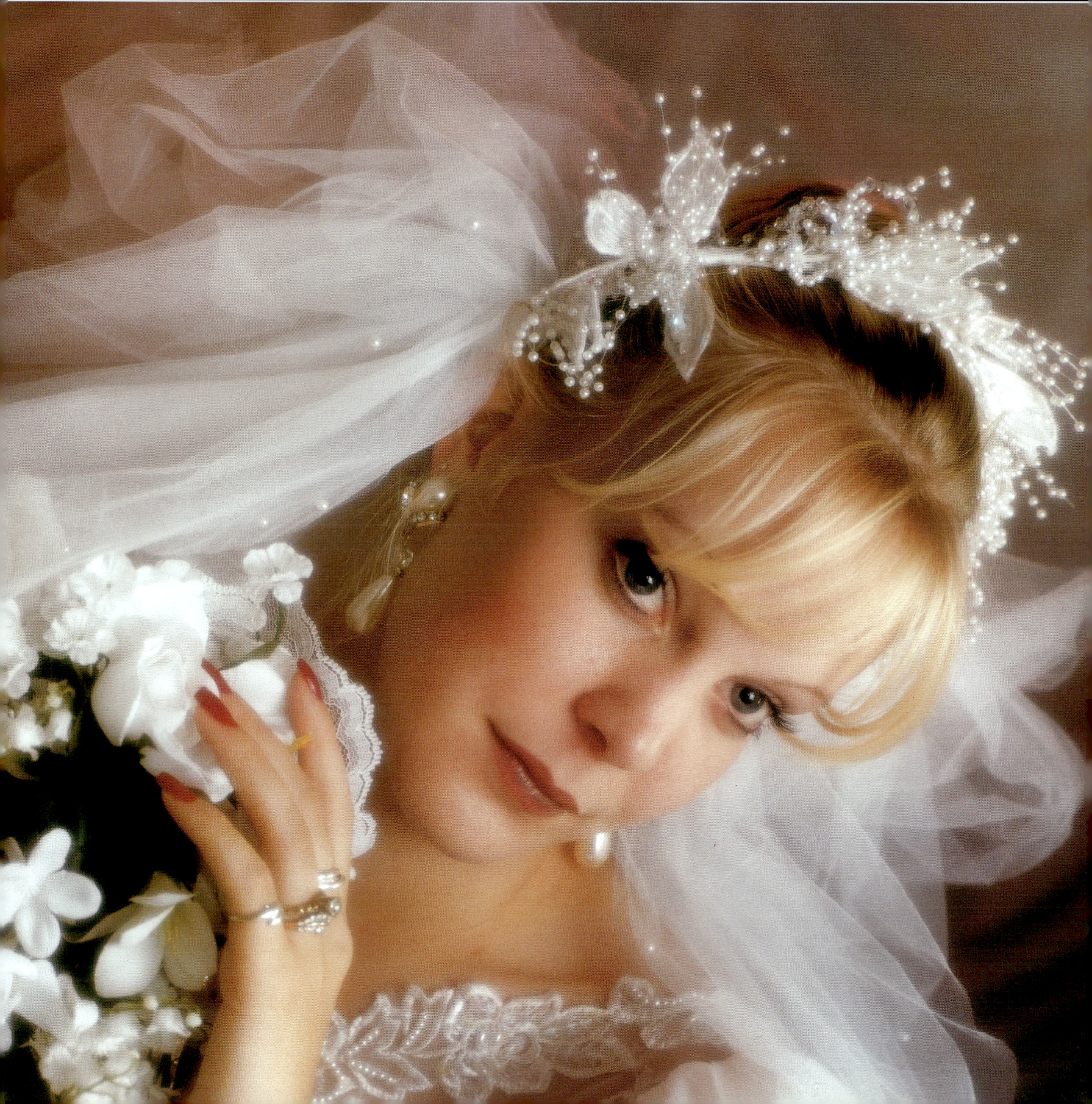

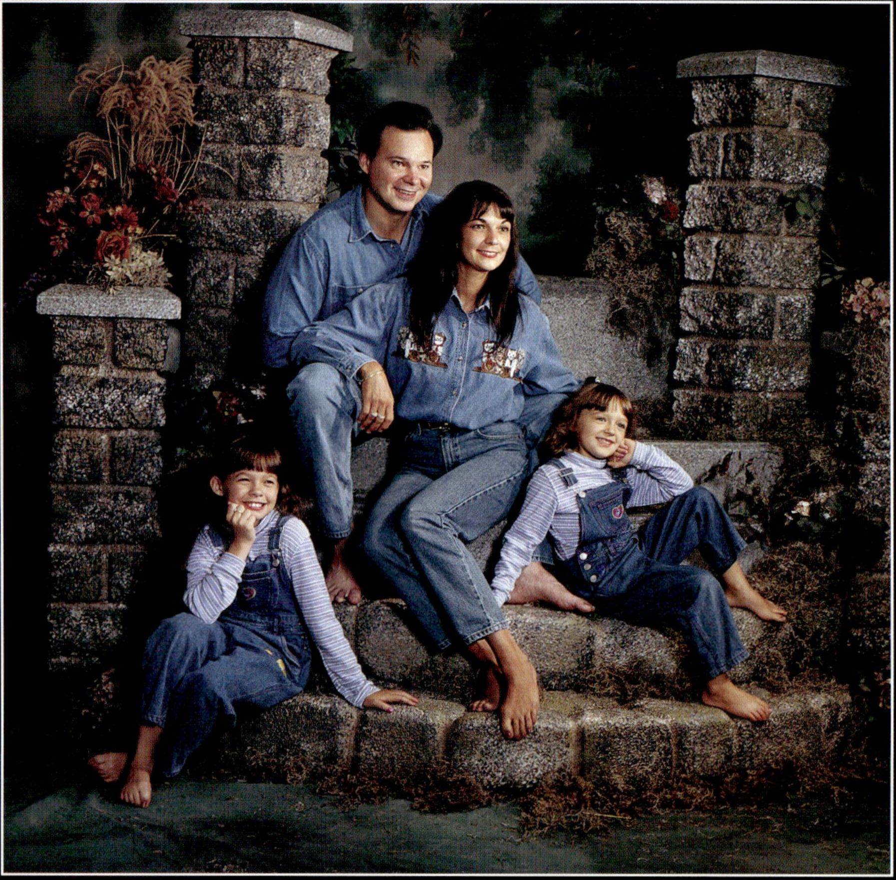

The way in which light falls off at the edges, drawing the viewer's attention to the central area of the photograph, makes punch-panel lighting ideal for group portraits such as this, made on an Off the Wall prop. The careful selection of clothes (by Mom, who wanted the family to look just right) is a unifying element. The wraparound lighting gives shape and texture to the family's bare feet and hands.

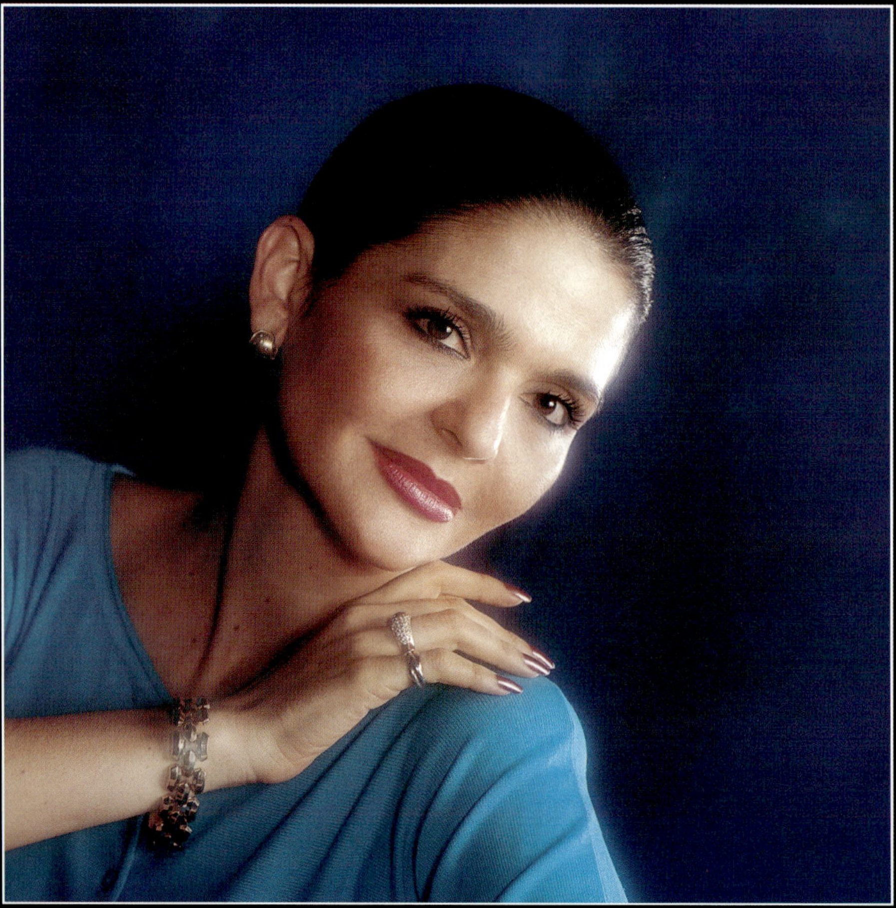

This classic portrait of an elegant woman was made in Villa Hermosa, Mexico. Don used a punch panel as the main light while his well-known garlic light provided just enough of an accent to outline the model's hair and shoulder. The graceful lines of the woman's hand and slightly separated fingers illustrate the importance of careful attention to hand posing.

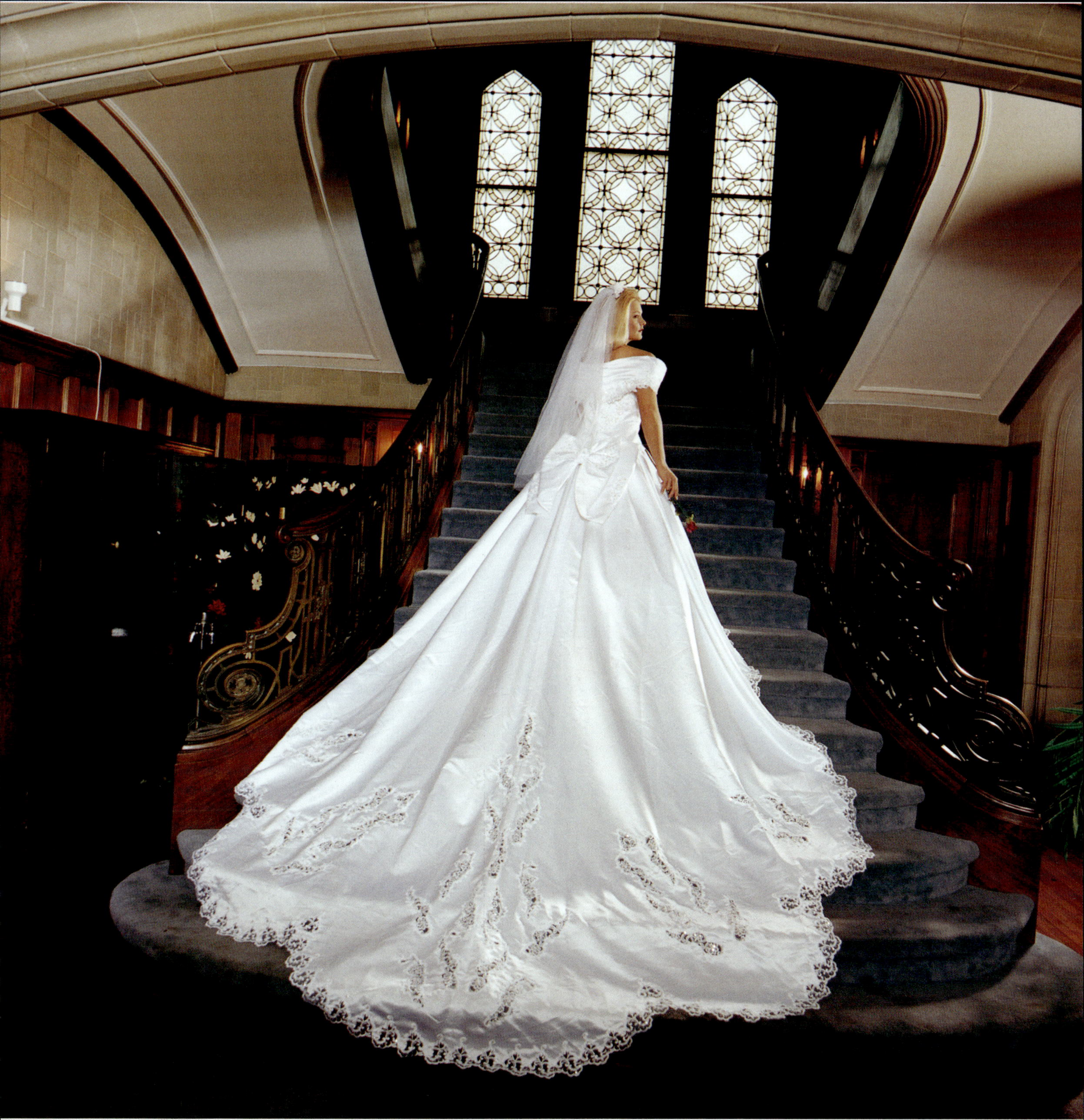

Depth of field, the fall of light to the edges, the flowing line of the gown and staircase, and the wonderful triangular composition (the staircase and window give an hourglass-like shape) are key to the impact of this shot. Note the beautiful texture and detail in the bride's sweeping train and how it was carefully draped over each step, further enhancing its flow and design. An accent light touched the edges of the gown, as well as the bride's shoulder and arm, and a slow shutter speed of about 1/15 second allowed the ambient light to contribute some shadow detail.

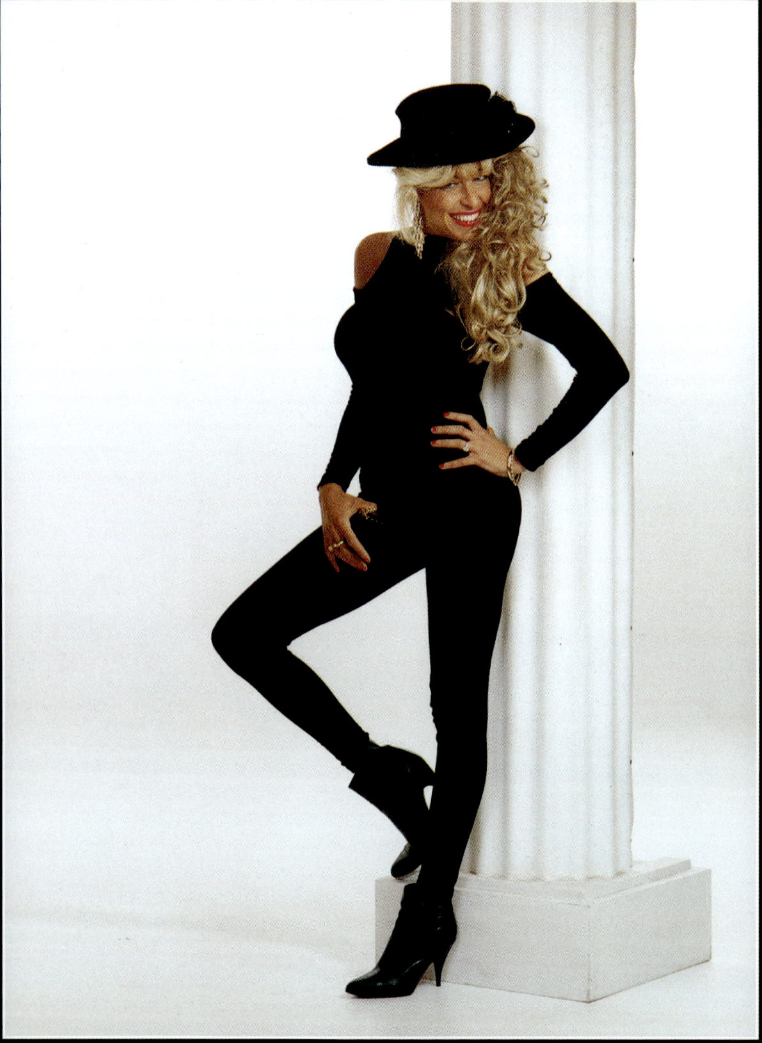

This high-key portrait of a black-clad model flirting with the camera shows the versatility of punch-panel lighting. The model's outfit adds contrast to the high-key scene, and Don points out that the background light for this look should be one f-stop brighter than the main light—sufficient to make it brighter but not burned out.

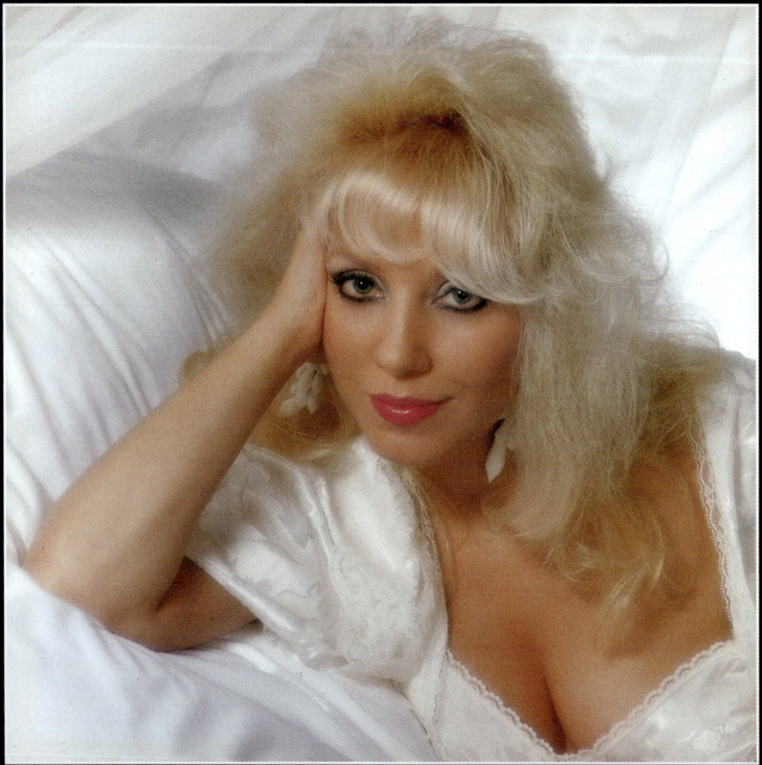

White on white can be a tricky combination to light. The key to success, in addition to accurate exposure, is to place the main light at an angle to the camera. That way, its direction ensures that the light wraps around the subject and enhances the shape and texture. In this soft-focus portrait, both the punch panel and accent light were to the left, while an umbrella fill at the lens axis gently filled in the shadow areas. A background light separated the model from the white background. The warm feel was created by feathering the light reflected from a touch-of-warmth reflector from the right.

This delightful portrait with the model's flowing blond hair seems simple, but it is demonstrative of both technical and compositional excellence. A punch panel and an accent light on the right wrapped around the girl's smiling face, giving shape, dimension, and separation. Her face, hands (edgewise to the camera), and long hair all flow to the left of the picture, adding motion. The camera was tipped slightly to accentuate the feeling of motion. Attention to detail and careful lighting ensure that even simple portraits are dynamic and effective.

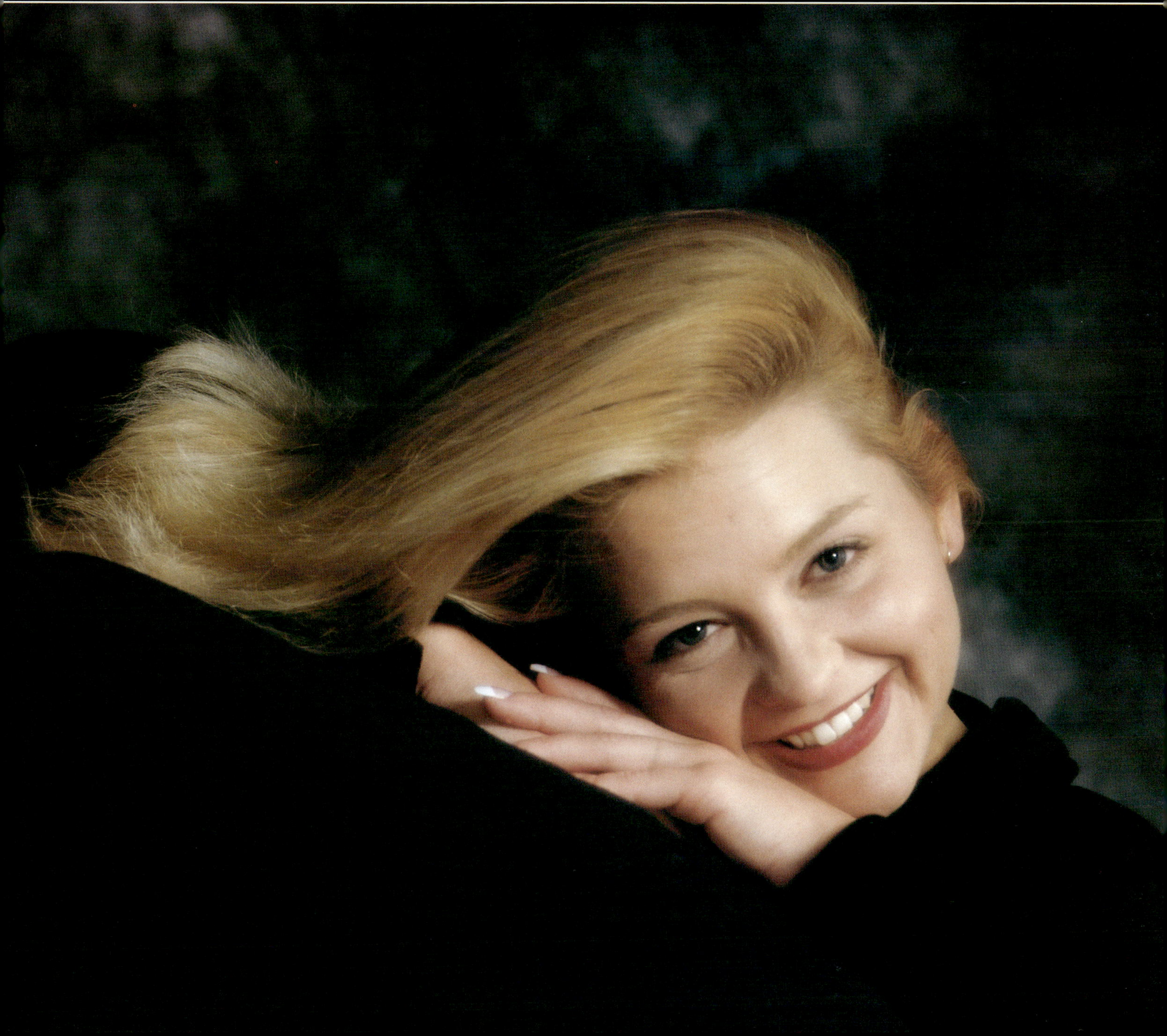

Well planned, well posed, well lighted, and skillfully executed—all that plus a beautiful bride ensures a delightful portrait. The lighting set consisted of a punch-panel main light; an accent light on the right; an umbrella fill with one f-stop less power than the main placed on the lens axis to gently fill in the shadow area; a hair light paced high and on the right; and a background light to provide separation. The slight tilt of the bride's head, the delicately posed hand just touching her chin, and the slight separation of the fingers (with the edge of her hand facing the camera) are key compositional elements.

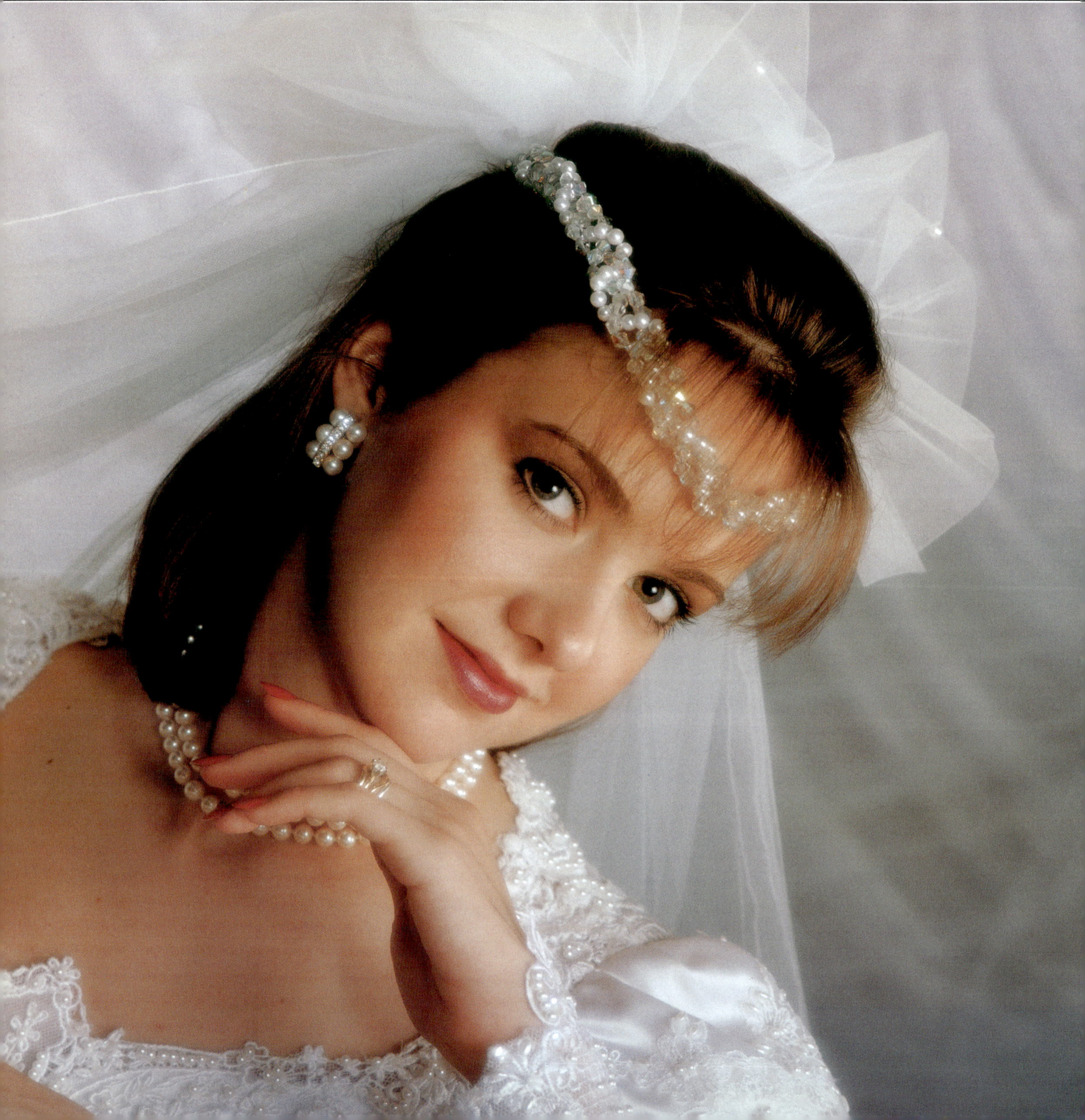

Notice who is the center of attention in this formal family portrait—man's best friend is really lapping up all the attention. The triangular composition of the family was based around the piano and the sweeping staircase. Only one light, the punch panel, was used. Dragging the shutter allowed the ambient light to provide shadow detail and separation. The image was made with an 80mm lens on a Hasselblad camera.

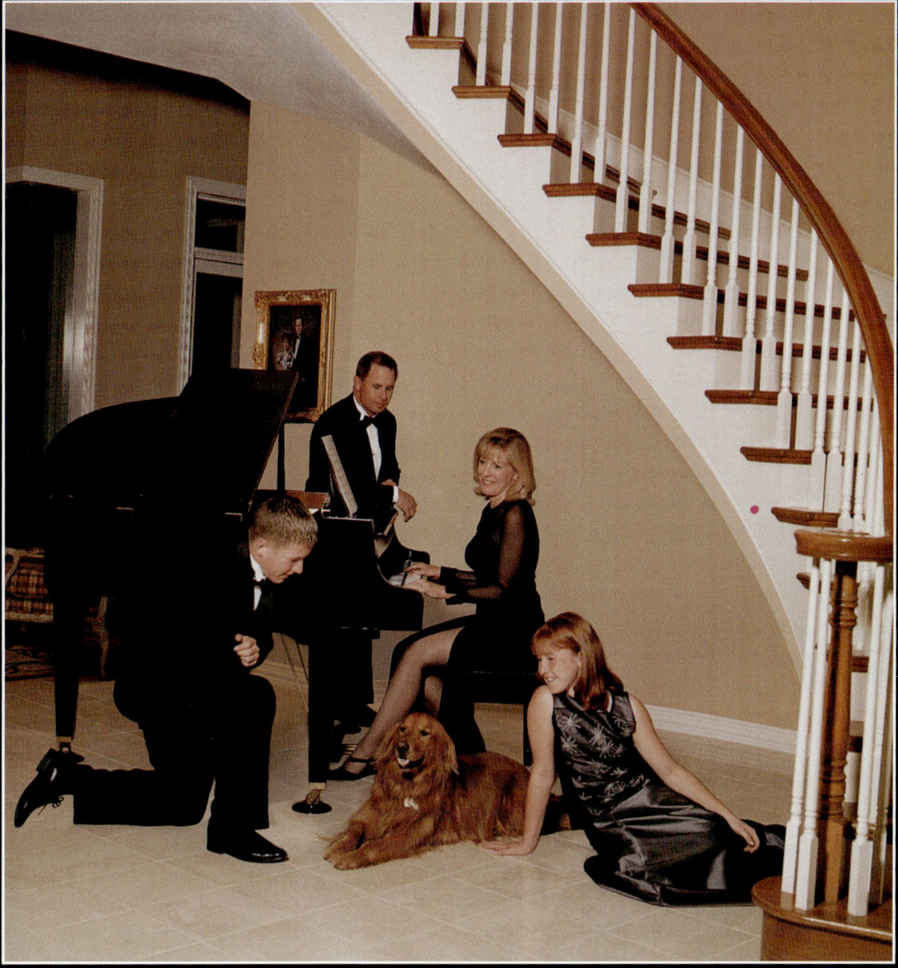

The natural falloff of light from the punch panel is clearly evident in this 30mm wide-angle image of a woman in a red dress leaning against a piano. Although a slower shutter speed was used to allow ambient light to influence the image, the ambient light is still subdued so as not to detract from the central point of interest. Note how the woman's body is turned away from the main light while her face is turned toward it, ensuring the viewer's eyes go straight to that part of the image. The sweeping spiral of the staircase complements the position of the woman's body.

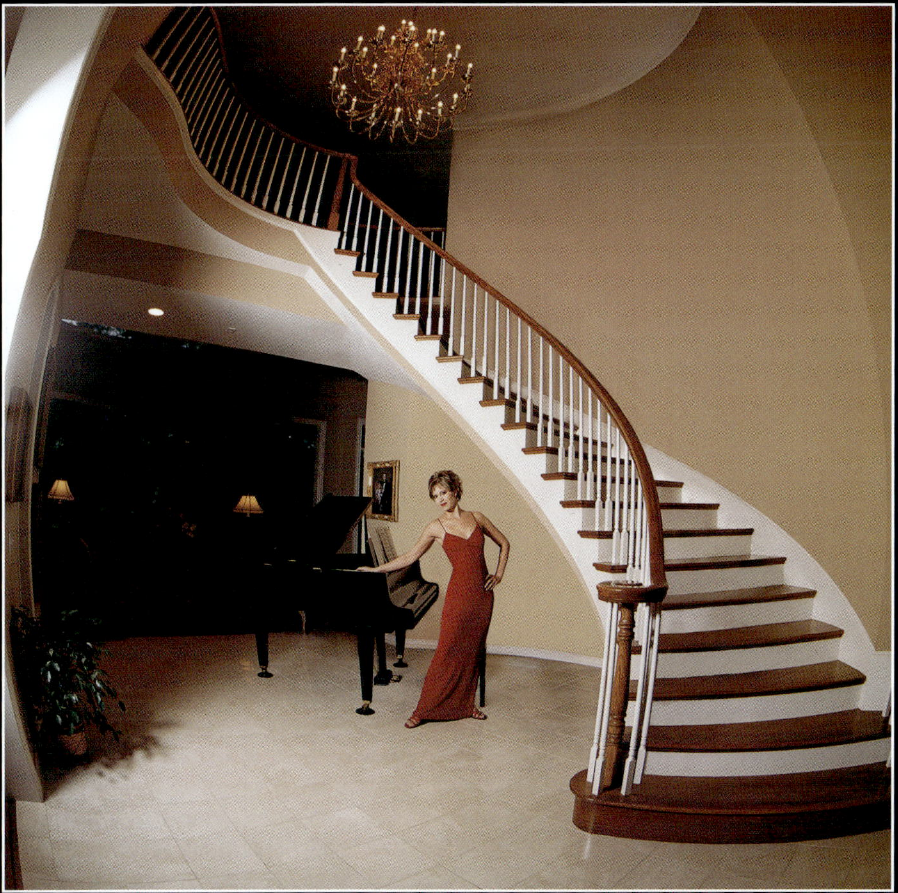

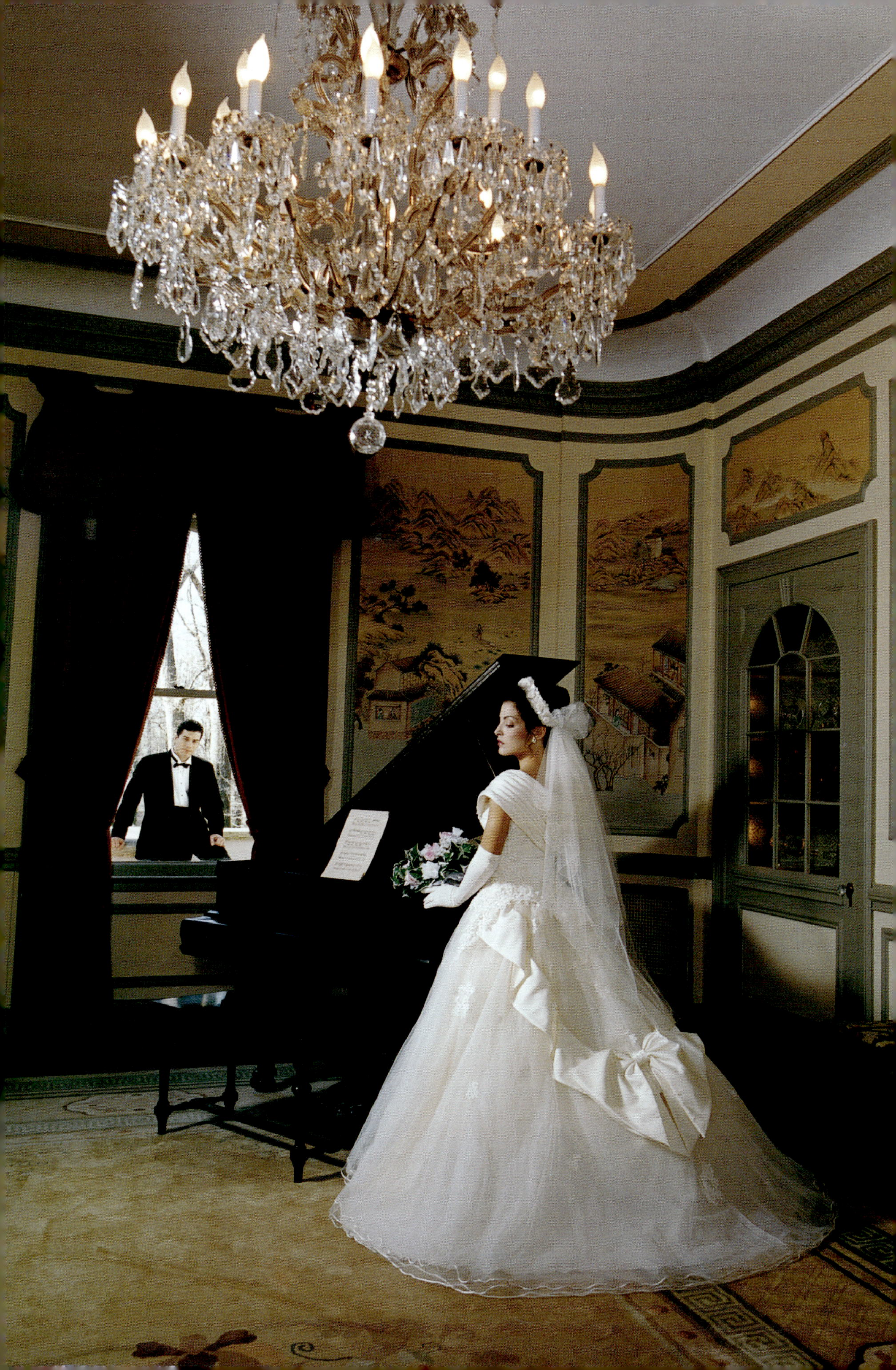

ACING PAGE—While a punch panel was the principal source of light, other lights and modifiers were employed in this complex setup. As Don points out, to do an image like this the right way is tough. The punch panel from the left lit the bride, while dragging the shutter allowed the ambient light and the chandelier to provide supporting illumination. An umbrella fill light on the lens axis accentuated the shadow detail in the bride's dress. The groom, looking through the window, was lit by daylight that was softened by an overhead diffuser to ensure that the highlights were not overexposed or burned up. A small but important compositional element is the sheet music, which visually connects the bride and groom.

BELOW—Punch-panel lighting, at about 45 degrees from the left side of the camera, was the main source of light. An accent light highlighted the ballerina's arms and gown while dragging the shutter let the ambient light in the background provide some shadow detail. It also separated the ballerina from the background. Don's tip for lighting in this kind of situation is not to have the main light too high.

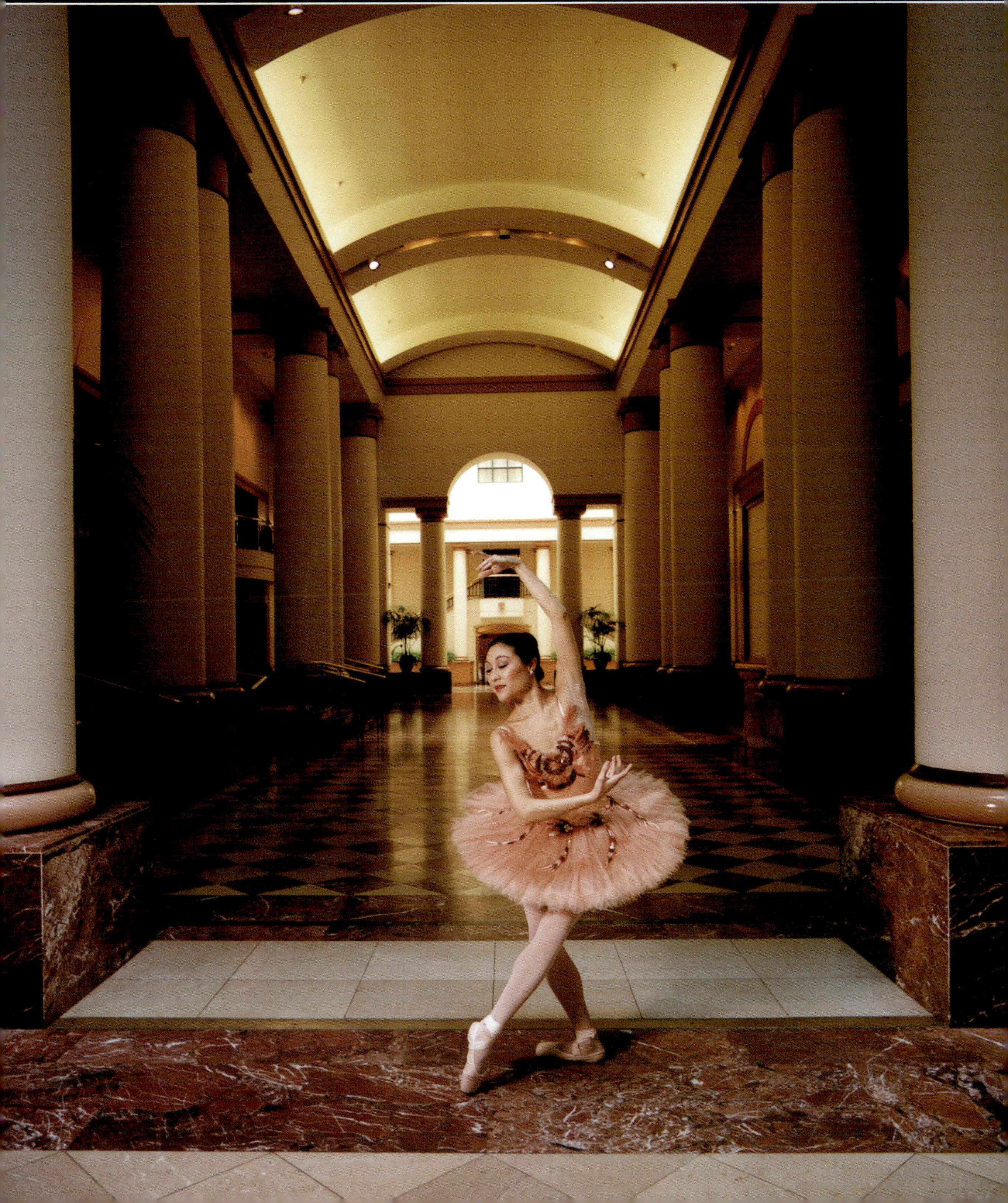

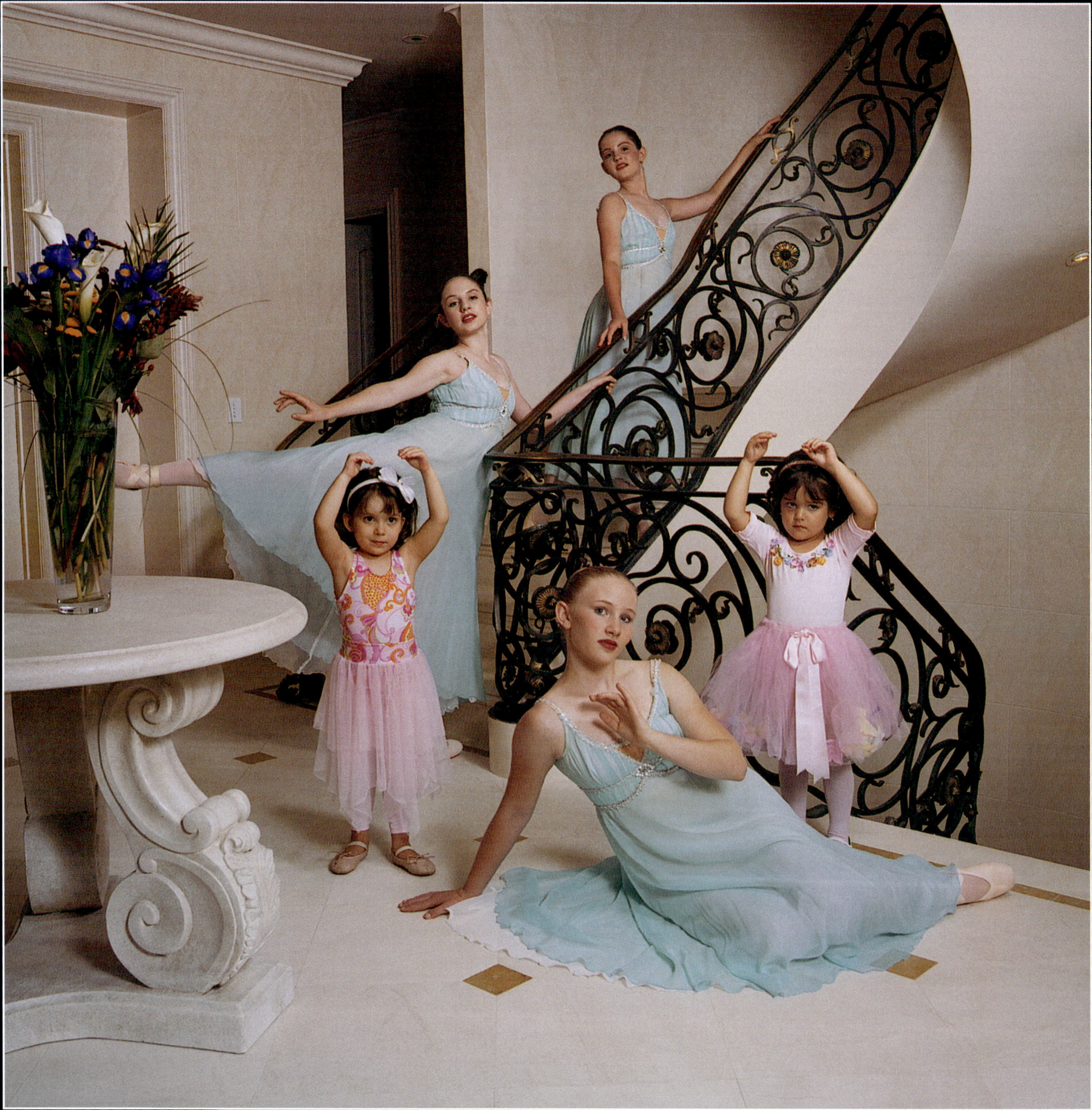

ABOVE—This group of young ballerinas was illuminated with a combination of light from a punch panel to the right of the camera and early evening summer daylight coming through a doorway to the left, which was supplemented by window light. Don, who had never seen the location before, spent about ten minutes assessing the situation and evaluating potential lighting patterns before deciding on the final set. He posed the older girls first—knowing they'd be able to concentrate longer—and then had the two little ballerinas in pink walk onto the set.

FACING PAGE—The rosy hue in this portrait (in keeping with the rose in the model's hand) was enhanced with a touch-of-warmth reflector from the front left. The other lights used were the punch panel, accent, and background lights, as well as an umbrella fill at the lens axis.

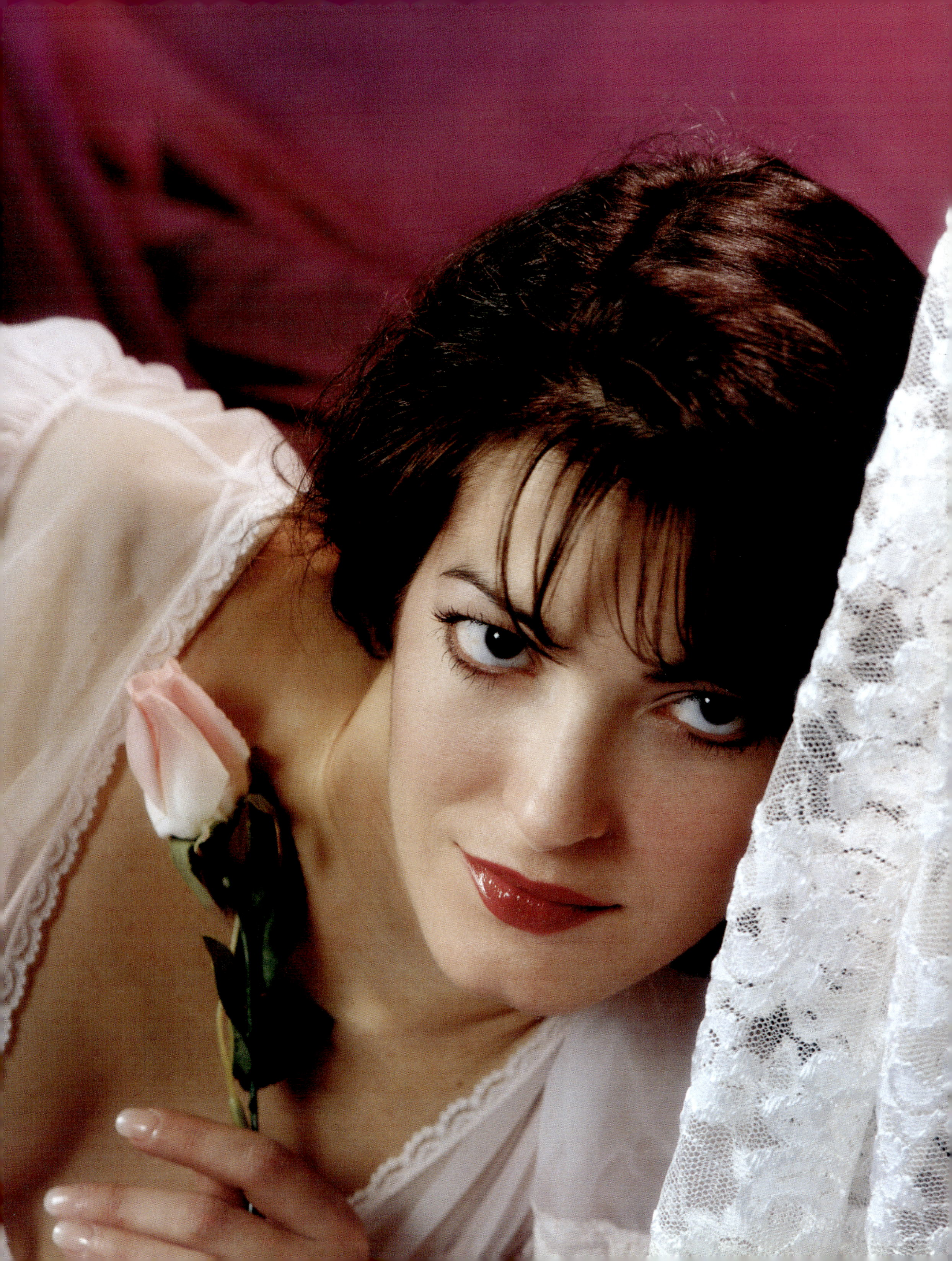

8. Parabolic Lighting with Barndoors

The tried-and-true tools for really controlling light and being able to paint with it are the aptly named barndoors. Designed to fit on parabolic reflectors to control the quantity and direction of light, barndoors have been around for a long time and most everyone is familiar with them. They yield a very controllable and dramatic light that is ideal for a variety of portraits. It's not for every subject, however, and is not recommended for children, since they tend to move around a bit.

When using barndoors, remember that you will be striving to use the edge of light, feathering it so that it literally skims across the subject. To do this with the barndoors, you have to pinch the doors way down, closing them so that there is only a small gap to let light out. Then, twist the doors so they are at a 45-degree angle, not vertical. This is very important. Use your modeling lights so you can see exactly what effect you are getting.

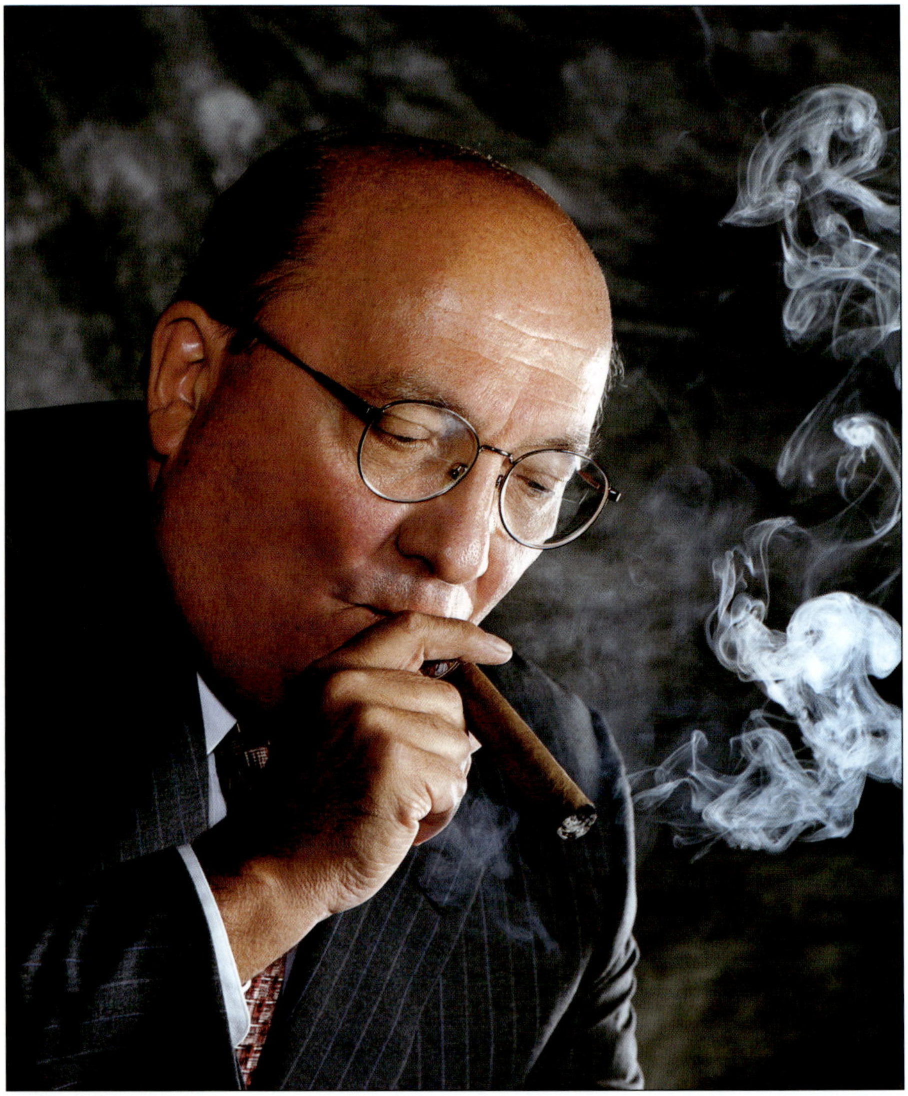

One of the keys to lighting bald heads is to use pinched-down barndoors on a parabolic reflector and feather the light so it skims the subject—it should not be directed straight at the subject. This was precisely the main light used in this portrait of a man puffing on a cigar. Umbrella fill was used to provide base density and shadow detail, while an accent light accentuated the cigar smoke.

If you use parabolics and barndoors correctly, you will be able to create a natural falloff of light that is very controllable. In addition to being an excellent tool for general portrait lighting, this means that barndoors provide a great way to light bald heads. You can also use the ratio of light and shadow to make larger people look slimmer and broaden thinner faces. If you

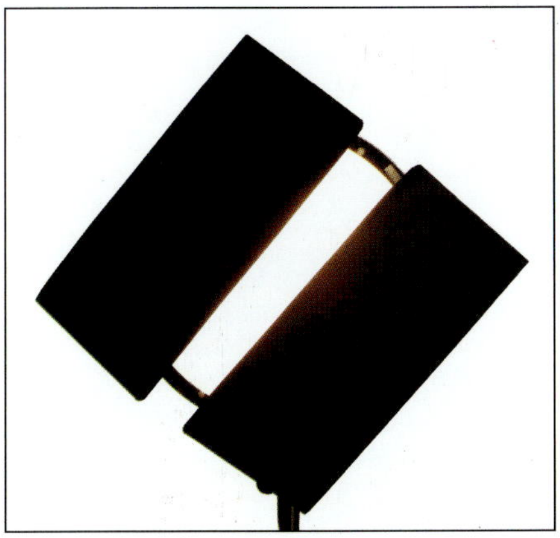

ABOVE—Parabolic with barndoors.

RIGHT—This portrait was created by balancing several light sources: daylight coming through the stained glass windows, lights inside the church (including a ceiling spot light that lit the background), and the feathered light of a parabolic reflector fitted with barndoors that lit the minister and railing. The organ pipes were illuminated with a parabolic and an umbrella, which provided a splash of fill light. Don used a faster shutter speed, in the order of $\frac{1}{60}$–$\frac{1}{125}$ second at f11, to control the daylight.

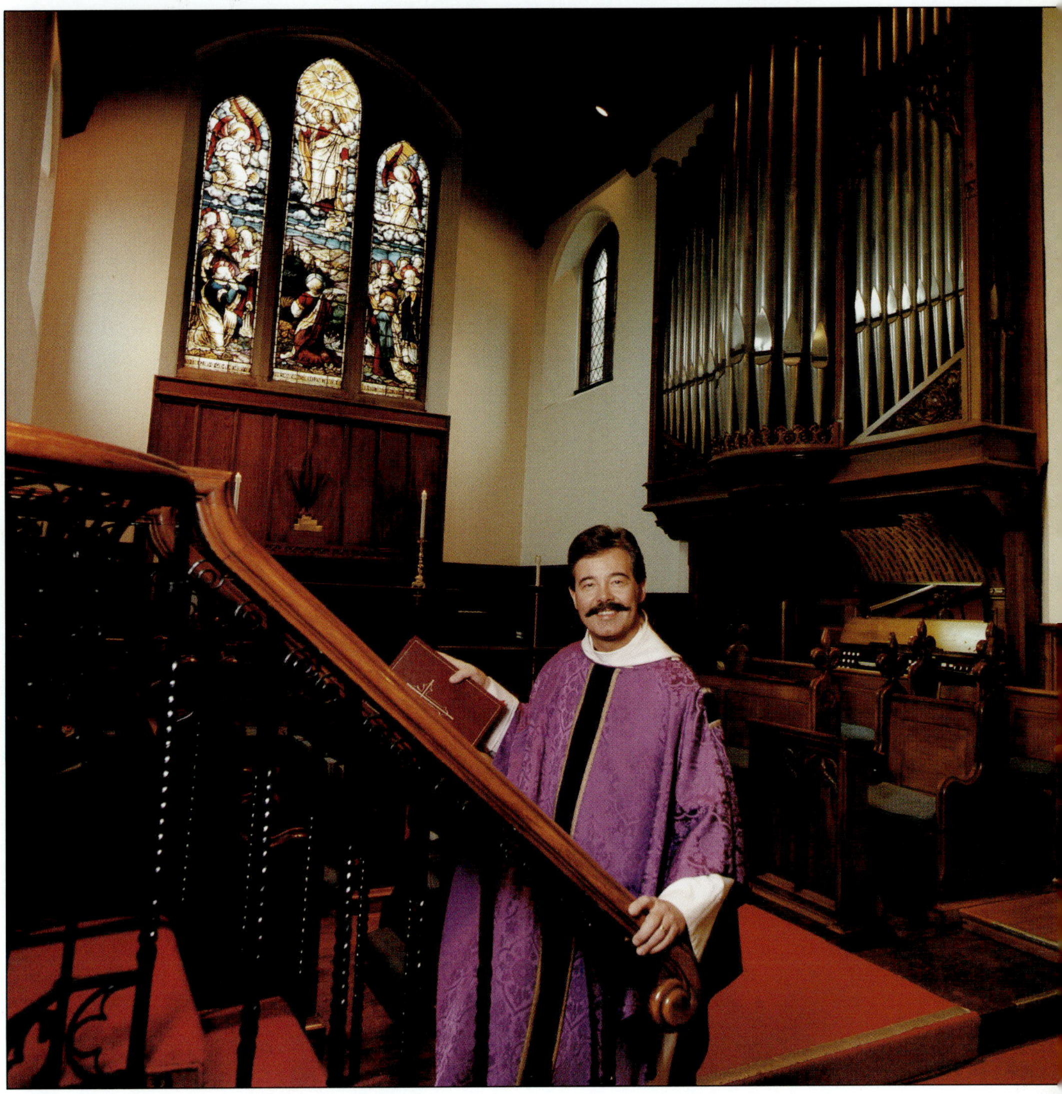

carefully adjust the direction at which the light hits the person's face, you'll be able to see the change in the lighting effect. The narrow point source of light created by the parabolic reflector facilitates this; the barndoors give you the control you need.

With these guidelines in mind, I think you'll be very happy with how you can control your lighting and make better portraits, both in the studio and on location.

Bank lobbies, like this one in Charlotte, North Carolina, are great locations. A 50mm wide angle lens on a Hasselblad was used to give great depth of field, ensuring that both the executive and the location were in focus. A parabolic with barndoors was the main light, an umbrella at the lens axis was used for fill, and an accent light provided separation. A slow shutter speed allowed the ambient light to illuminate the background.

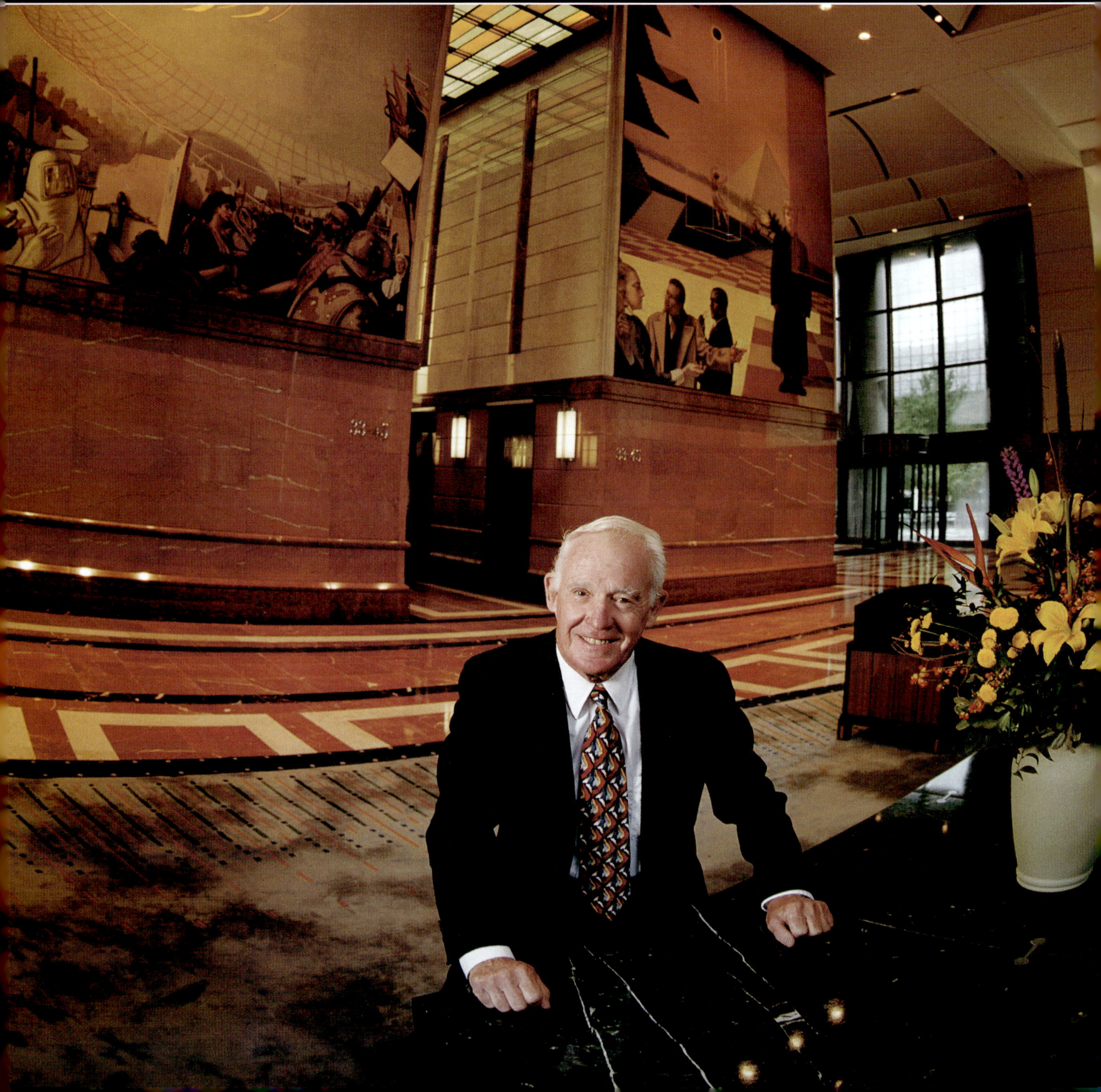

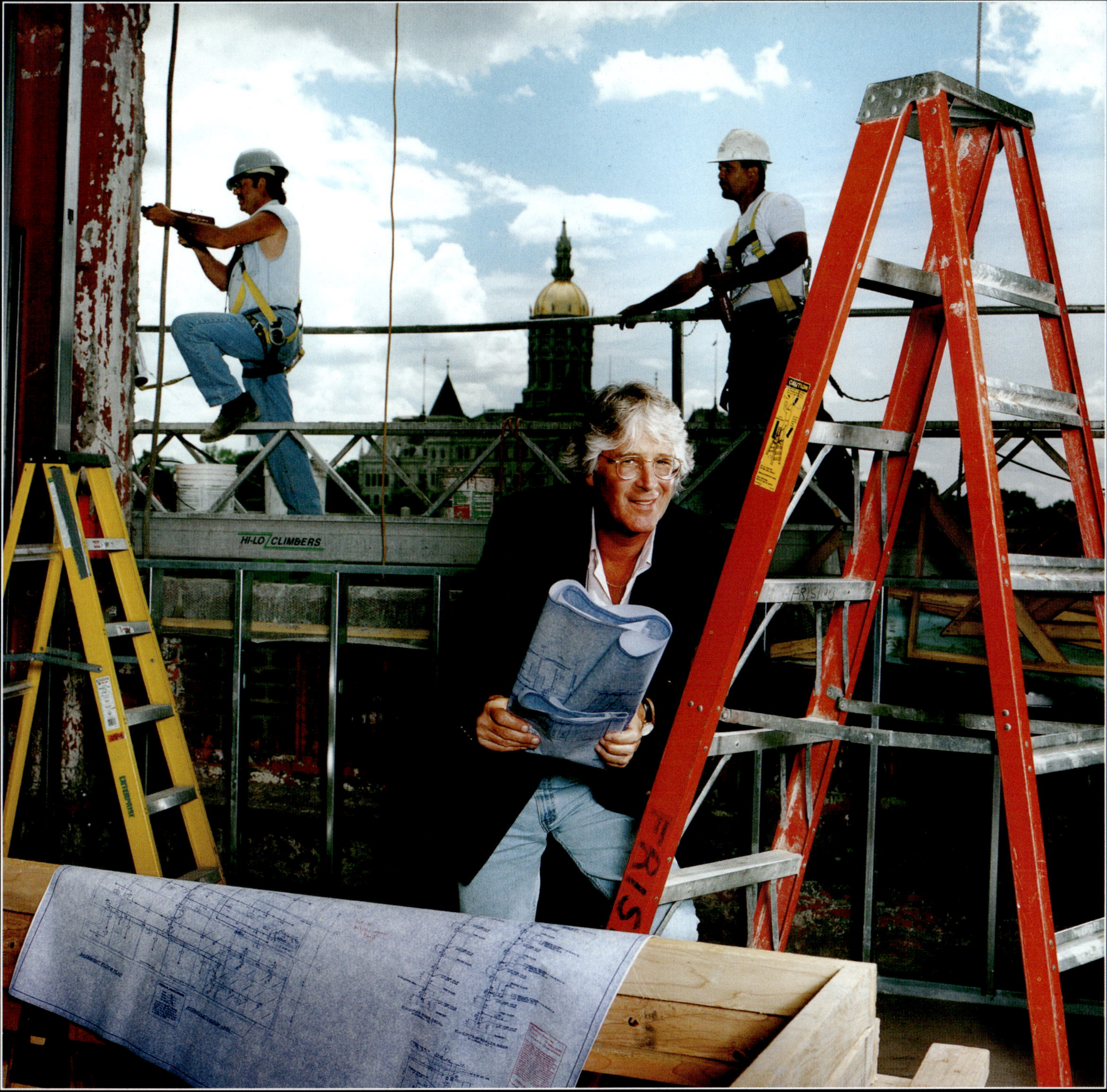

This shot of an architect on location posed many challenges. Space was tight, and the frame in the foreground couldn't be moved, so a carefully placed blueprint turned a distraction into a key element. The red ladder was balanced by a smaller, less conspicuous, yellow ladder on the left, while the two workmen on the scaffold in the background added a secondary point of interest. Lighting the architect and the red ladder was done with a parabolic reflector and barndoors, while an accent light (placed on the same side as the main light) helped separate the subject from the darker background. The main light had to be elevated sufficiently to avoid throwing shadow on the architect's face. An umbrella fill light provided shadow detail. Finally, a shutter speed of about $\frac{1}{125}$ second was used to balance the main light with the blue sky.

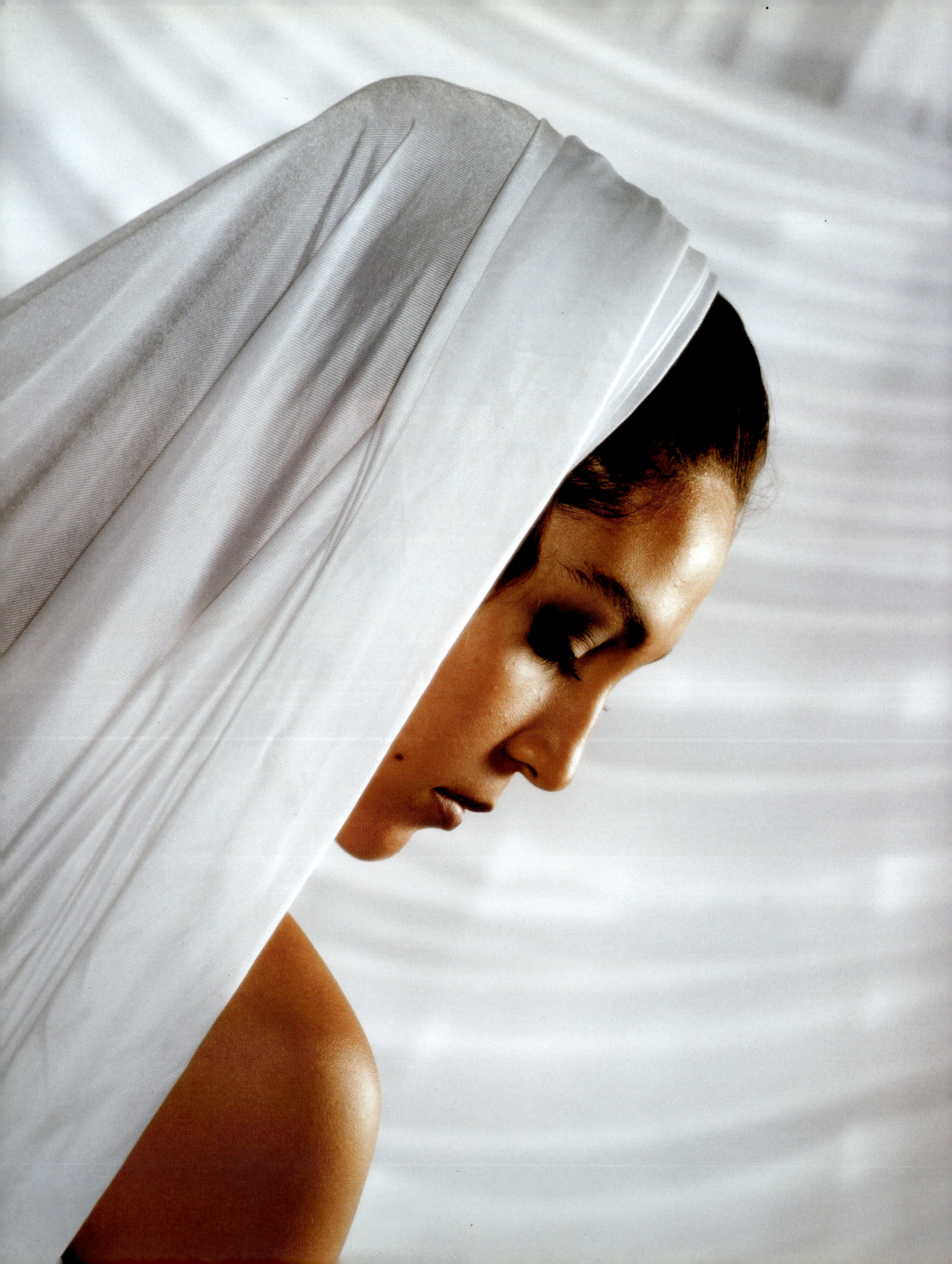

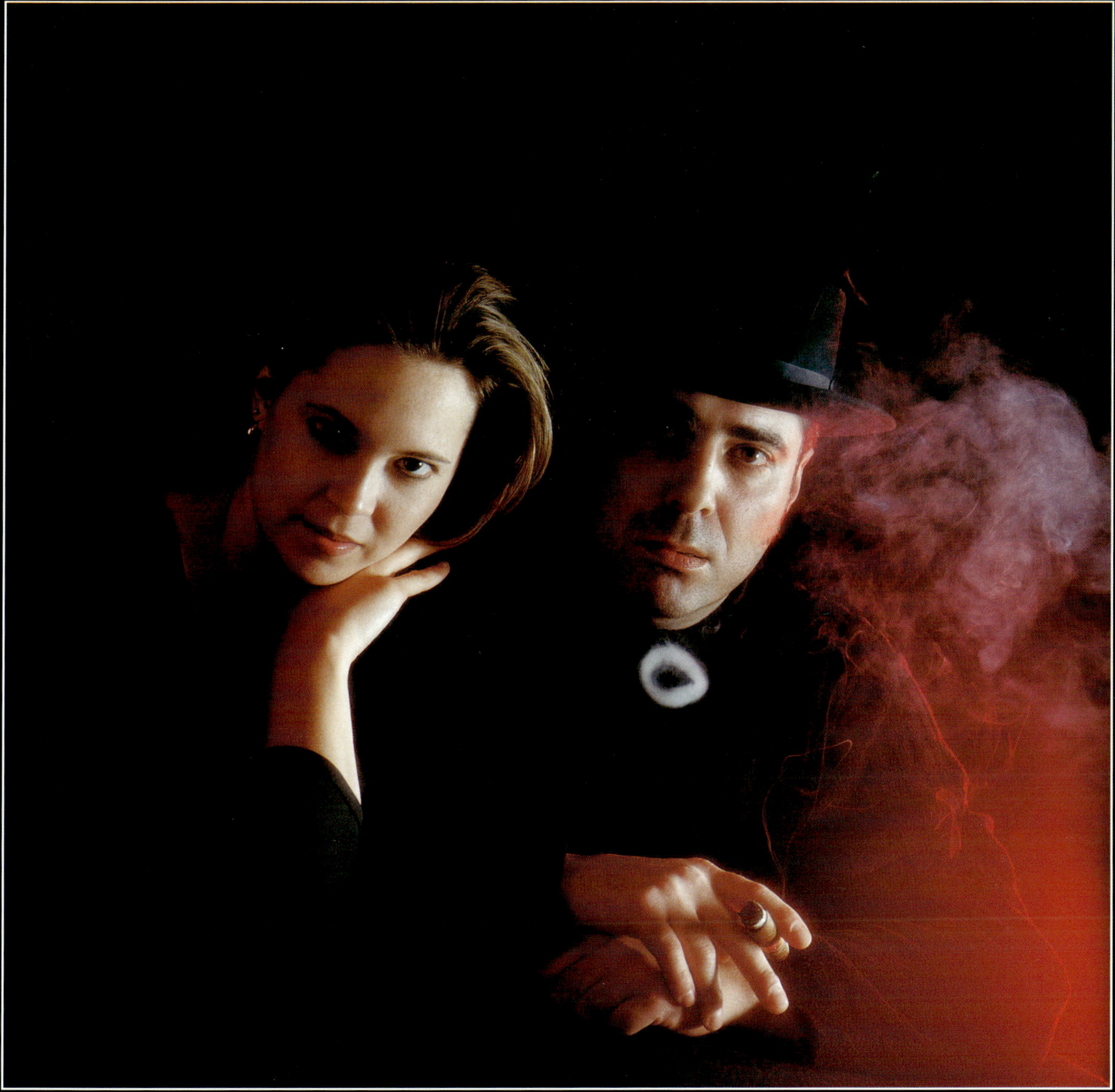

ABOVE—This moody, smoke-filled image (great timing with the smoke ring!) was made during one of Don's seminars. An umbrella fill light gave the base density to the image, while a parabolic reflector with barndoors, placed at the right, was the main light. A red gel enhanced the mood. An accent light outlined the man's hat and backlit the cigar smoke.

FACING PAGE—The flow of the material and the tilt of the camera give a feel of motion and light to this portrait. A parabolic with pinched-down barndoors—with no more than a ½-inch opening—was the main light source, the carefully controlled light skimming the model's face. Fill lighting was from an umbrella, while an accent light, placed on the right, separated the model from the background.

Roundness, shape, and texture are the hallmarks of this image. Note how the sweep of the light gives roundness to the girls' arms and brings out the texture in the backdrop and their dresses. The principal light source was a parabolic with barndoors. An accent light illuminated the edges of the models' arms and provided separation. Gelled spotlights helped light the background in a red glow.

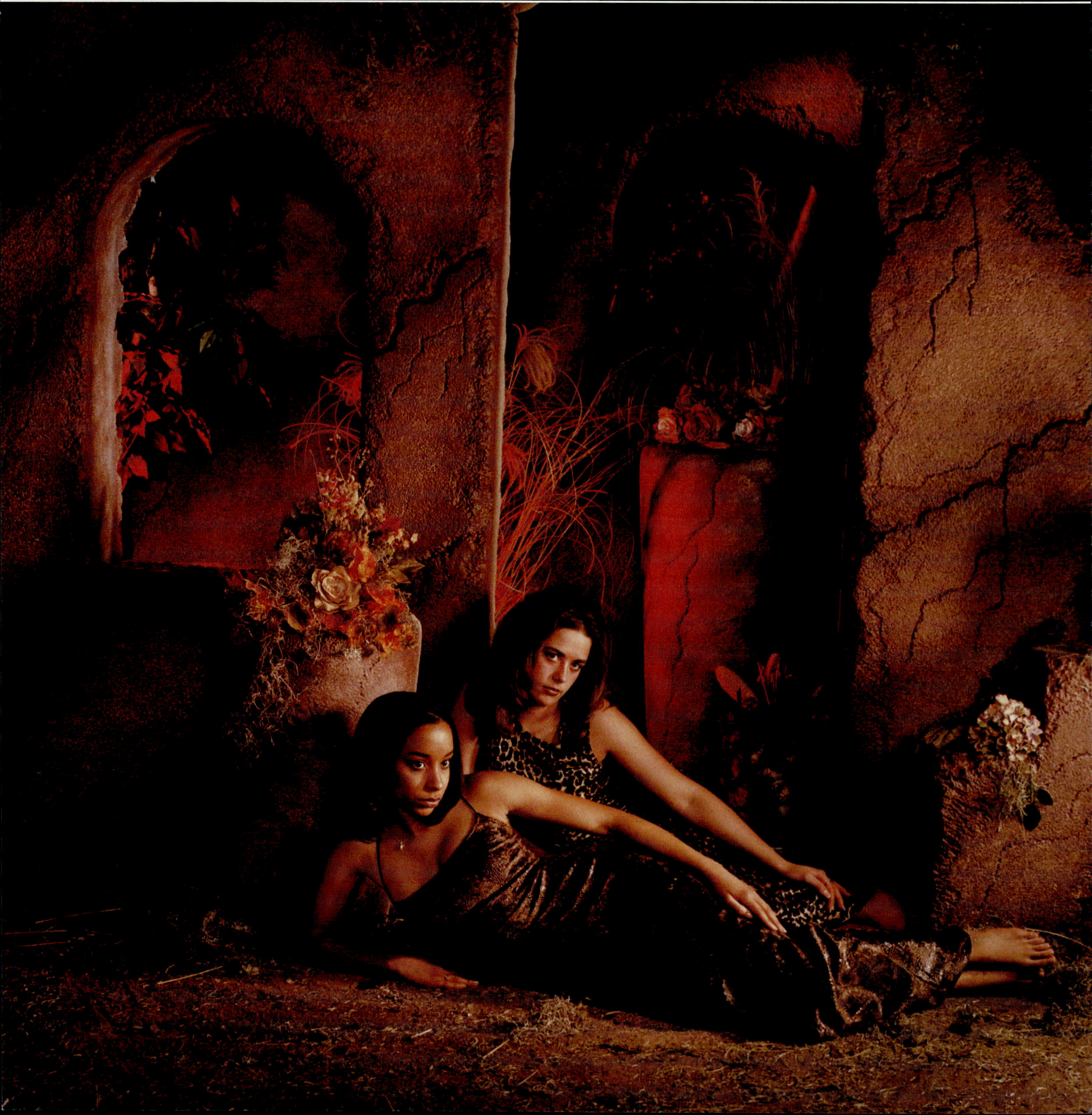

9. Posing and Problem Solving

As portrait photographers, our job is to make the subject look as good as possible. And let's face it—people are different, and not everybody's features will be perfect. However, there is no such thing as an unattractive person and, by skilful lighting, careful posing, and an ability to bring out the sparkle in somebody's personality, we can solve these "problem areas." As you get more experience in working with people, you will be able to make all your subjects look their best. In this section I will cover some of the situations you are likely to encounter. You may also wish to consult my guide to lighting and posing called *Body Parts* (Marathon Press, 1999), which I produced with well-known industry personality Skip Cohen, president of Rangefinder Publishing.

POSING BASICS

Let's talk about posing. A few simple things can be done to dramatically improve the way a person looks in a photograph. Keep in mind that the subject might not feel comfortable in front of a camera—not many of us do—and it's important to remind them that a pose that might feel awkward actually looks very natural in the final image.

One basic guideline for all posing is to avoid having the head and body turned in the same direction. Invariably, a pose like this results in a flat, static, and not very attractive photograph. While photographs like this can serve a documentary purpose—family albums are full of these "firing squad" images—our job as portrait photographers is to be more artistic and creative.

One basic guideline for all posing is to avoid having the head and body turned in the same direction.

By simply turning the head and the body, an ordinary photograph can be transformed into a dynamic image. This doesn't mean you have to twist the person's head at some unusual angle—the slightest turn or a lean might be all that's needed. Try turning the person's body to about 45 degrees to the camera and slightly into the shadow side of the frame. Then, have the subject turn their face back into the main light.

COUPLES AND GROUPS

Couples and groups have to be posed with care—and the more people there are in the photograph, the harder it is to get everyone to work in concert. Above all, as mentioned above, avoid the static, square-on "firing squad" look, with all the subjects standing in a line and their heads at the same level. The following are some simple guidelines. With couples, try to have the woman's eyes at about the man's lip level or chin level, and keep the man and the main light on opposite sides of the camera. Have him lean slightly forward. Put the light on him and feather it across her. If the people in a couple are of vastly different heights, have the taller one sit and the shorter person lean into the partner or stand or kneel behind.

With larger groups, the basic tenet is to avoid having all the heads at the same height or the faces stacked on top of each other. Positioning the faces at different levels avoids the "firing squad" look and makes the photograph far more interesting. On location, rocks, walls, logs, and other natural settings can be used to your advantage

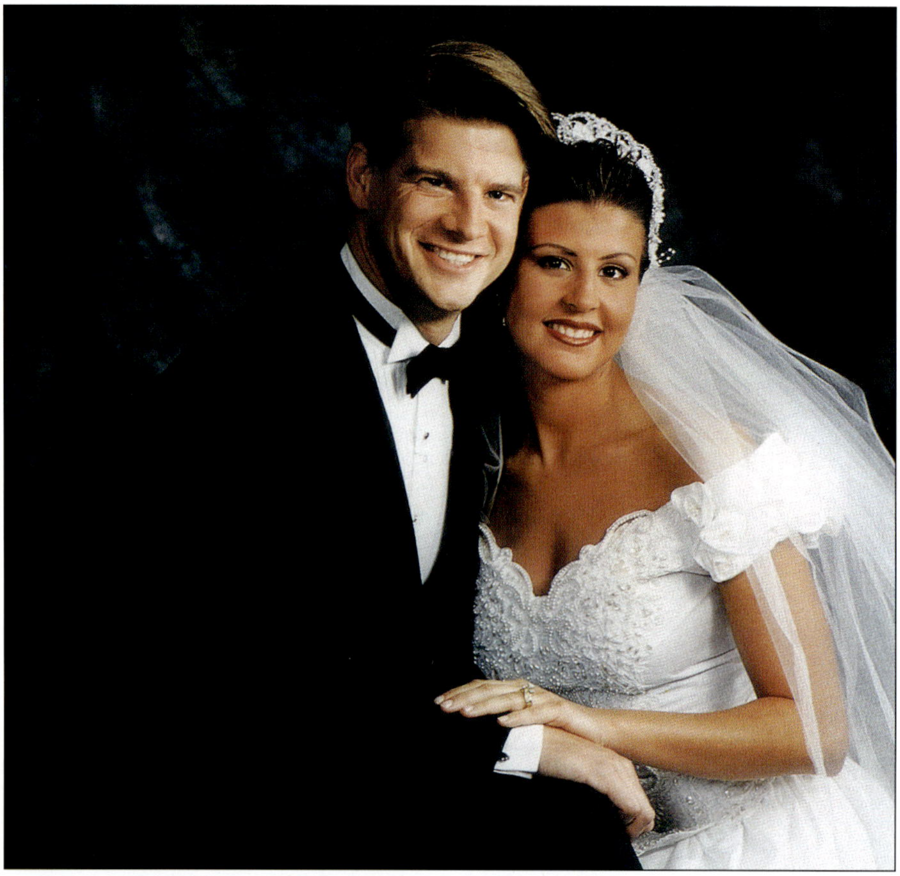

With couples, try to have the woman's eyes at about the man's lip level or chin level.

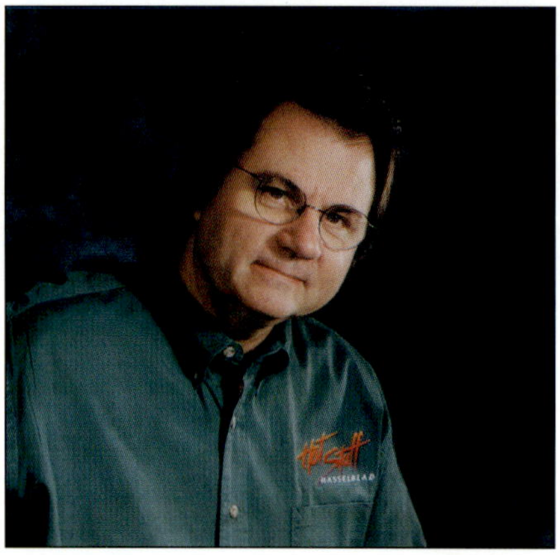

When the subject wears glasses, have them turn their face toward the main light and tip their head slightly forward.

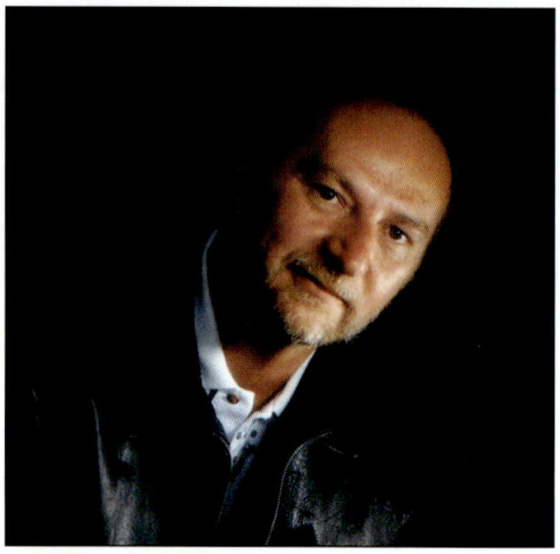

Lighting the face and leaving the top of the head in shadow helps to minimize the appearance of baldness.

in positioning the subjects at different heights. One of the keys to successful outdoor group photography is to scout a location beforehand so you can take advantage of the environment.

At times, the composition of groups is best accomplished by dividing the main group into several smaller ones, which are then composed separately. One of my favorite compositions is based on the triangle, and this can work very well for family groups—especially indoors when you can photograph into a corner and use the converging lines to enhance the overall composition.

THE EYES

It's been said that the eyes are the windows to the soul, and in portrait photography the eyes play a very important role. Your lighting should have that catchlight, the sparkle or glint in the eye that brightens it up. You can avoid photographing into the whites of the eyes by ensuring the subject's eyes are turned toward the camera. Even if their head is turned slightly away, have them look back to the lens.

When photographing someone with spectacles, simply remember that the angle of incidence equals the angle of reflection. Have the subject turn their face toward the main light and tip their head slightly forward. That way, the light hitting their glasses will reflect down toward the floor and not back into the lens. You can also tip the glasses slightly forward, using your modeling lights to preview the effect.

It's that simple. If you get the light right the first time, you can save a lot of time and expense in post-production cleanup in custom print retouching or Photoshop.

BALDNESS

Now, on to the man with the bald head. Lighting is the key to solving this problem. Using barndoors and feathering the light is a good way to make sure you are concentrating the light on the person's face and not on the top of that highly reflective bald head. Just remember to light the front plane of the face and let the light fall off on the top of the head.

THE HANDS

The placement of the hands and their position in relation to the camera can make or break an image. In general, you should have the edges of the hands toward the camera and avoid having too much of either the back of the hands or the palms facing the camera.

Women's fingers in particular should be extended so they are long and graceful, not curled up, which can cause them to look claw-like. Even with men's hands, where grace and elegance are not as important as they are for women's, the fingers should look relaxed and the hand should not be clenched. Usually, I recommend that men's hands should not be brought together. However, there might be times when you want to accentuate masculinity and power; in cases like this folded hands can be a feature, but they should still be relaxed.

Also, if there is anything the hands could or should be doing, let them do it. Adding a prop—something to hold—can be very effective. If it's an executive, give him or her a book or another appropriate prop. You can also add a touch of natural elegance to a bridal portrait by having the subject hold her bouquet or a single flower.

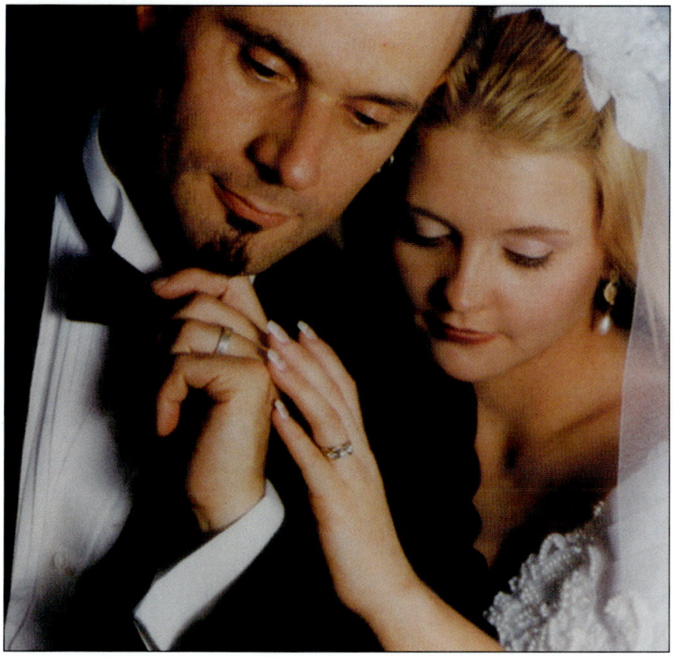
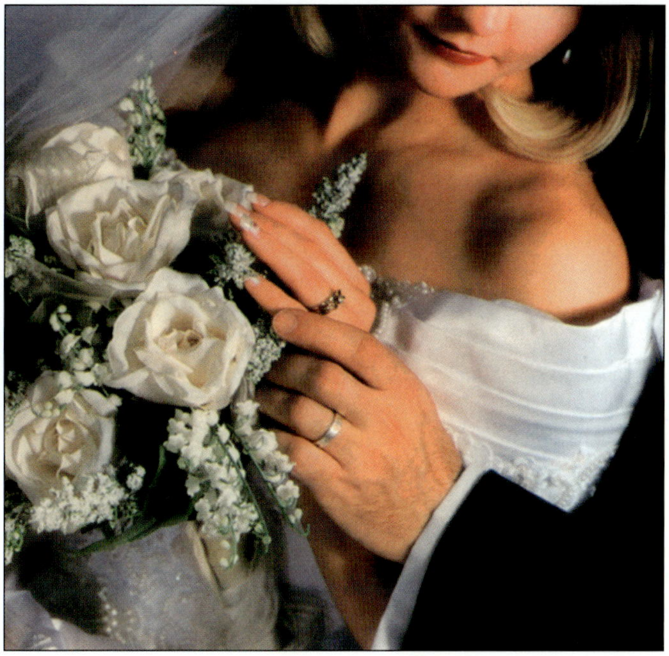

Hands look best when the edge (rather than the back of the hand or the palm) faces the camera. If possible, give the hands something to hold.

10. Environmental Portraiture

As you study the photographs in this section, you will notice one common and very important element: the direction of light. As I mentioned earlier, avoid light that is at 90 degrees to the subject. Similarly, light that comes from directly behind the photographer tends to be flat and uninteresting. Even if the quality of this light is good—as it is in the early morning or late afternoon—its direction makes for uninspiring images.

One very simple solution is all that it takes: move the camera position about 15 or 20 degrees to the subject, and the effect is immediate and obvious. Light and shadow will work together to create exciting, dynamic, and visually pleasing

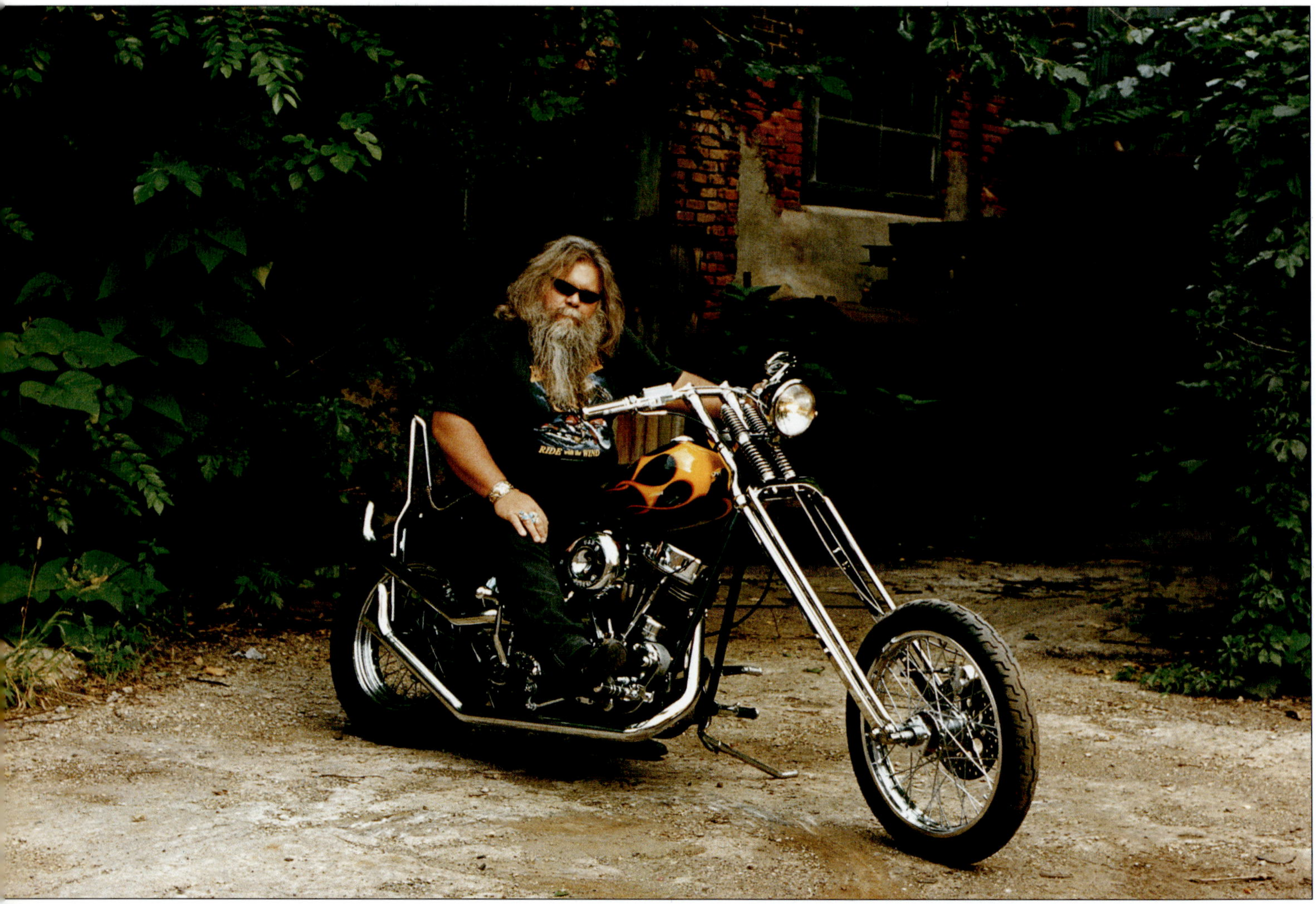

This simple but powerful image of a biker says "attitude." It was created using ambient light with the bike's headlight turned on for added effect. The triangular composition of the bike and rider blend well with shape of the dark background area.

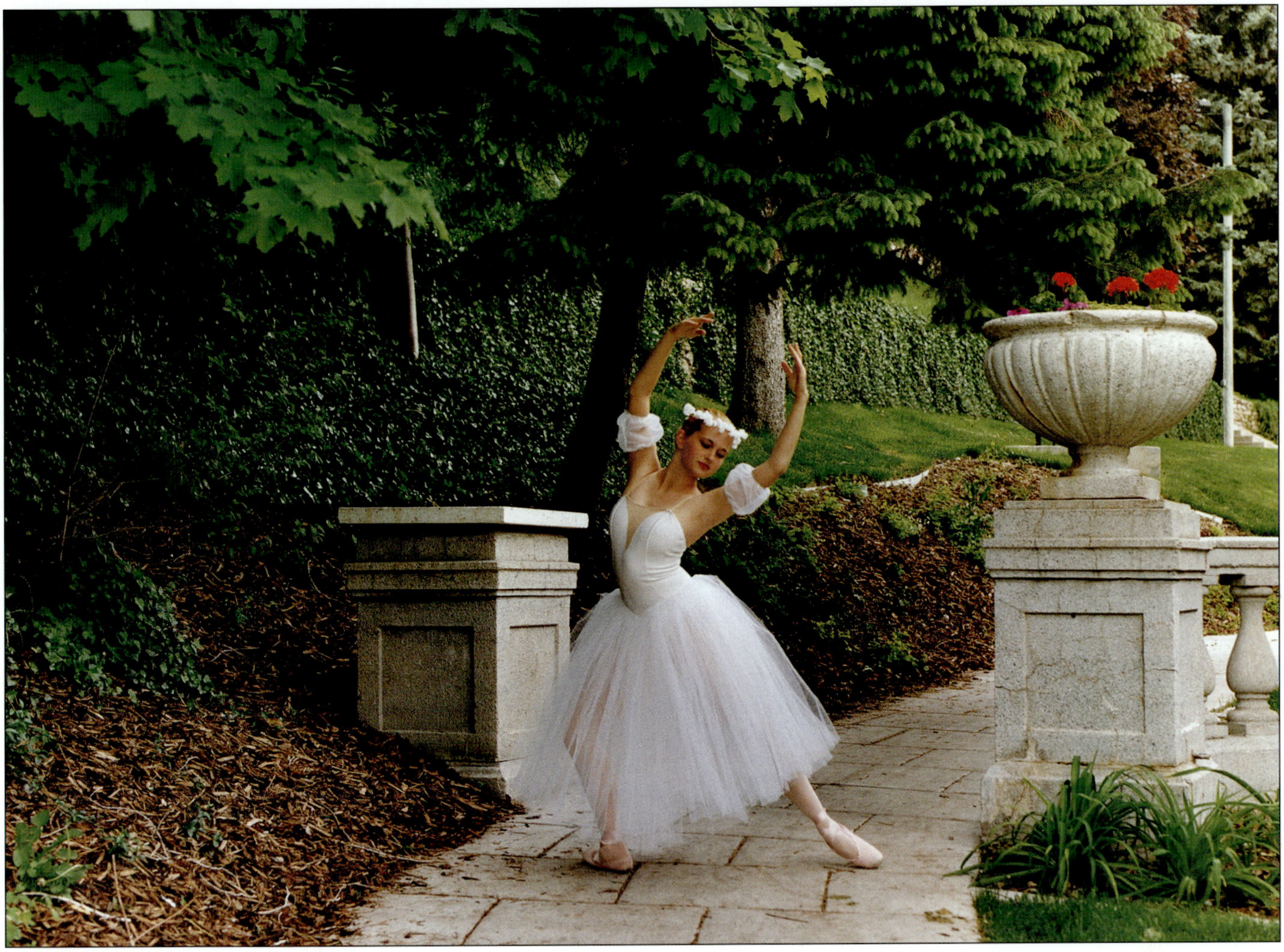

Soft, diffused daylight outlines the ballerina's dress, enhancing its translucence while wrapping around to light up her face. The classic pose emphasized the triangle composition created by her body and arms.

images. The intensity and quality of the light will be the same, but the resulting photograph will be very different and vastly improved.

TIME OF DAY

Without a doubt, the best time to photograph people outdoors is in the early morning or late afternoon when the light is softer. For the most flattering results, you should avoid photographing people during the middle of the day. If it's unavoidable, you will either have to move them into shaded areas, diffuse the light with translucent material, or employ some other means of improving the light. However, I advise you to make every effort to use those optimum times of day when you can take full advantage of "sweet light."

LOCATION LIGHTING

For years, I have specialized in the creation of environmental portraiture and I have learned that the best place to photograph is on the edge of the light. I have found that the edge of a tree line is ideal. Here, the daylight creates a nice ratio between the highlight and shadow areas, and the subject is well lighted with detail retained on the shadow side

As I pointed out earlier, I favor a 4:1 ratio of light, but a 3:1 ratio is also ideal for environmental portraiture. Keep in mind that your eyes can handle a wider range of light than film or digital capture can, so the ratio must be low enough so that the highlights are well exposed and there is detail in the important shadow areas.

In settings where there is open sky in the background, such as at the beach or in wide-open spaces, the color of sunset, dramatic clouds, or some other natural phenomena can really make a photograph. Look for the subtleties and nuances in natural light to enhance the principal subject matter in particular and the overall photograph in general.

Many elements must work together to make great portraits, but often these elements are so well blended that none stands out to overpower the others. If you can create photographs like that, you have mastered the environmental portrait.

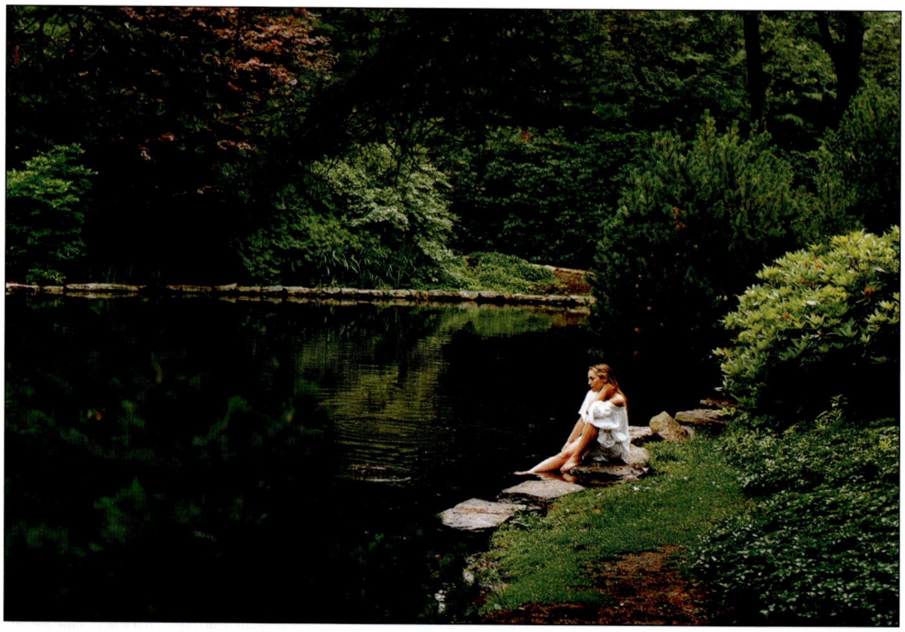

Tranquility is the hallmark of this delightful photograph. Natural light entered the frame from the left (and at an ideal angle relative to the camera position), and produced a 4:1 ratio. A spot meter was used to read the shadow side of the model's face. A good rule of thumb is to expose for the shadow side and print for the highlight.

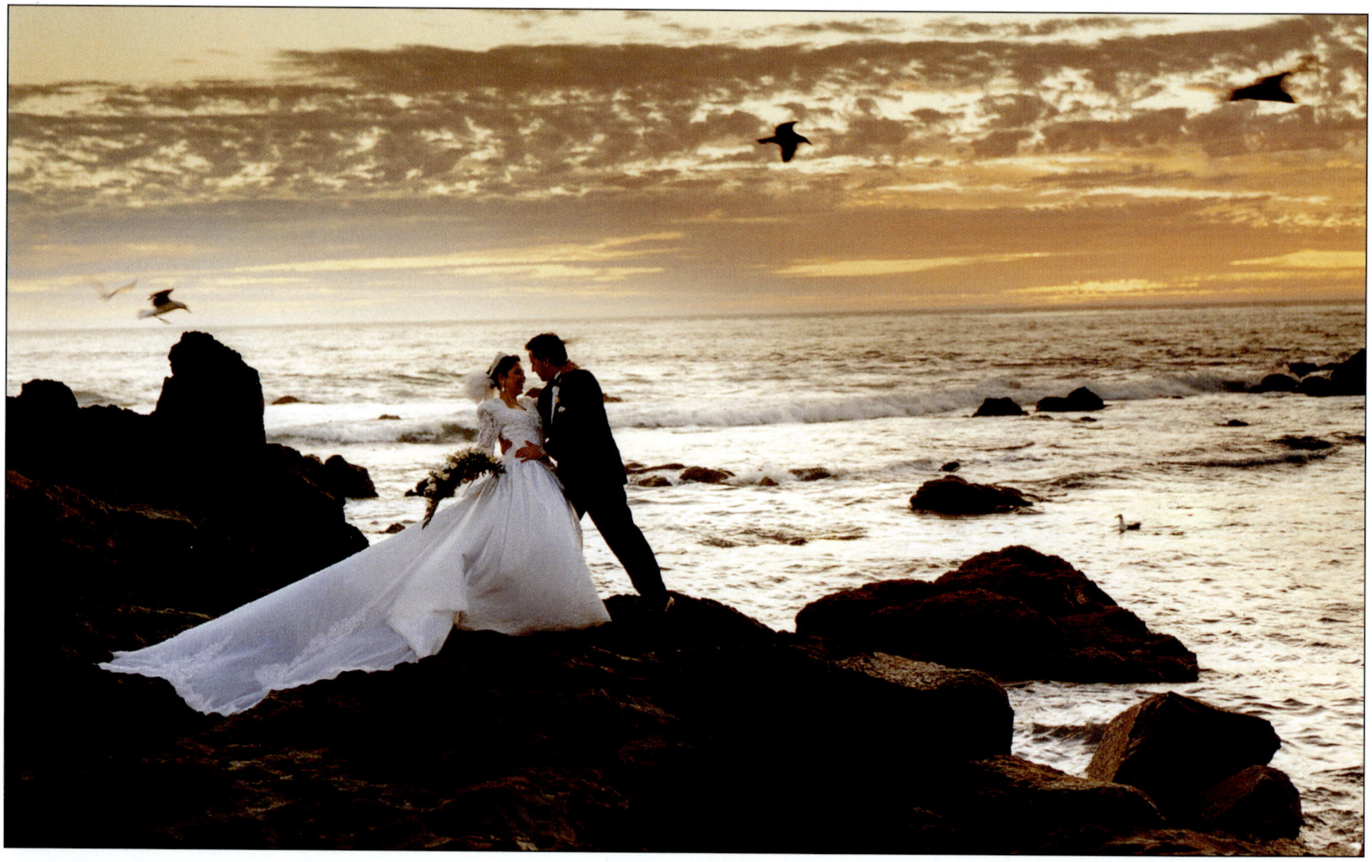

Picking the right time of day and including some natural elements, like the seagulls, truly enhances a photograph. In this situation, late afternoon daylight skimmed across the sea, rocks, and the bride's gown, which was spread across the rocks to create the base for a triangle composition. It's simple and effective, the result of careful planning and skilful execution.

complemented by the light and surroundings. The ambient light, coming from the right, accentuated the bride's gown, which is highlighted against the dark water and rocks.

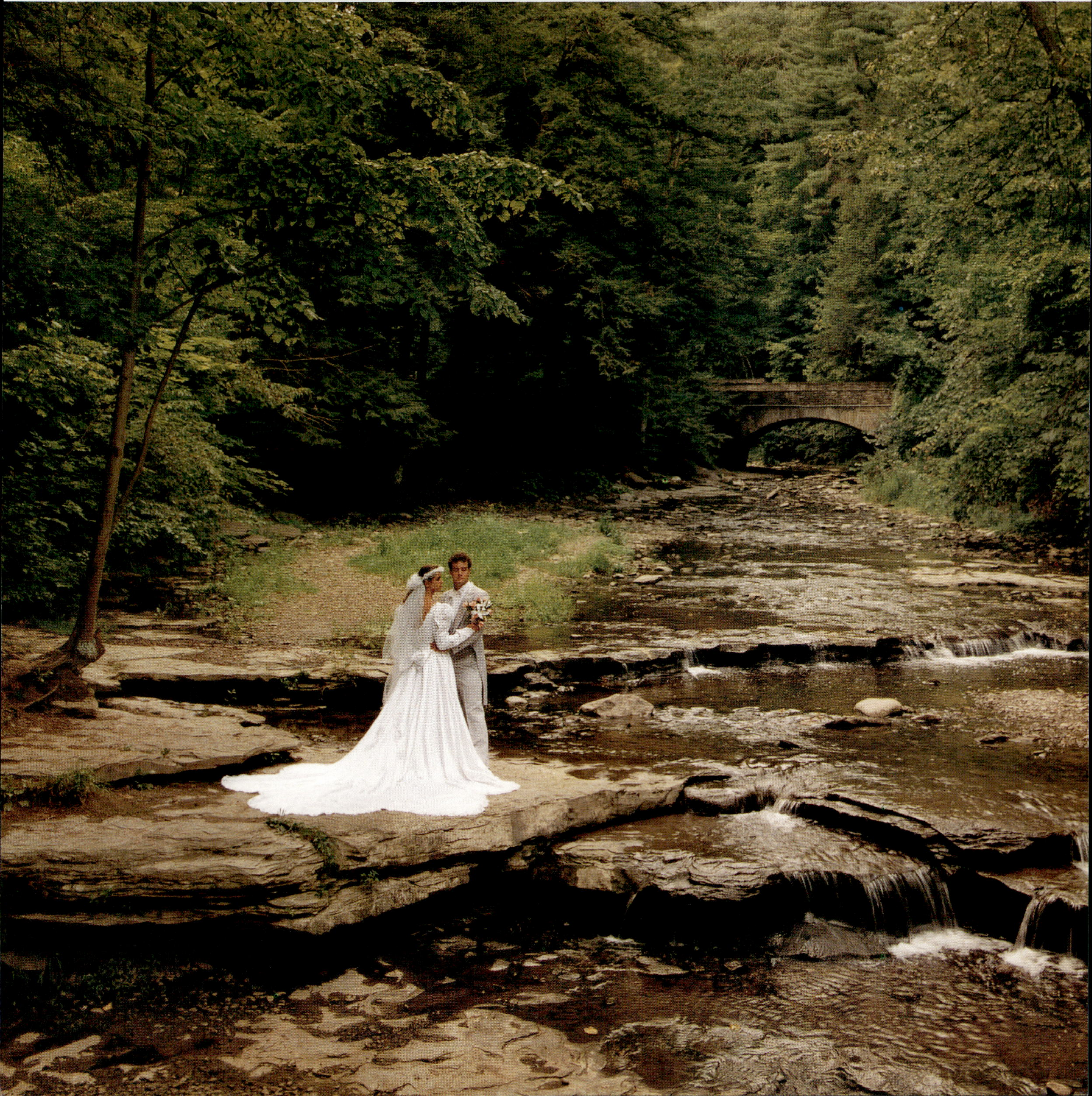

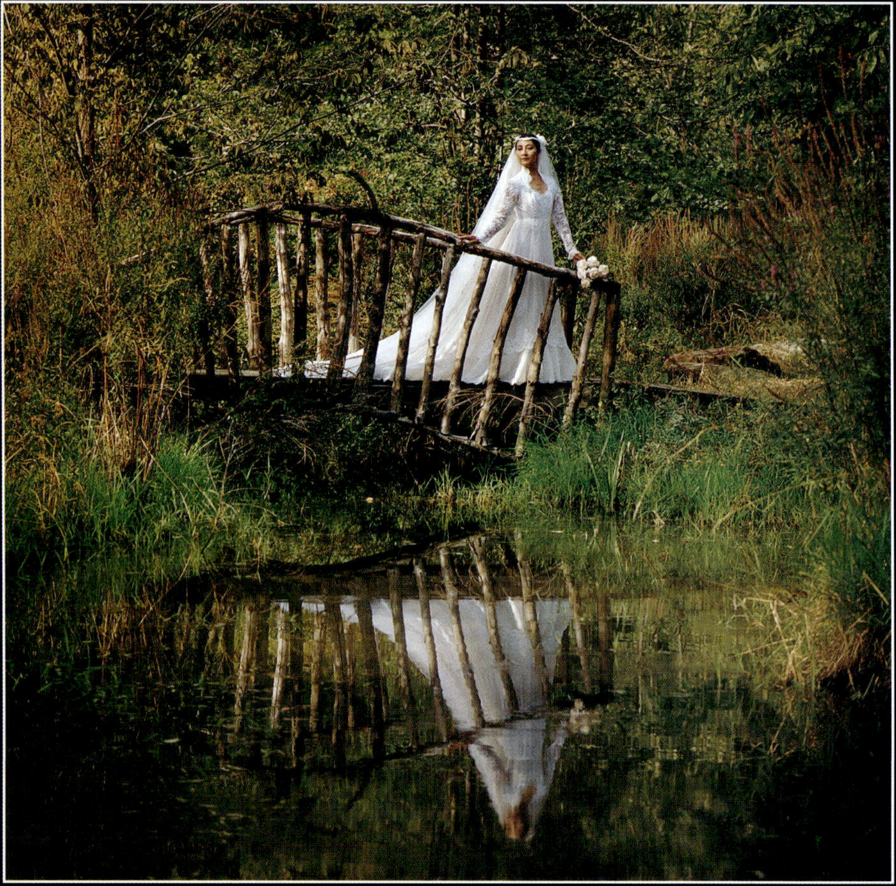

On a prior occasion, Don had seen and made a note of this picturesque setting in upper New York state. So, when the opportunity arose while teaching a workshop, he made full use of the location's potential. The natural light virtually spotlighted the bride and bridge, while the gentle movement of water created a diffused reflection that complemented the composition.

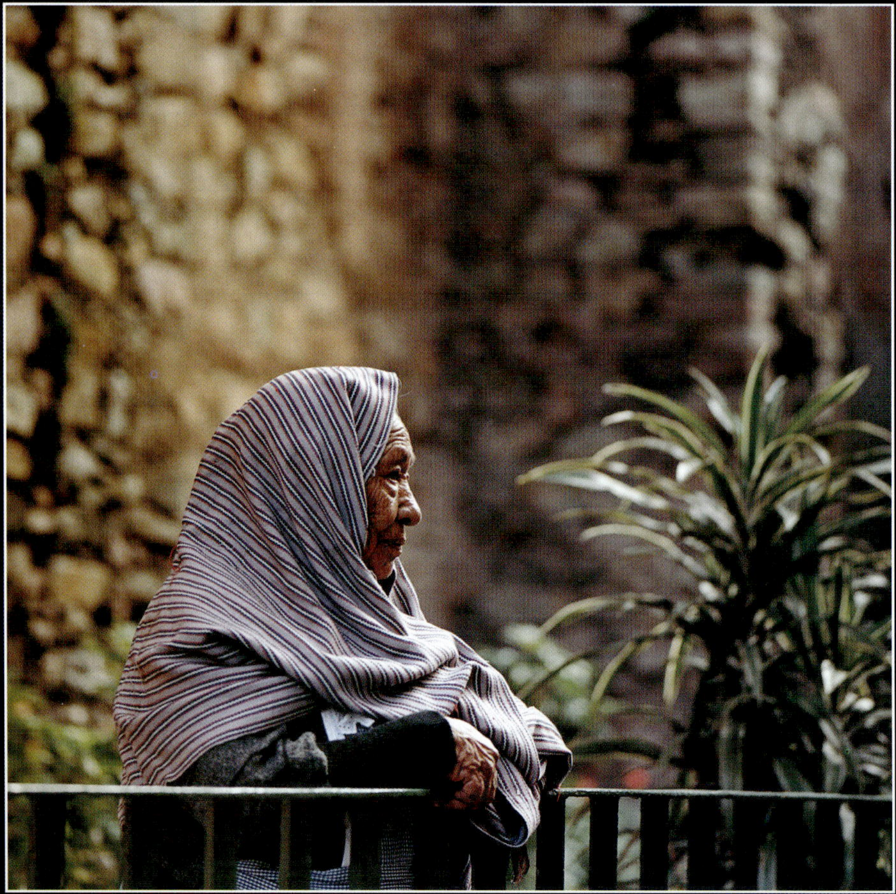

A 180mm lens was ideal for this portrait of an old Mexican woman whose strong facial features are accentuated by daylight from the right. Note how the light caught the top rail of the fence she was leaning on and gave texture to her head covering while also illuminating the out-of-focus background. Having the subject off-center adds to the mood of the image.

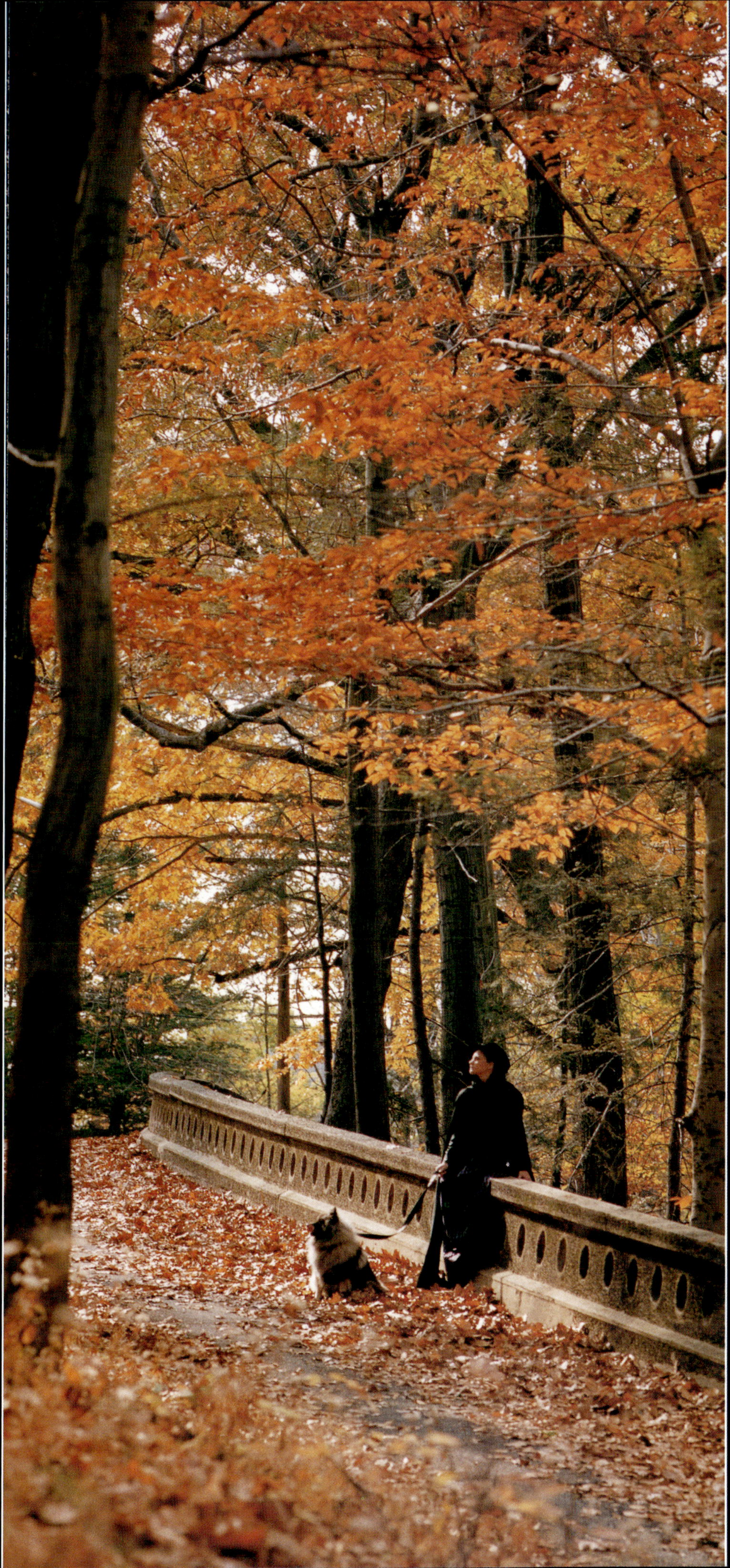

Late afternoon light thro
age spotlighted the wor
her dog and also provi
preferred 4:1 ratio of li
shadow.

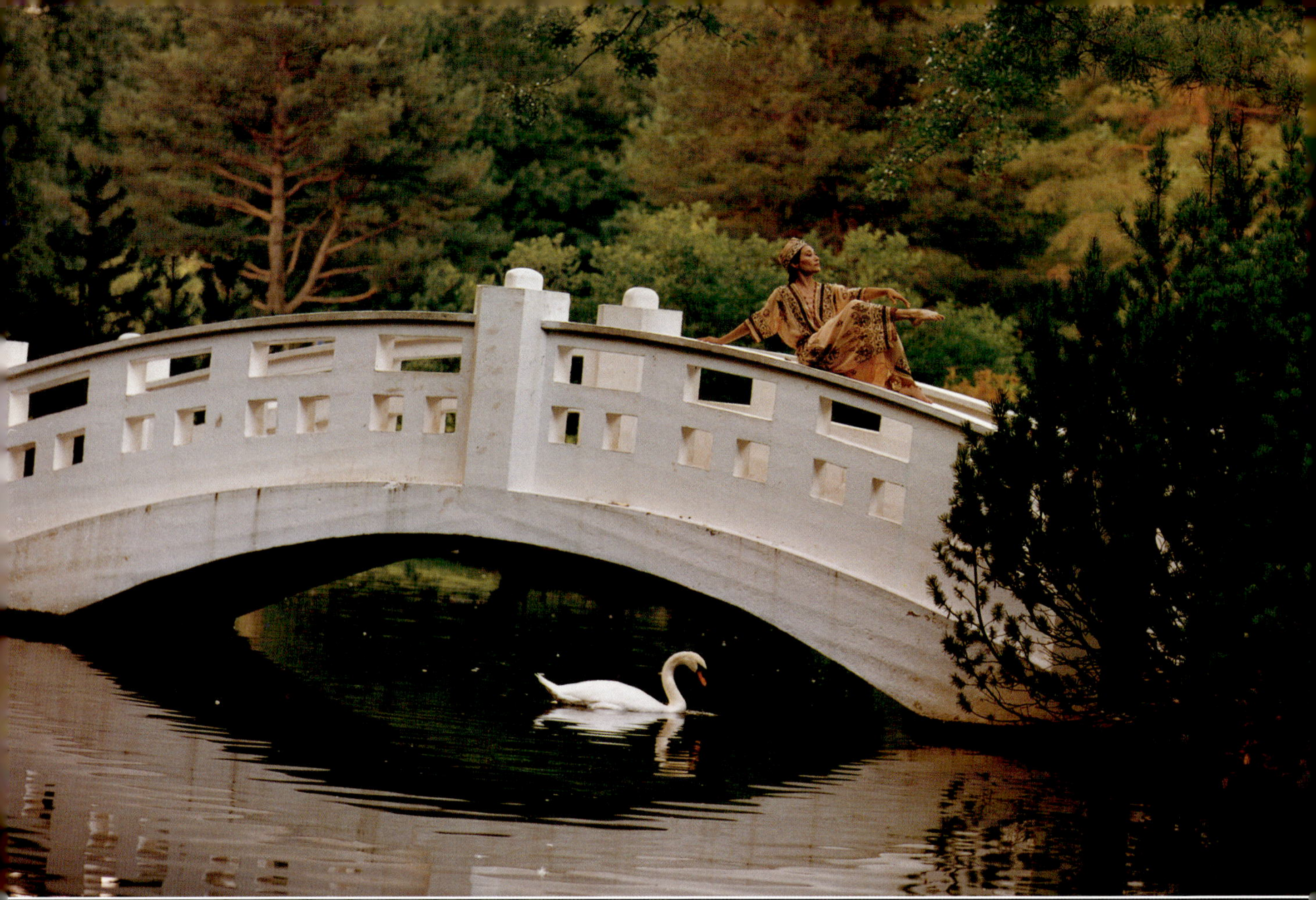

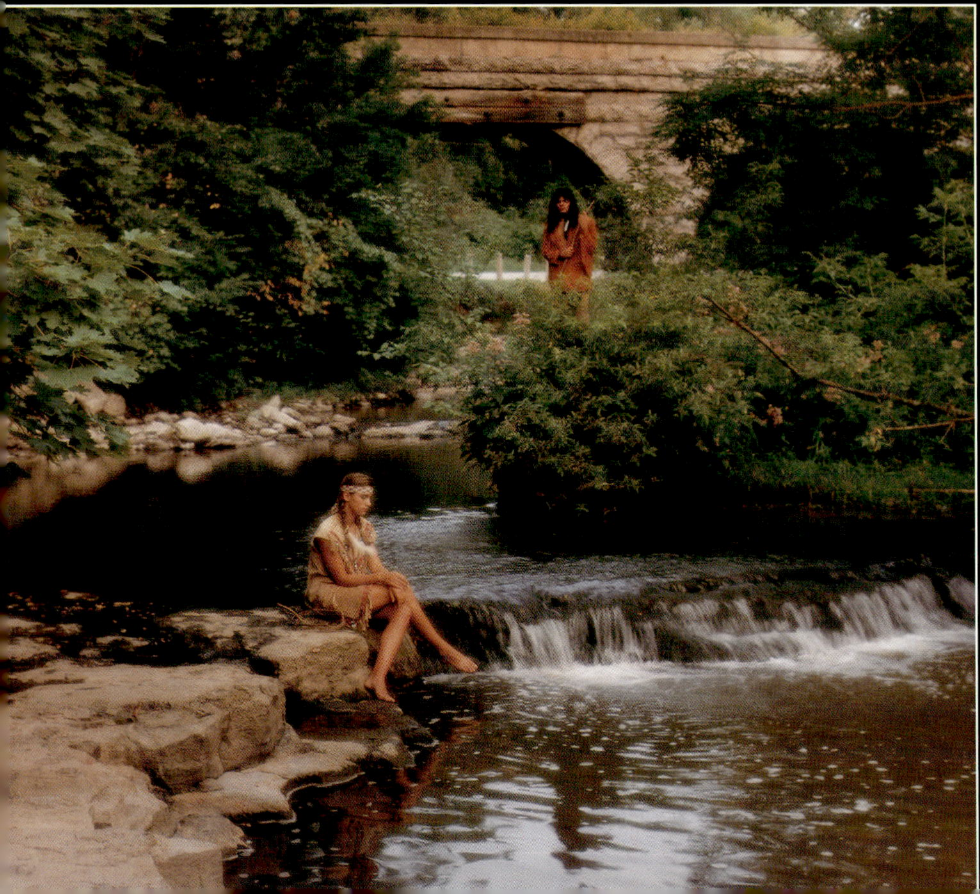

ABOVE—The elegant pose of the womar on the bridge and the graceful figure o the swan combine to perfection. Late afternoon daylight coming from the righ was all that was needed to provide c main light and separate the principal subject from the background.

LEFT—The time spent finding the righ location can pay off—just ask Don Blair Teaching workshops makes any instructo think on their feet and Don will often tel his students, "Don't talk to me for abou ten minutes while I work out a shot." Ther he'll come up with a winner. This tranqui image, with a Native American feel, uses a variety of natural elements that work ir harmony with the bridge in the background. Mother Nature provided all the right light for the occasion.

The edge of the tree line is an ideal location for late afternoon outdoor portraiture. In this portrait of a high school senior, the light sweeping across her face and gown is similar to a feathered studio light. A touch of humor is added with the statue of the cherub.

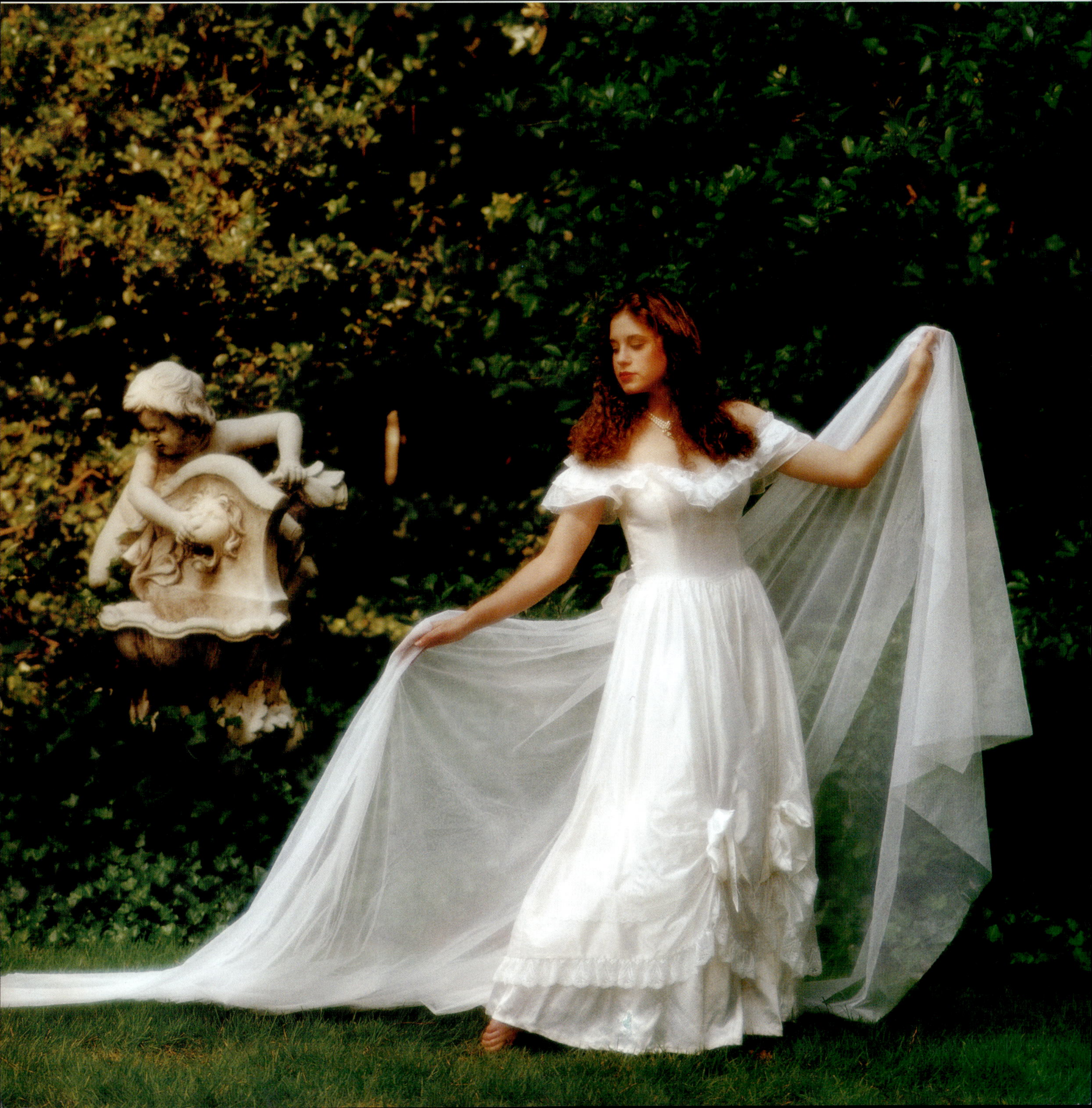

Here's another striking image made during that moment of "sweet light" at day's end. A Lindahl zoom lens on a Hasselblad camera was used to create the zoom effect with soft edges, so the viewer's eyes go immediately to the center of interest.

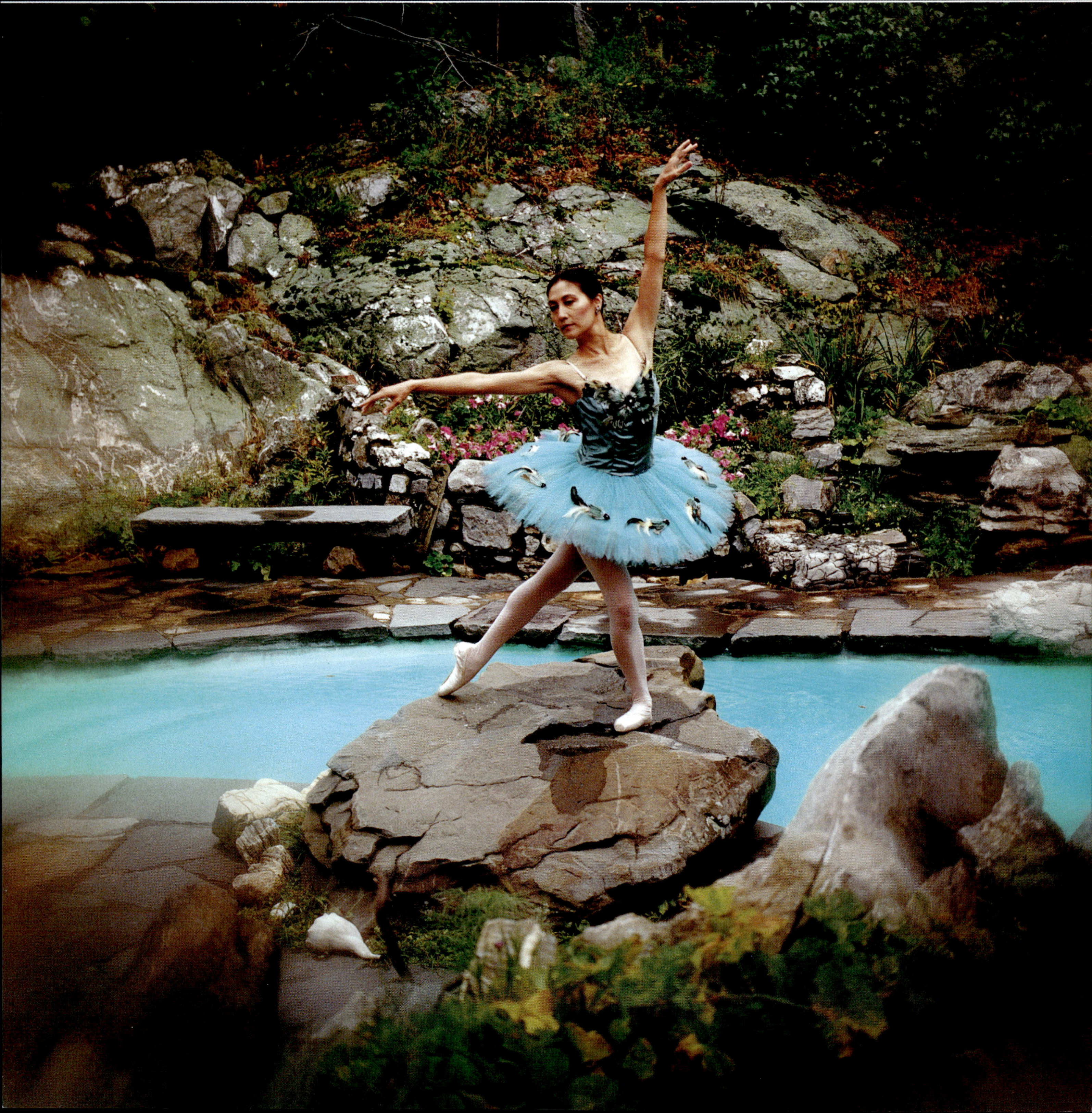

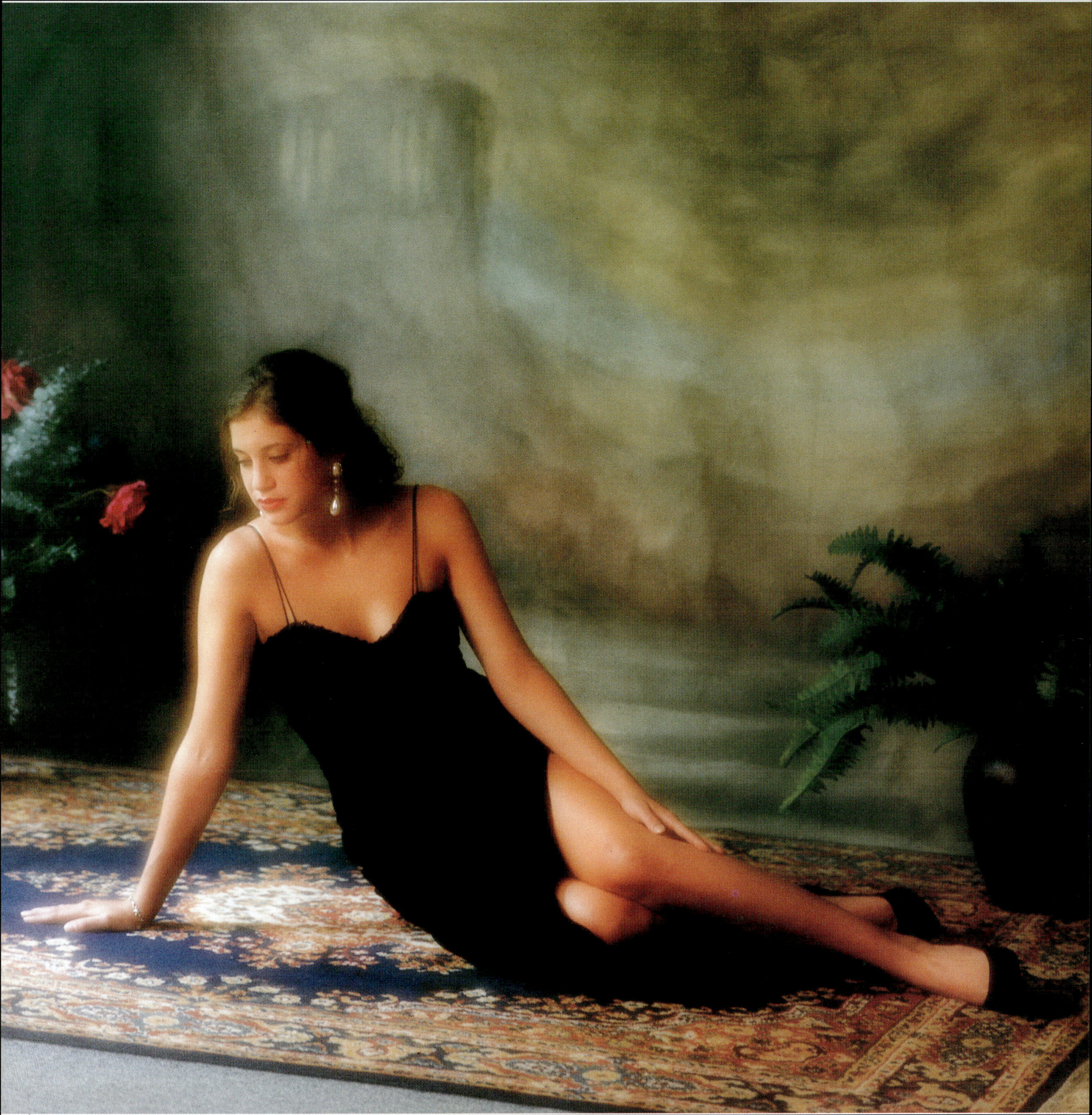

Simple and elegant. Window light from the left illuminated the model's face, arms, and legs, as well as the painted canvas backdrop. A touch-of-warmth reflector wrapped light around from the right to separate the subject from the background. The out-of-focus plants on both sides enhanced the composition.

12. *The Versatility of Spotlights*

Tungsten lights have their advantages. You can see exactly what you are getting in quality, quantity, and direction—and, when used properly, the lighting is hard to differentiate from electronic flash. In fact, few people could tell the difference when looking at prints. A blue filter over the lights balances the tungsten light source to daylight color temperature, but using tungsten film (or setting the white balance to tungsten on a digital camera) is a good alternative.

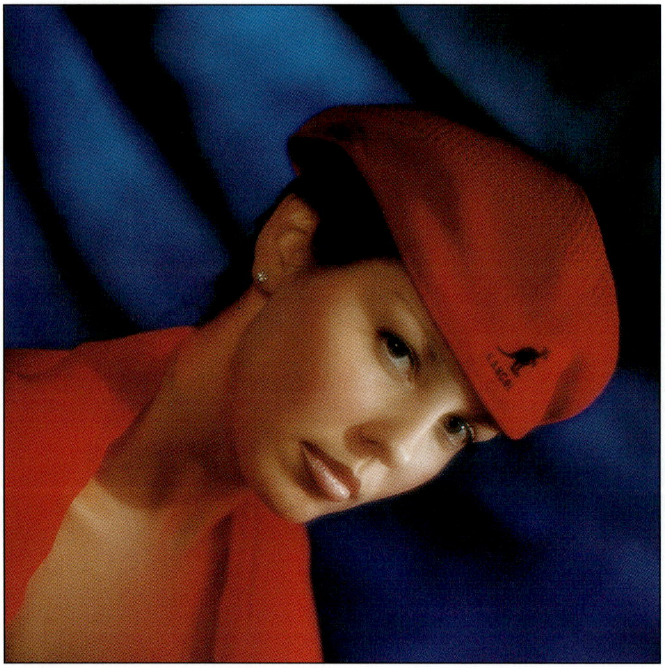

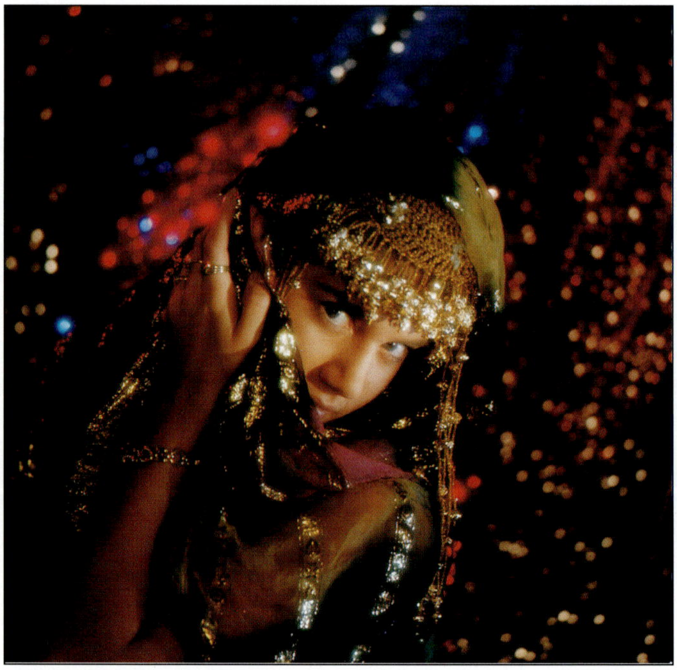

LEFT—This captivating portrait of a high school senior was created using a diffused main light and a mini-spotlight as an accent light. The background lights were tungsten lights with barndoors, one of which was gelled. A color correcting Wratten filter was used to balance the daylight negative film to the tungsten light source. (Don often uses Kodak Portra 800 color negative film when working with tungsten light sources.)

RIGHT—This is another of Don's "playtime" photographs, and the beguiling model and her sparkling jewelry really suit the mood. The main light was filtered for daylight film and a filtered tungsten mini-spotlight was used as the fill.

FACING PAGE—The lighting control possible with hot lights and barndoors is well illustrated here. The main light was at a 45-degree angle from the right, and a fill light next to the camera illuminated the shadow area. A touch-of-warmth reflector, on the opposite side but also close to the camera, was also used. Colored gels add to the mood of the image. Note the soft focus effect on the model's hands, which help draw the viewer's gaze to the girl's attractive face.

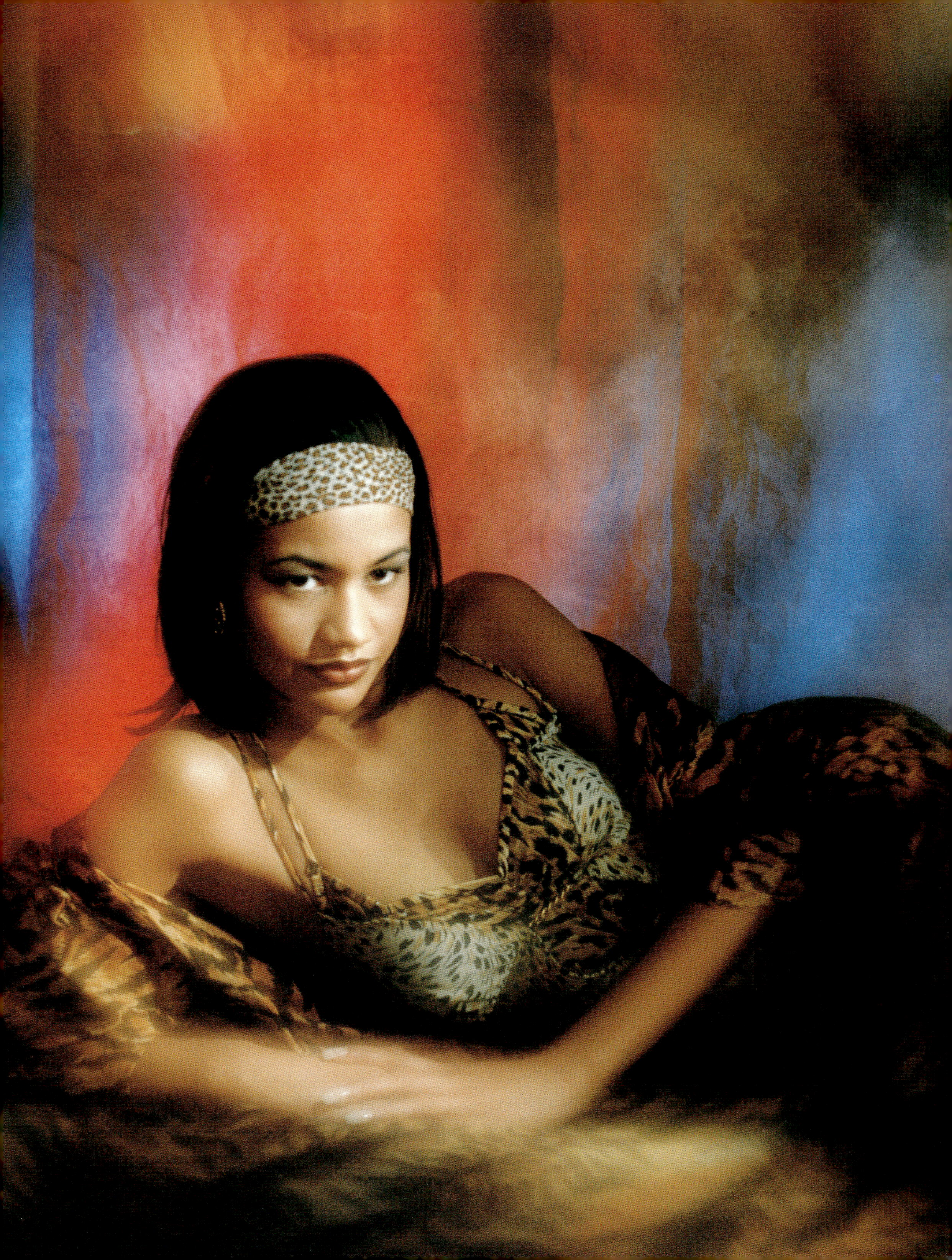

A slow shutter speed added motion to the swinging string of pearls and the red fan (note the blurred effect on both). Barndoors were used on both the main and accent lights to create the spotlight effect, while colored gels on the background complemented the red fan. A touch-of-warmth reflector feathered light into the shadow area.

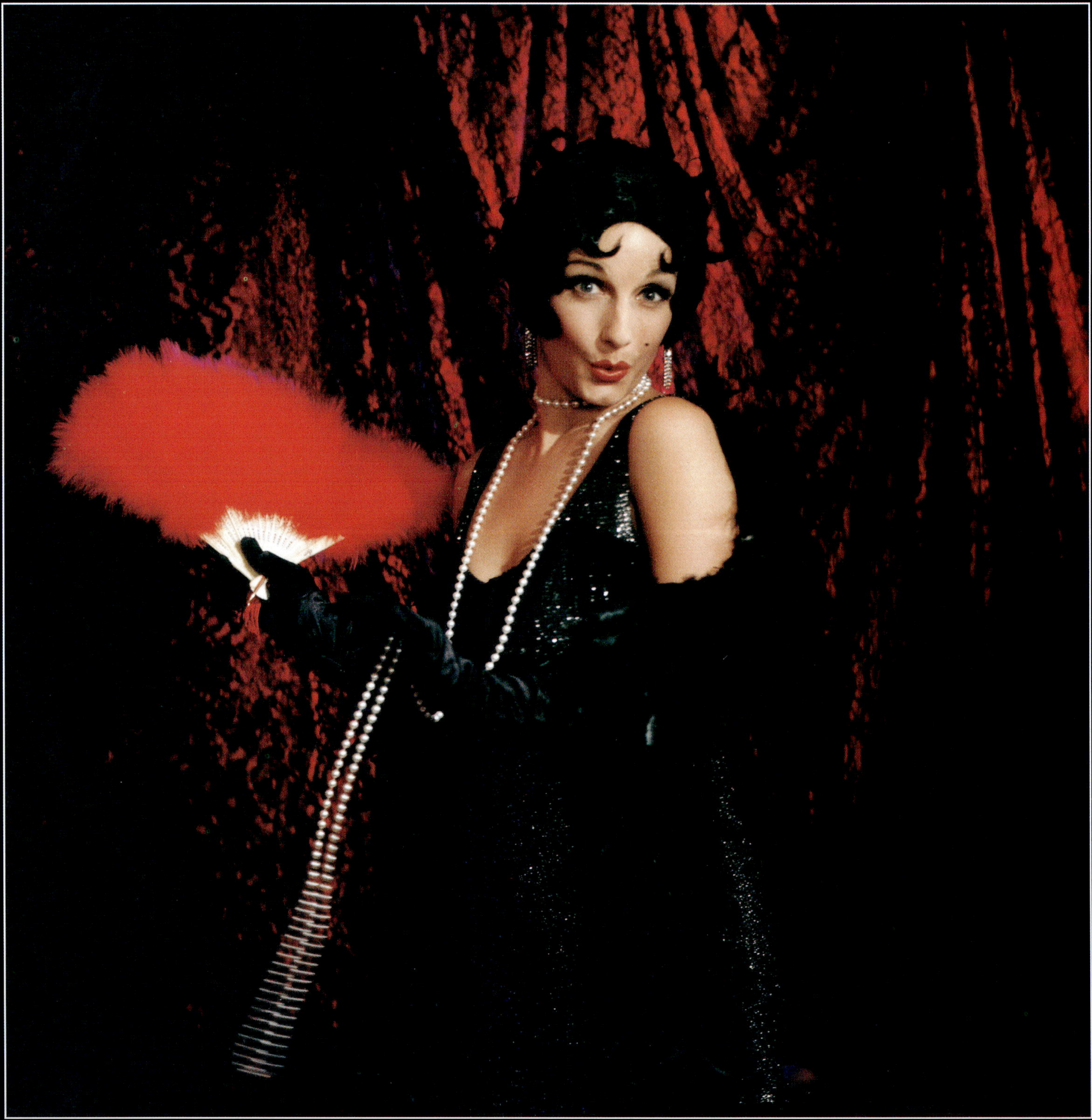

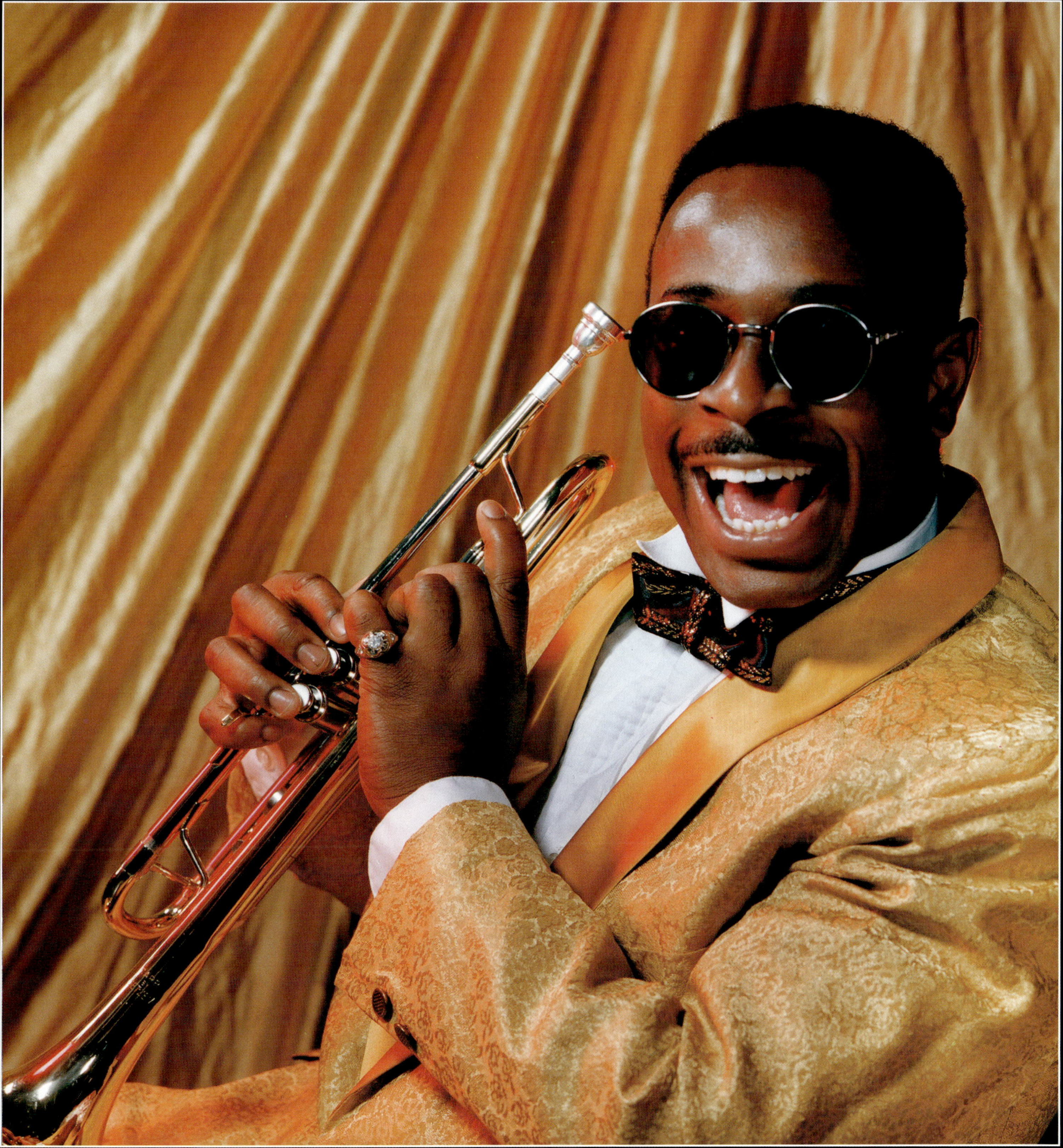

Bold, bright, animated, and exciting are apt terms to describe this action-packed portrait of a jazz musician. The lighting setup included numerous hot lights with a touch-of-warmth reflector on the left to add that extra measure of dazzle. The main light and one accent light were on the right. A second accent light and a hair light (high and behind the musician), two background lights, and a broad umbrella fill light at the lens axis completed the set. All the lights, apart from those on the background (Don wasn't too concerned about the additional warm color on the gold material) were filtered to balance with daylight film. The model's head was tilted down slightly to avoid reflection on his sunglasses.

13. Digital Photography

Many professional wedding and portrait photographers have embraced digital photography and are creating excellent work. You can too.

Manufacturers have made great strides in digital technology and, as with anything to do with computer technology, any new product will be superceded by an even newer one in a short time. However, this does not mean you should wait on the sidelines until the perfect camera arrives on the scene. You'll be waiting forever.

Digital photography has a language of its own, and that in itself can be confusing, and perhaps even intimidating. Having been a photographer for over fifty years, I have seen many changes and advances, and I learned a long time ago that old dogs *can* be taught new tricks—as long as the old dog is enthusiastic and curious. My advice is to get your feet wet, attend classes, go to trade shows, read magazines, speak with other photographers, and learn what digital can do for you. Above all, don't be afraid of it.

Good lighting is the key to great portraits, so if your lighting skills are good, you'll be able to make the most of digital photography. I have not changed a thing in my lighting techniques as I have made the transition from film to digital. Therefore, every lighting tip I offer in this book can be applied to digital photography. With digital, you also have the advantage of being able to see the image immediately—and that is a huge asset.

Recently, I have been using digital capture a lot and have photographed with Kodak backs on my Hasselblad 555 ELD and also with the Kodak 14n SLR with superb results from both. The following images, for a Kodak promotion, were all made with the Kodak DCS back on the Hasselblad 555 ELD with a 120mm lens.

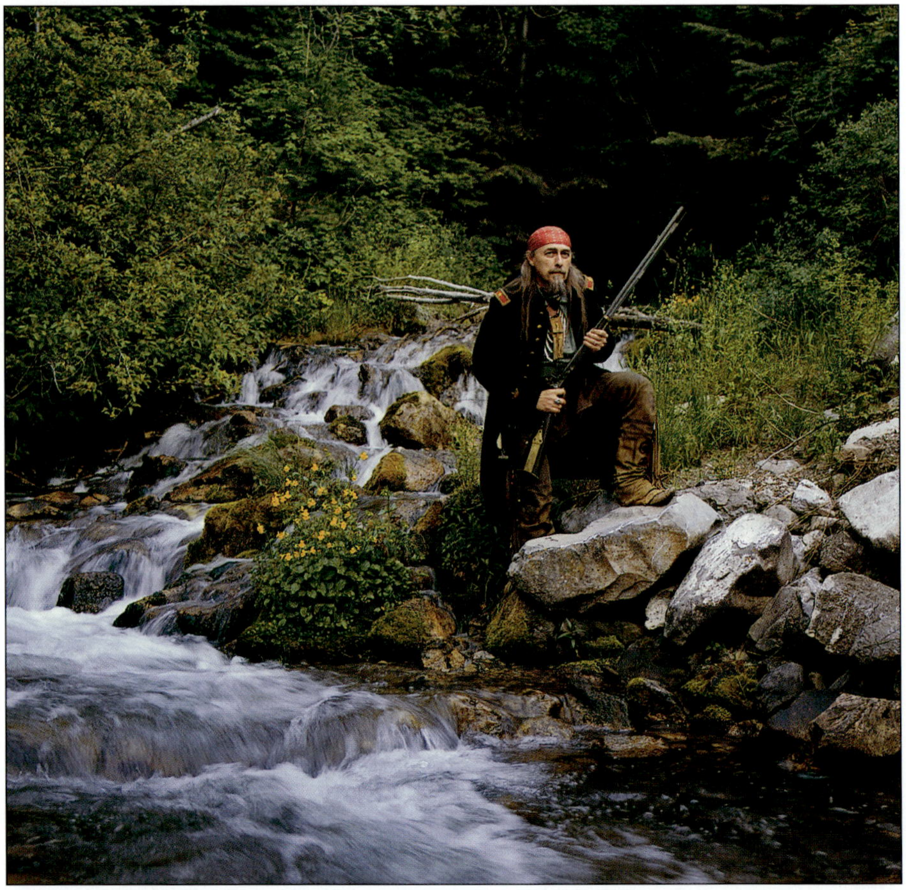

This environmental portrait of a musket-bearing frontier man was made with natural ambient light as the only illumination. A slower shutter speed was used to show the movement of the stream.

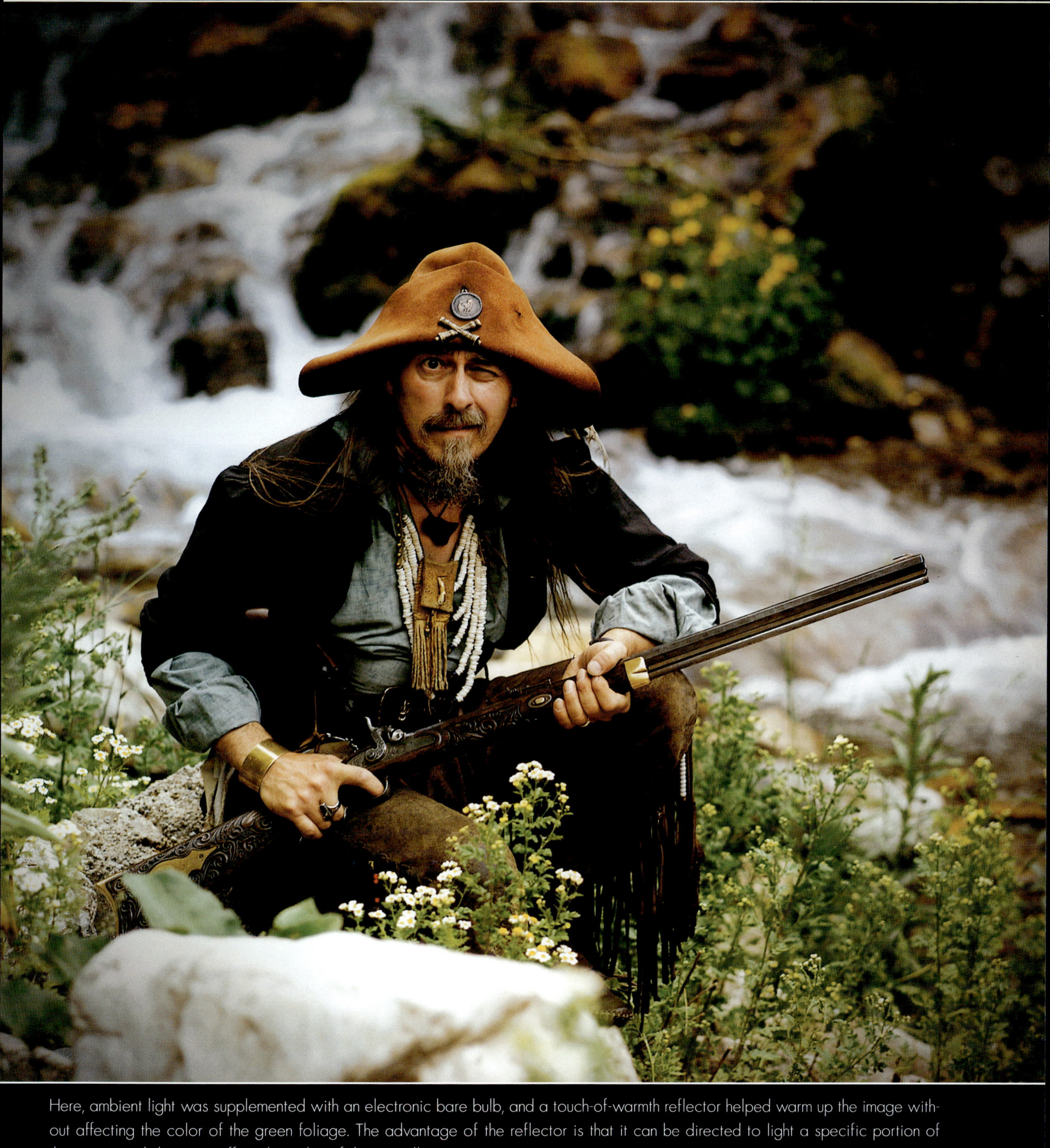

Here, ambient light was supplemented with an electronic bare bulb, and a touch-of-warmth reflector helped warm up the image without affecting the color of the green foliage. The advantage of the reflector is that it can be directed to light a specific portion of the image and does not affect the color of the overall scene.

Light and shadow are important compositional and visual elements in this portrait, which was lit with a punch panel. Light sweeping from the right enhanced the subject's shape and texture, while an accent light separated the model from the background and highlighted her hair. Note the posing of the arms and hands with the edge of her hands turned toward the camera.

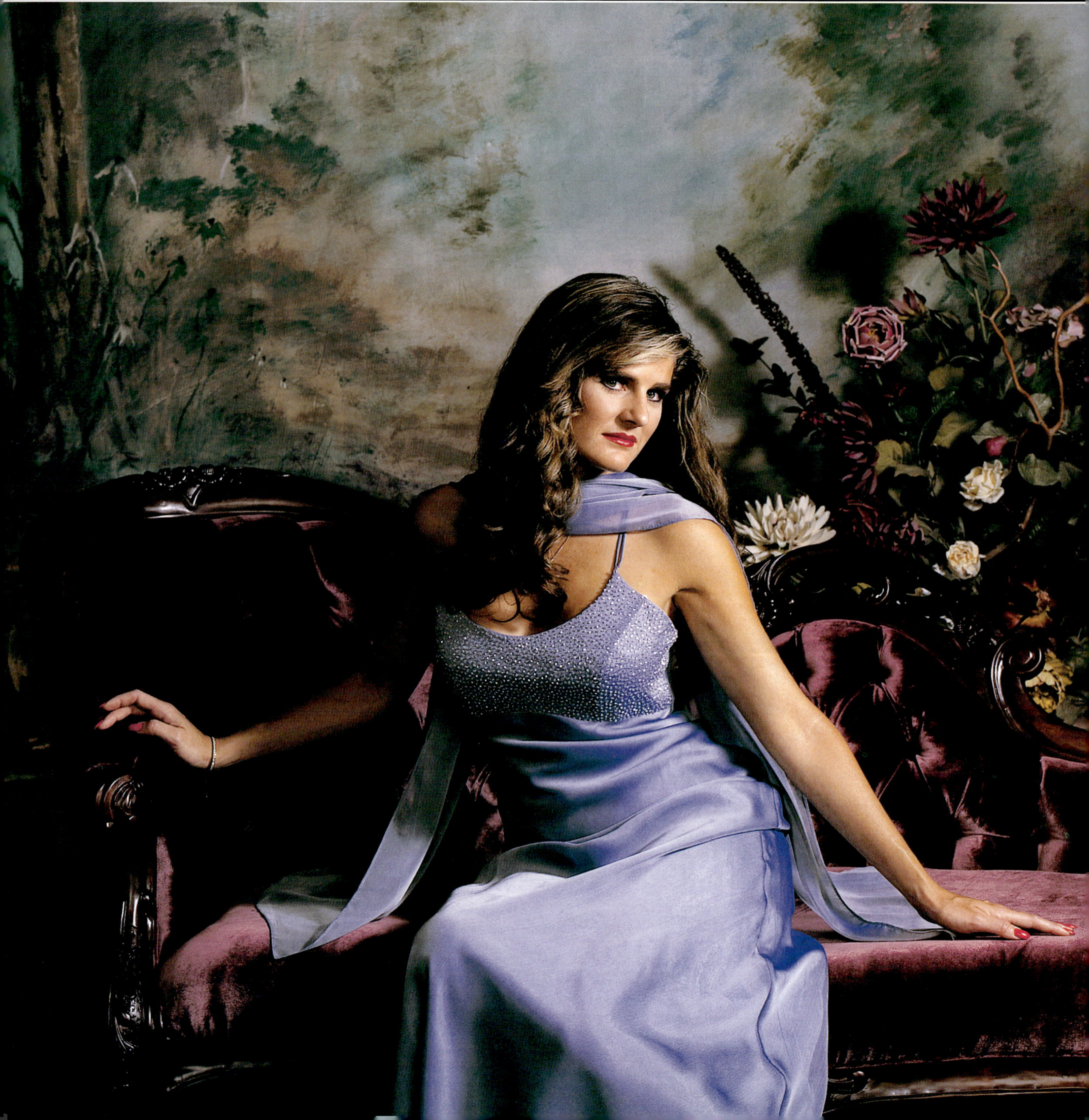

This character portrait was captured digitally and lit conventionally. A parabolic reflector with barndoors was the main light, an umbrella provided fill, and an accent light played its part in separation while adding highlights. A small background light illuminated the archway and also provided separation. A touch-of-warmth reflector added extra sparkle.

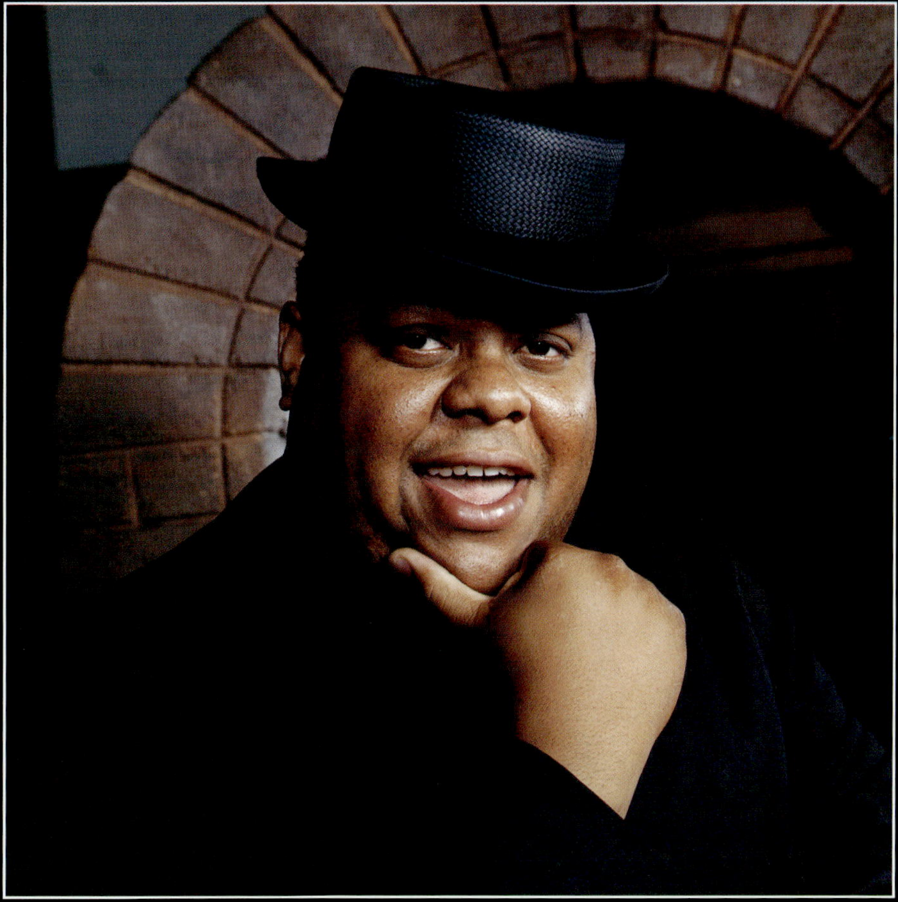

The ballerina, posed precariously on the boulder, was lit by a combination of ambient light, electronic bare bulb, and a touch-of-warmth reflector. A slow shutter speed was used to show the motion of the running stream. Careful selection of the subject's position ensured that her dress would stand out against the dark background

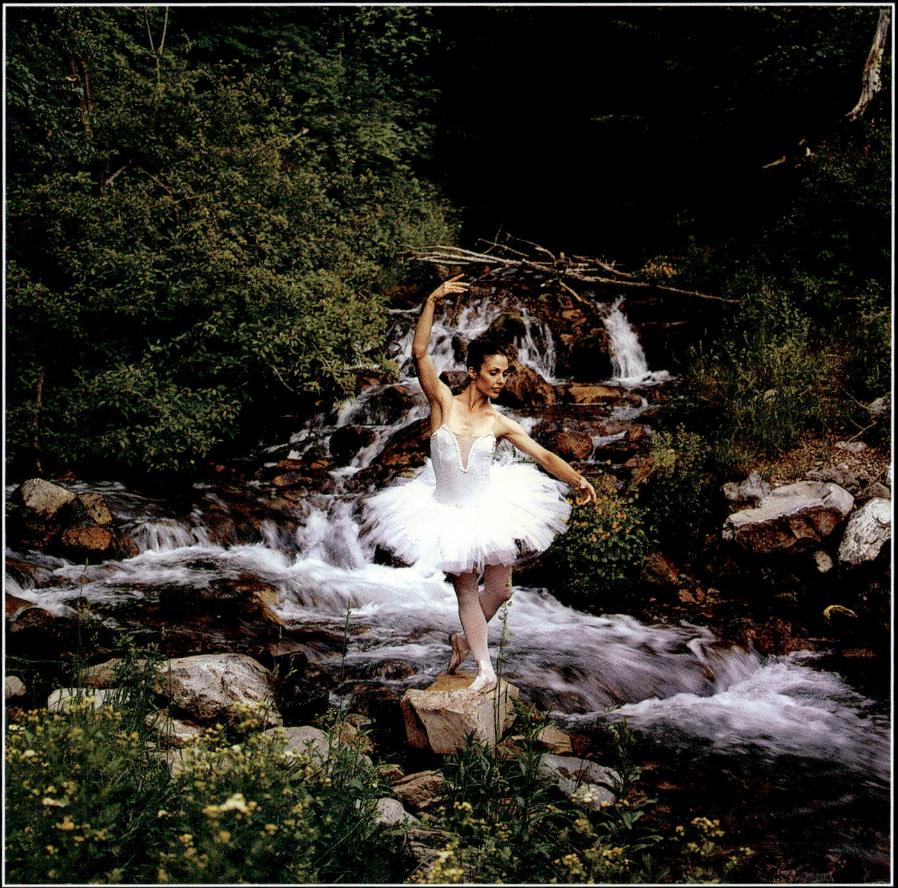

14. The Scene Machine

Backgrounds and props are important elements in portraiture. While the right background can certainly enhance the image, it should never overpower or detract from the principal subjects. Over the years, much of my work has been environmental and on-location, and I have created many memorable images in natural settings. In fact, if I were to choose the ideal location for a portrait, chances are I would select one of my favorite outdoor settings.

However, we all know that Mother Nature does not always cooperate for an environmental photography session—especially if you live in an area where winter weather limits the amount of time you and your clients can spend outdoors. During those colder months, much of our work has to be done indoors. And, in such circumstances, it's not always easy to find the ideal background.

However, there is a high-technology solution, and it's one that I have been using recently. It's accomplished by creating virtual backgrounds, something that has been made easy with the Scene Machine projection system. This

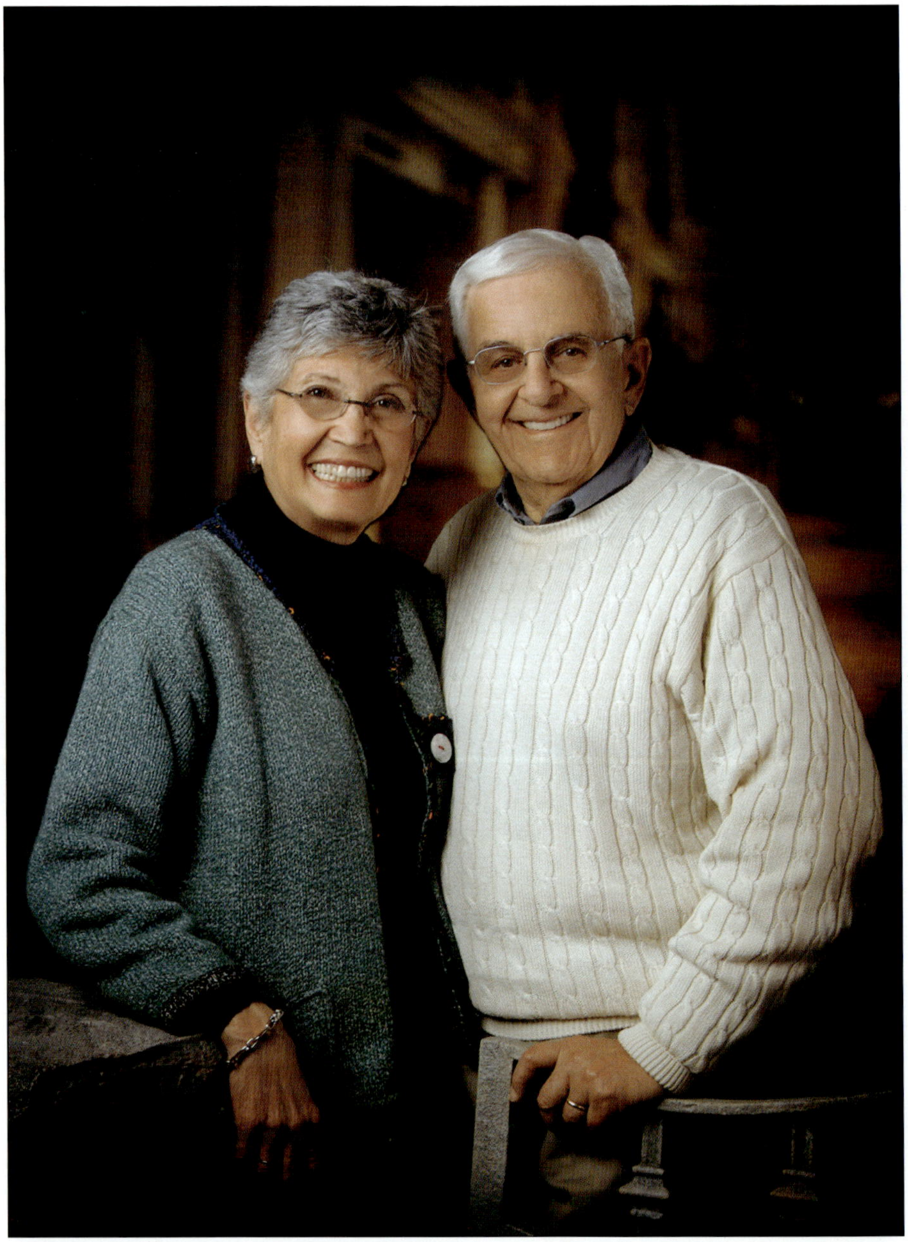

ABOVE AND FACING PAGE—Portrait lighting using the Scene Machine is essentially the same as for traditional portraiture. The one exception is that the fill light is moved slightly off the lens axis so it is not reflected in the Scene Machine's screen. These delightful portraits of the woman and the couple were lit with punch-panel main and fill lights on the left, accent and hair lights, and a touch-of-warmth reflector on the right.

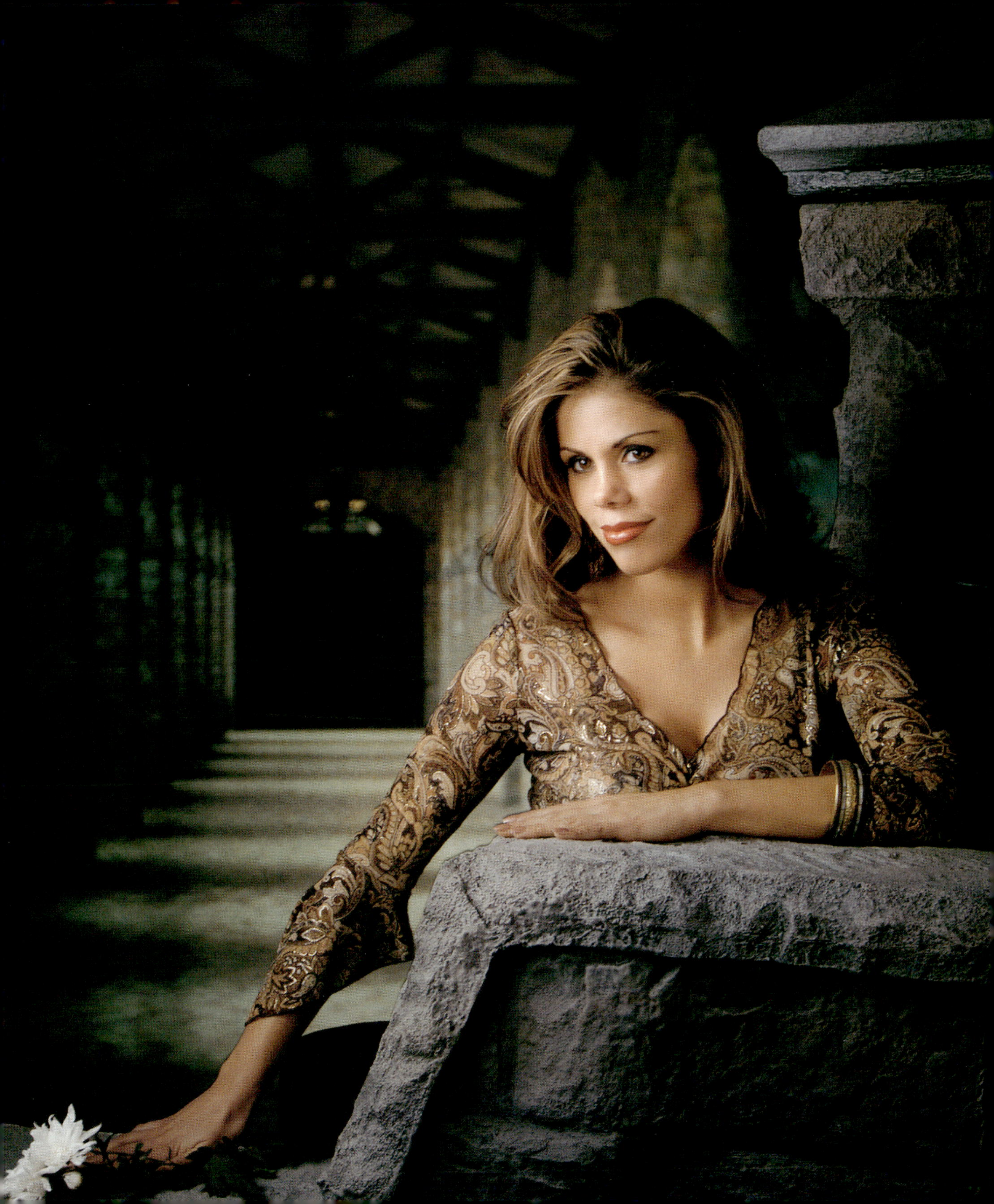

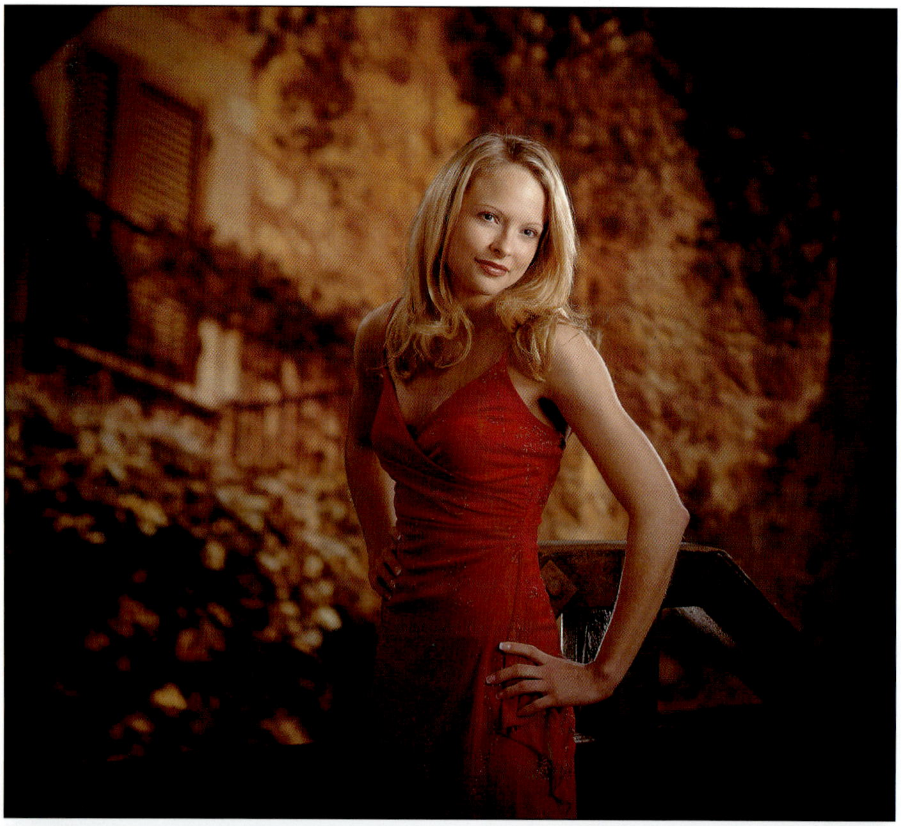

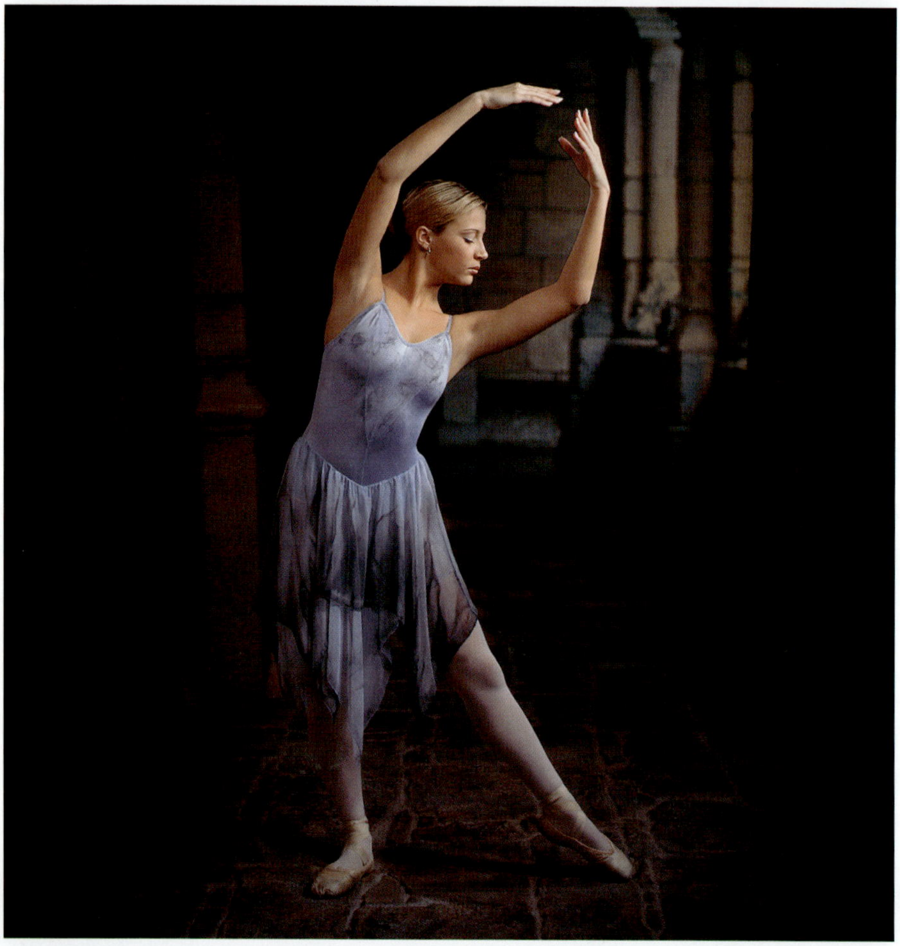

remarkable equipment was developed by Dr. Henry Oles and, depending on the kind of studio you are operating, has the potential to put you into a league of your own and greatly increase your revenue stream. You can learn more about this company, their products, and their training programs by visiting www.vitualbackgrounds.net.

To use the Scene Machine, you simply insert any ordinary transparency or slide. Making use of a beam splitter and a specially coated, retro-reflective screen, the image is then projected behind the subject. The image is flashed simultaneously with the studio strobes used to light the subject, creating a backdrop during the exposure. The background is captured on film or digital at the exact same moment the subject is photographed. Due to the highly reflective quality of the background screen, the projected image appears only on the screen, not on the subject. With only a small amount of light from the projector, the Scene Machine produces a background that records as bright

LEFT AND FACING PAGE—The wide range of virtual backgrounds offered by the Scene Machine is illustrated in these three images. These portraits of attractive young women were all lit with the same setup but with different backgrounds. Illumination was from a punch-panel main light, fill light, and accent light all placed on the right, while an elevated hair light provided separation. In a nutshell, there is virtually no limit to the variety of background possibilities.

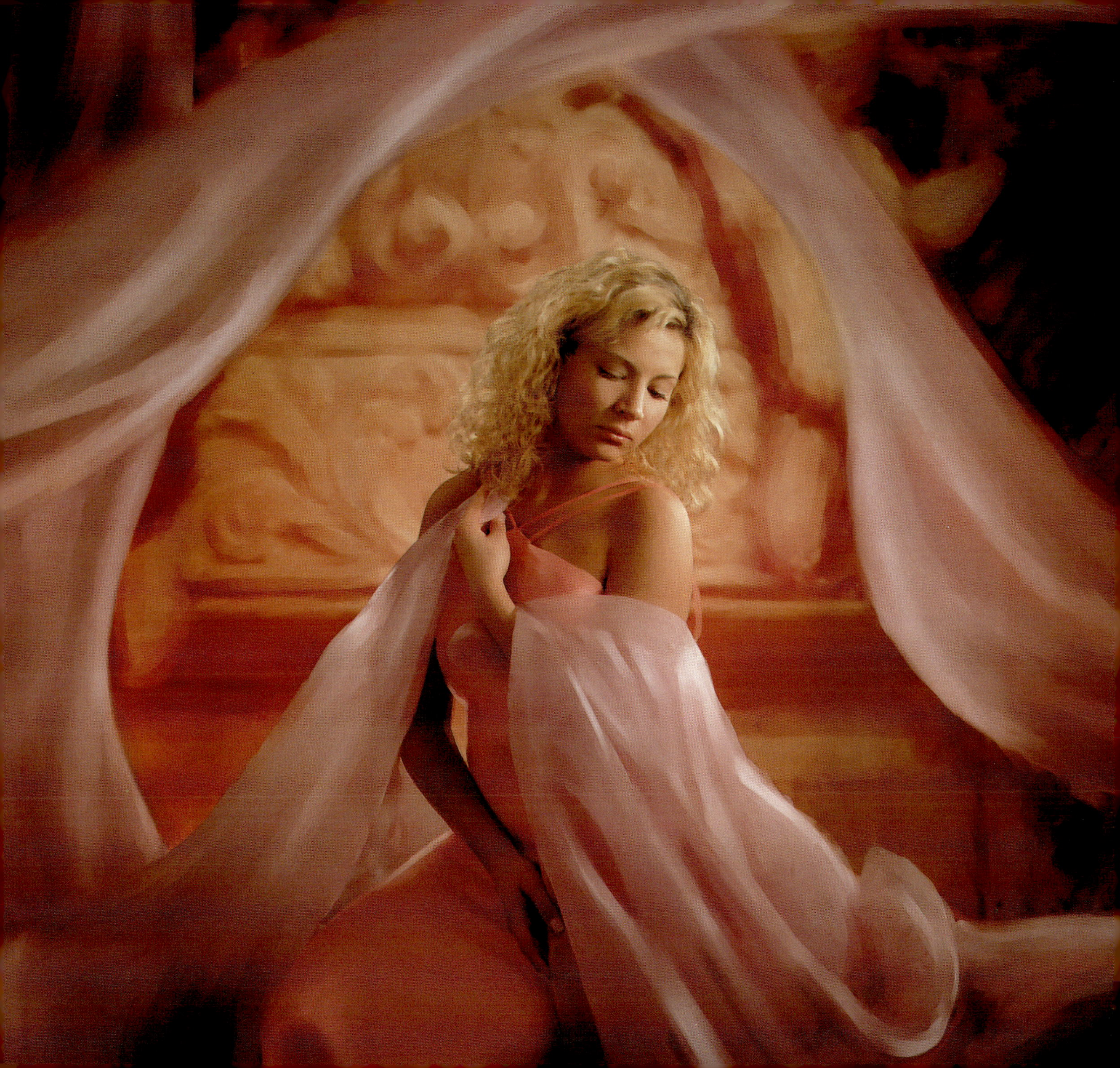

and saturated, yet is produced with too little light to show on the subject's skin or clothing.

When using the Scene Machine, you can light your subject as you normally do, as long as you don't position your fill light directly behind your camera (which would affect the screen). I know that many photographers using the system add barndoors and louvers to their lighting so they can be even more creative. Since I really like using barndoors to feather the light, I find this works well for me too. Obviously, the lighting you use should have the same color, direction, and feel as the background you have selected.

The choice of backgrounds is virtually limitless. The manufacturer has a gallery of about one thousand generic backgrounds that can be purchased, or you can use your own slides. The latter choice is ideal if you prefer to incorporate local scenes into your environmental images. For example, you could photograph local schools, churches, and monuments to use in special promotions. When you go on vacation, take along a camera and some slide film to create background slides. Keep in mind, however, that the background slides must be carefully composed so they do not distract from the subject.

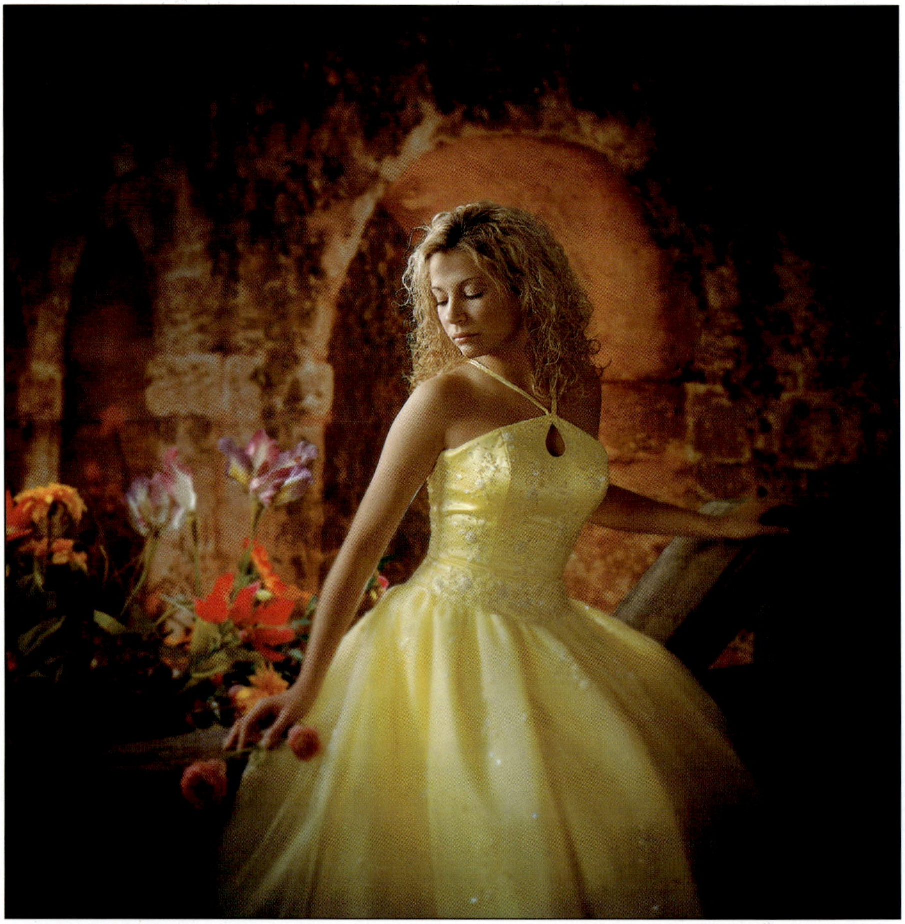

ABOVE AND FACING PAGE—These portraits were lit with slightly varying setups. For both images, the main light was a parabolic 16-inch reflector with barndoors. An umbrella fill light and an accent light, placed to the left of the subjects, completed the setup. A hair light was incorporated in the image of the woman whose outstretched arm gracefully follows the line of her dress, and a touch-of-warmth reflector was placed on the right.

Whether you shoot film or digital, the virtual background system gives you total control over the background. It can also boost your efficiency, allowing you to quickly change from one background to the next. More variety spells more customer satisfaction, which translates into more profit. It's really that simple.

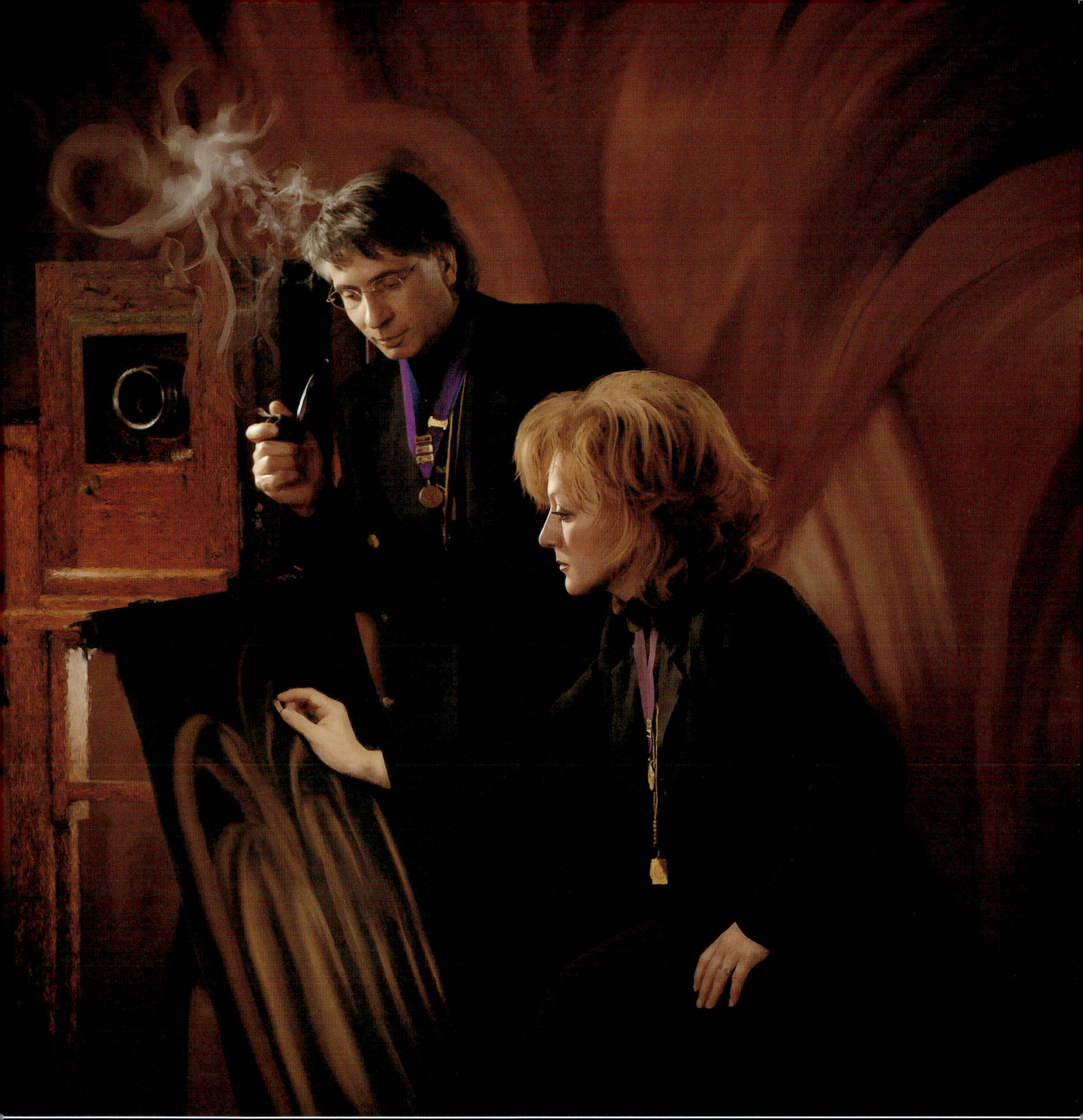

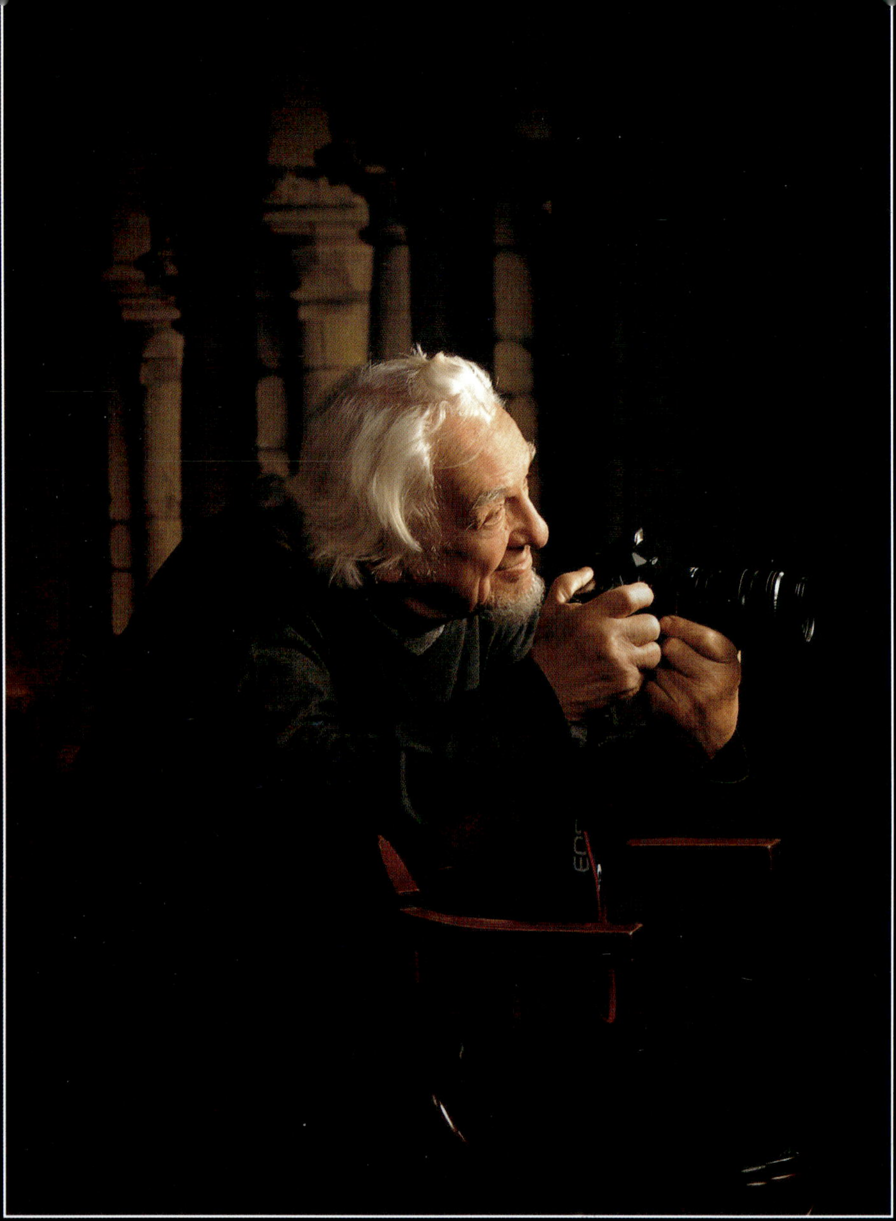

THIS PAGE AND FACING PAGE—Simplicity, character, elegance, and craftsmanship resonate from this series of portraits, all lit with a three-light setup against an array of virtual backgrounds provided by the versatile Scene Machine. Study these images and you will see that the main parabolic light with barndoors, the umbrella fill, and the accent light were all placed to the right of the subjects. It should be stressed that the fill light must be slightly off lens axis to avoid reflection. Apart from that, creating portraits with the Scene Machine virtual backgrounds is no different from traditional portrait lighting.

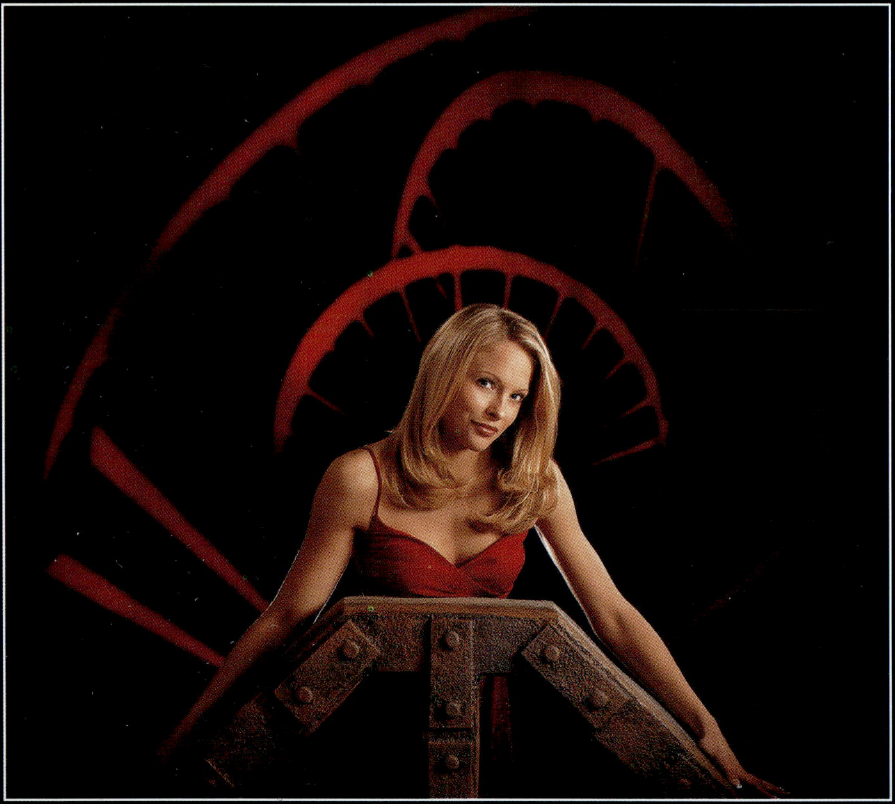

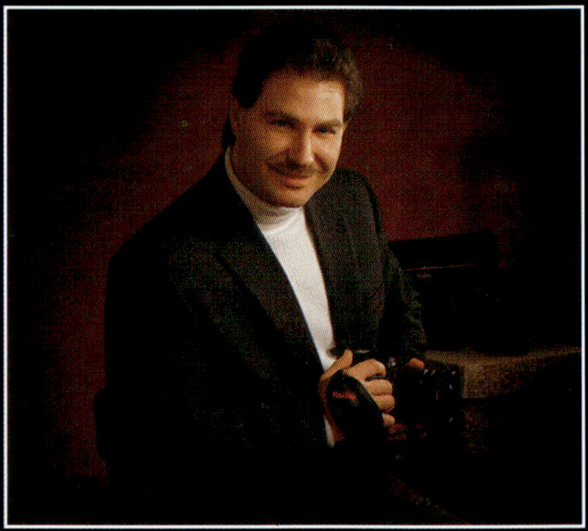

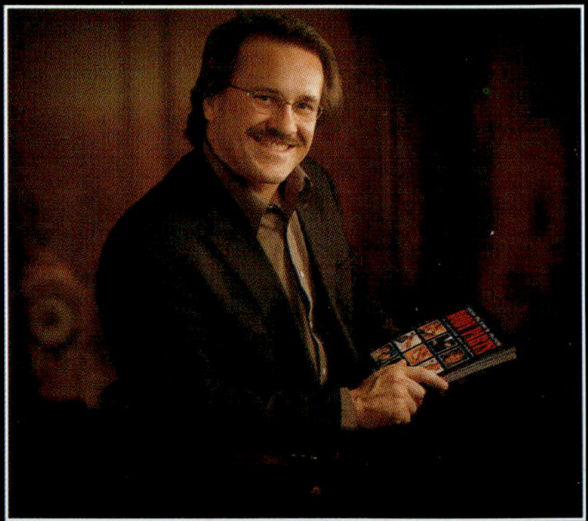

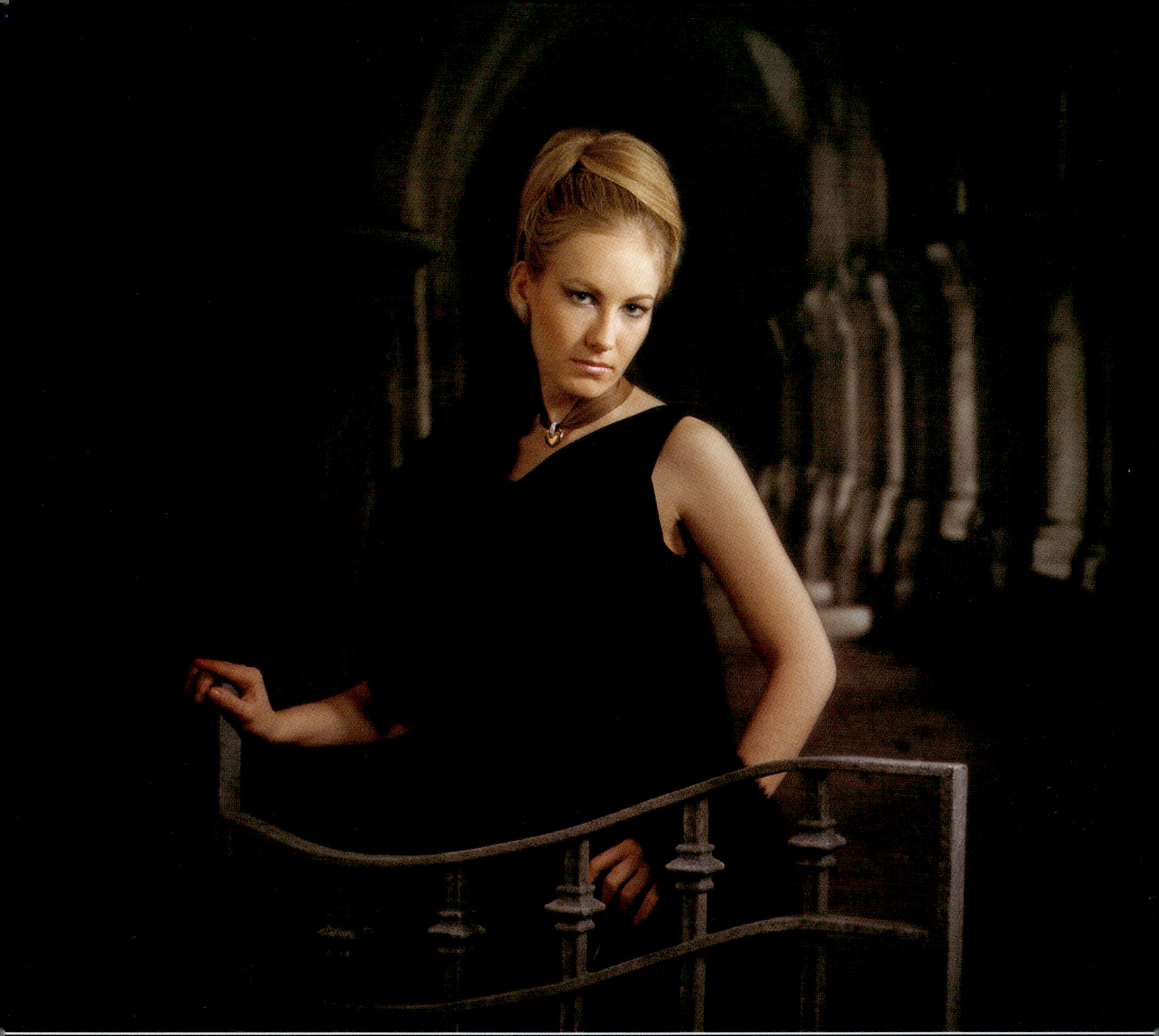

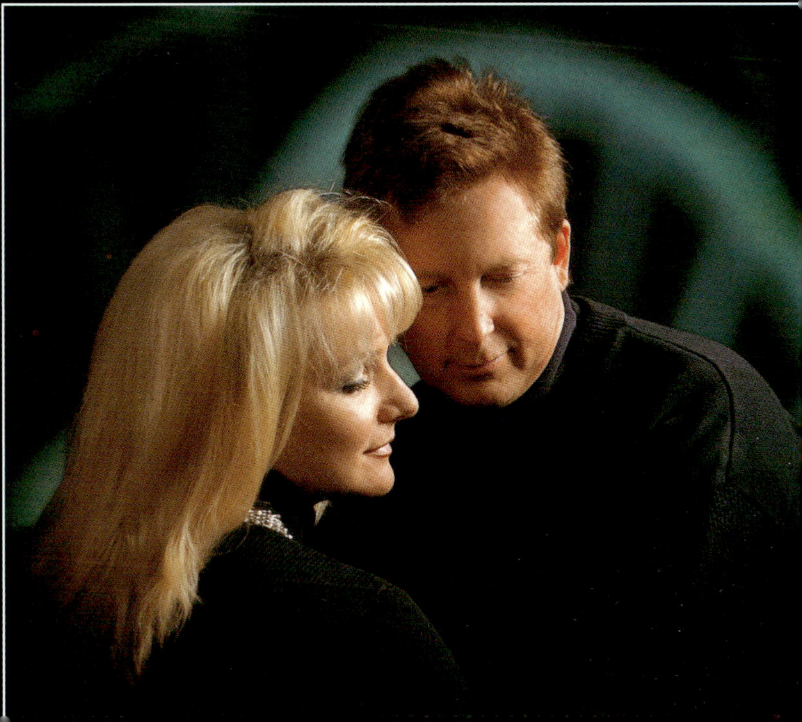

14. Special Effects and Having Fun

Don't be afraid to experiment with lighting or special effects. You never know when something great will emerge from your efforts. It's also a good idea to keep notes of what you did so you can repeat the technique in the future. Most "experiments" are based on a solid foundation of technique, so you should have a pretty good idea of the final result before you start. Visualize what you want and shoot for it. In some cases it's just a matter of trying something fun and zany. The images in this section are just some of my own experiments from over the years and each has its own background story, which adds to the memory. So, my advice is to go ahead and have fun with your photography, add a few colored gels to the lights, try some extra-long exposures with movement and action, or experiment with a few multi-exposure images.

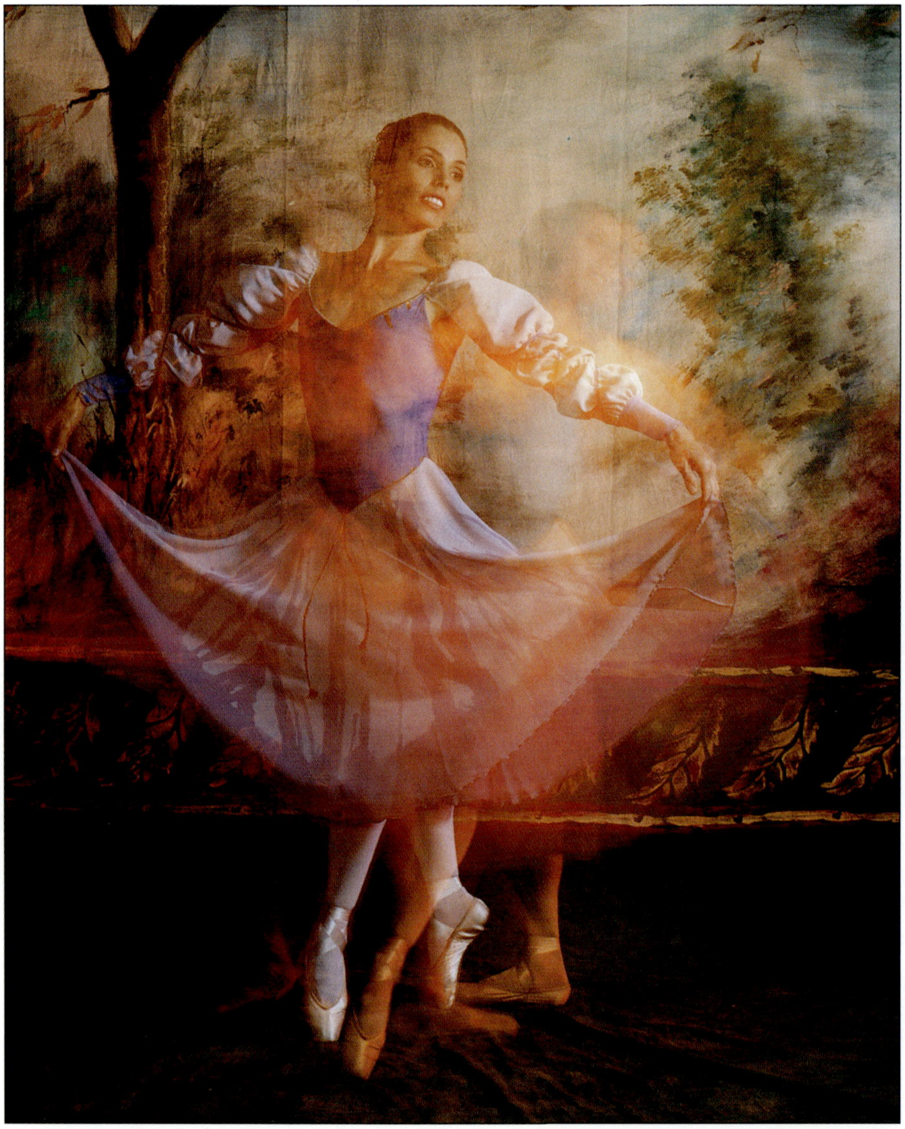

The first exposure of the ballet dancer was made with a flash. Then, while she kept dancing within a defined area, the shutter was left open for 12 seconds. The only illumination during the latter part of the exposure was from the modeling light, which resulted in the warm look to the image.

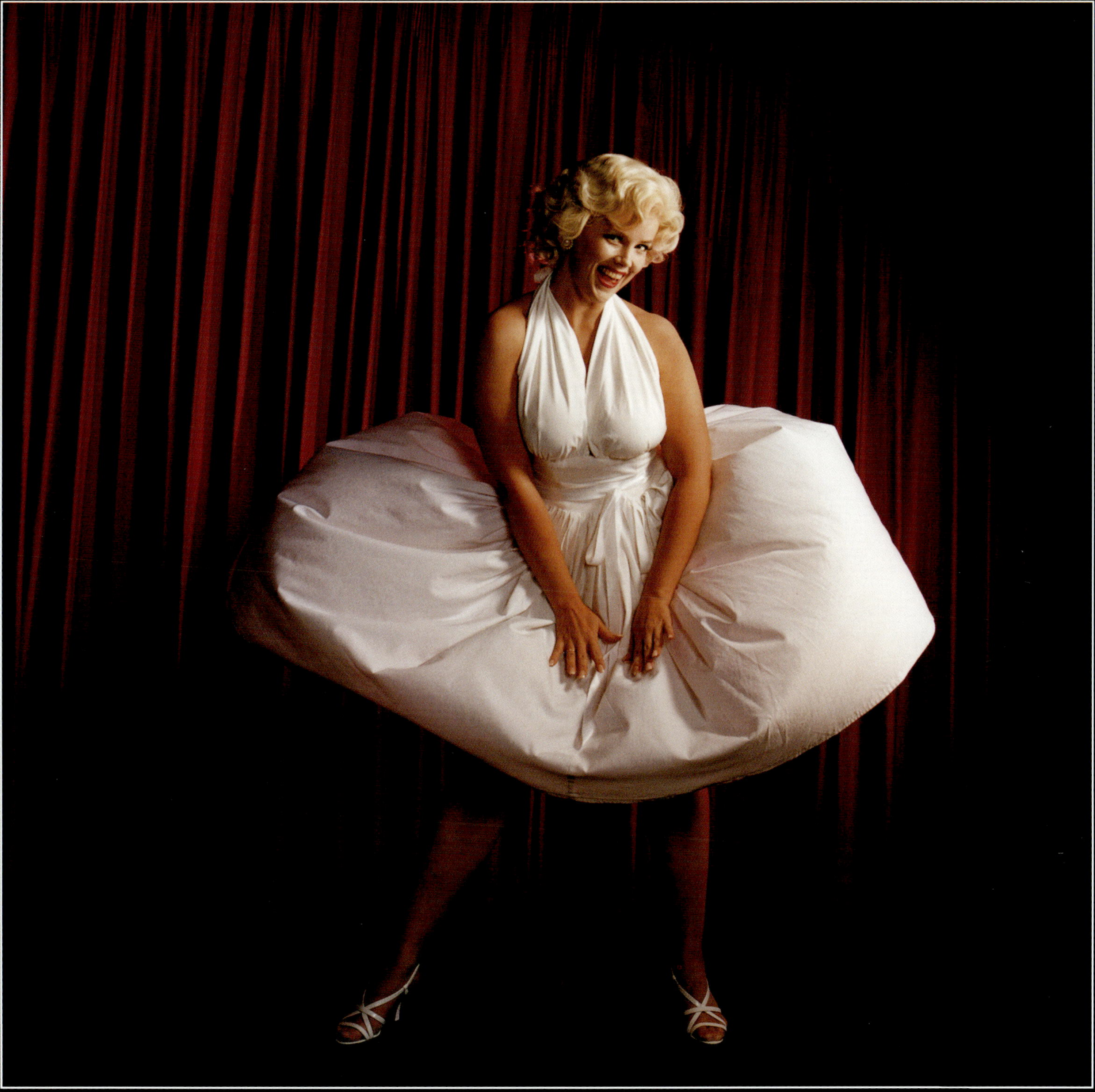

This Marilyn Monroe look-alike was having as much fun with this adaptation of the famous original image as Don and the audience were. To concentrate the light, and the viewer's attention, on the model's face and body, a parabolic light with barndoors was used as the main light. Barndoors are a great tool for feathering light, as long as you pinch those doors way down! A colored gel was used on the background light, giving it a theatrical look. Finally, a leaf blower under the stage was used to fill "Marilyn's" dress with air. The model was standing on milk crates, hidden from view by the feathered light.

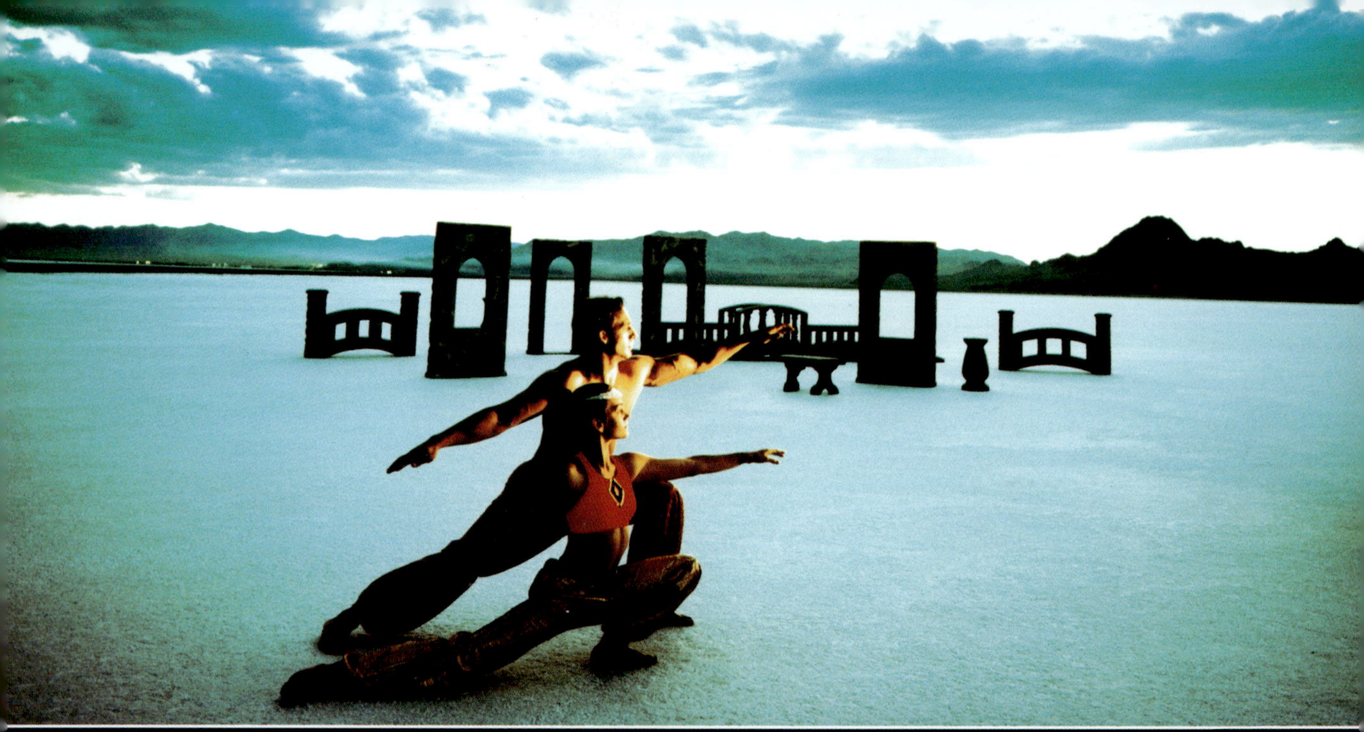

ABOVE—Cross-processing and unusual lighting were used to give a combination of warmth and coolness to this image of dancers on the salt flats near Salt Lake City. Transparency film (normally processed in E-6) was run through C-41 processing (for negative film). The headlights of a van provided the warm lighting on the dancers. "This was a playtime shot," Don said of this very dramatic looking image.

RIGHT—Two ballet dancers held their pose on pointed toes while a third dancer twirled around the set during this 12-second exposure. The photograph was lit with tungsten spotlights fitted with red gels, while an overhead room light was left on low to supply soft illumination from above.

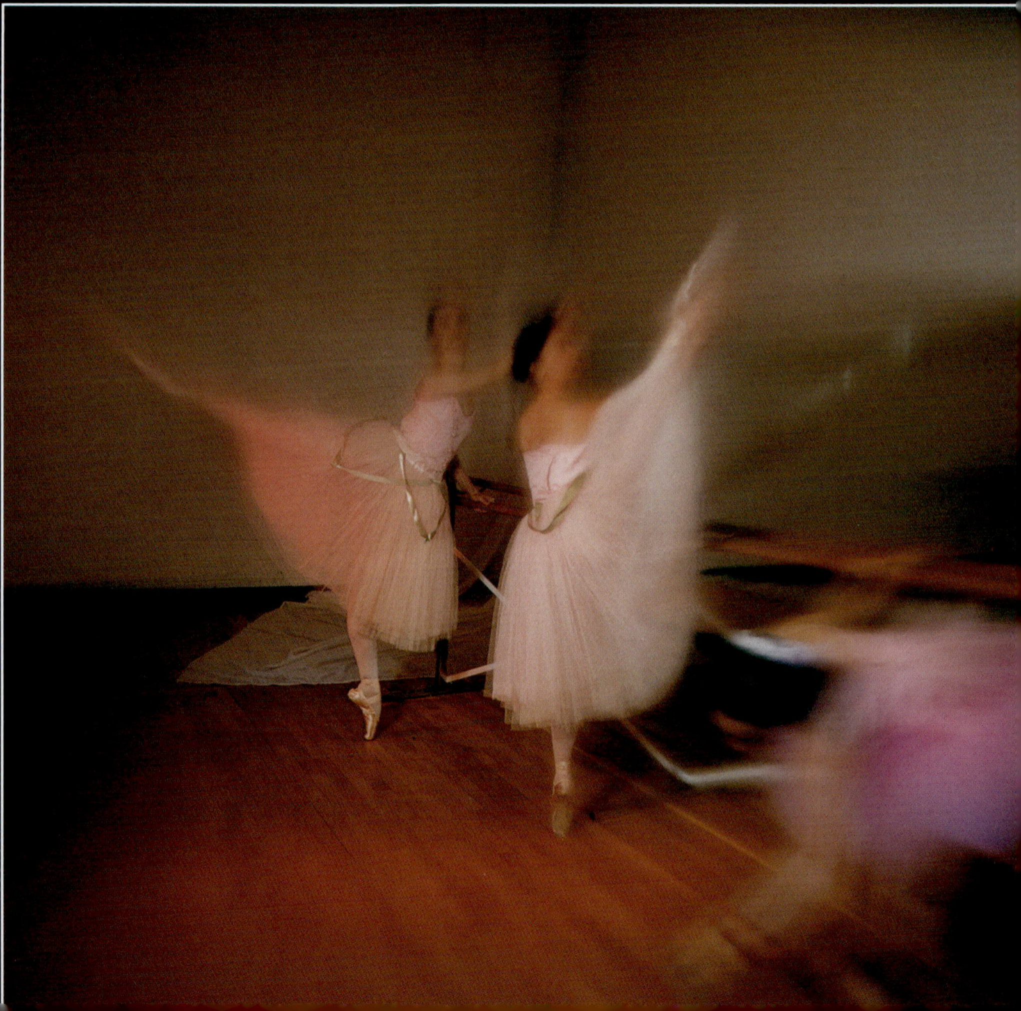

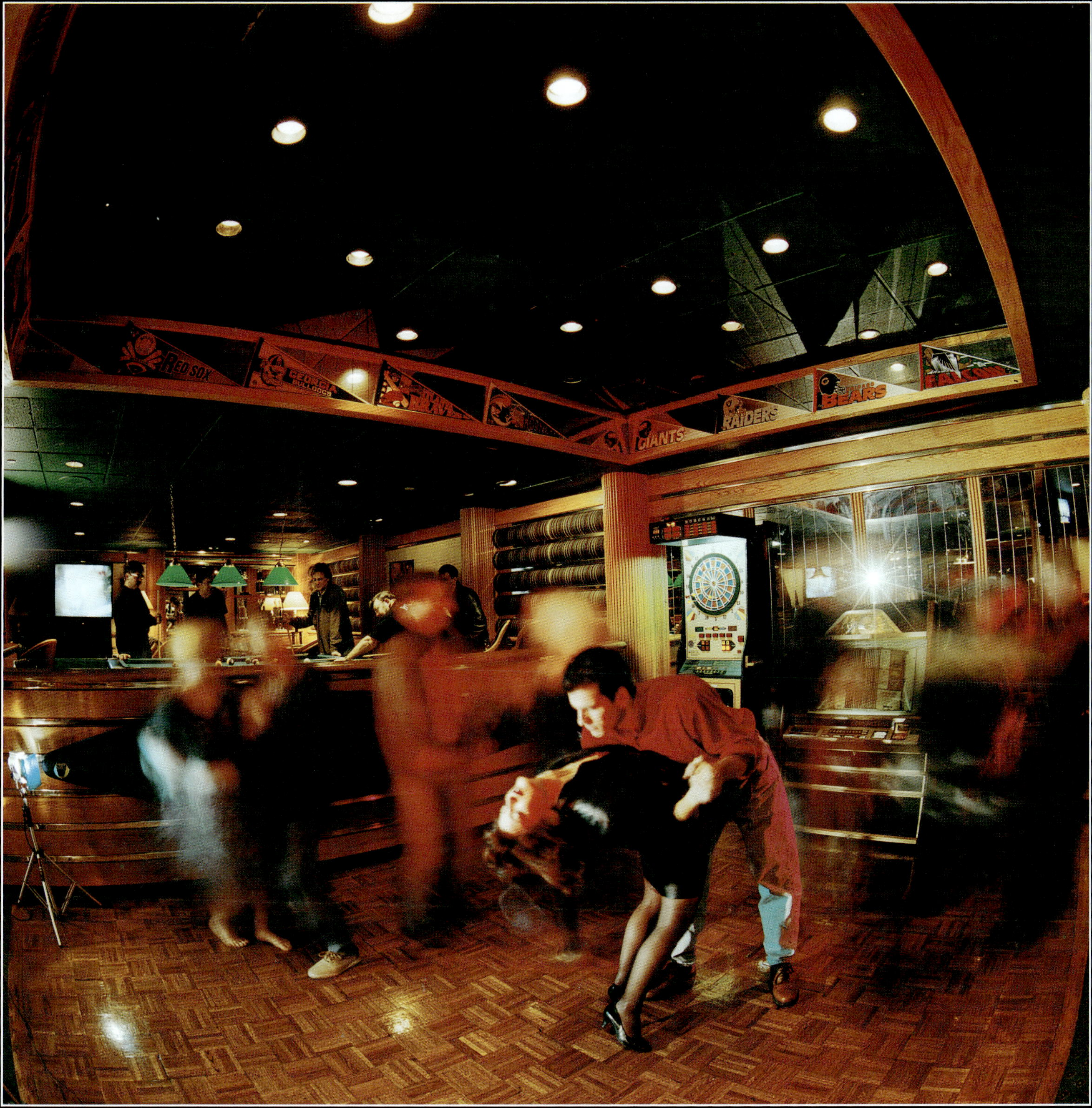

Pool players in the background watch while dancers gyrate to the beat of rock 'n' roll music in this long-exposure image. The couple in the foreground remained stationary while the other subjects danced throughout the 12- to 15-second exposure. Illumination was a combination of the pool table lights in the background and two spotlights on the dancers, one of which was gelled to give the red glow on some areas of the image. The photograph was made during a Winona School workshop.

15. X-Pan Images

The following environmental portraits were made using Hasselblad's X-Pan 35mm camera with a 45mm lens. I really liked the panoramic look of these wide-angle images. I have put the X-Pan to the test by making some 60-inch wide prints and was very impressed with the overall sharpness, especially at the edges.

In these images, the overall effect of the main subject being a small but principal element in the composition shows that portrait photography is much more than tight shots. Don't be afraid of making your main subject quite small in the overall scene; careful composition of the subject within the environment, choice of clothing, perspective, and lighting all combine to produce great images.

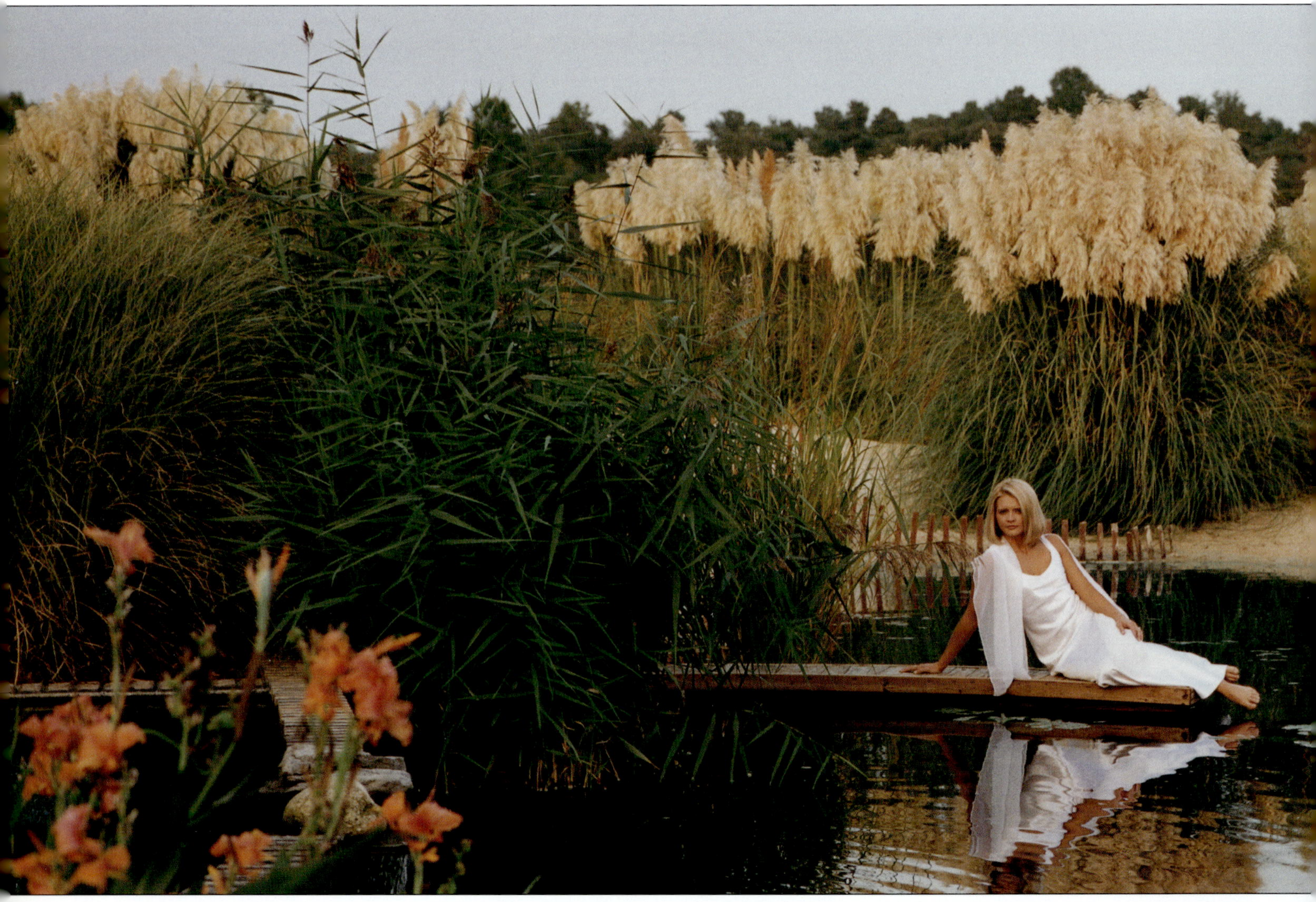

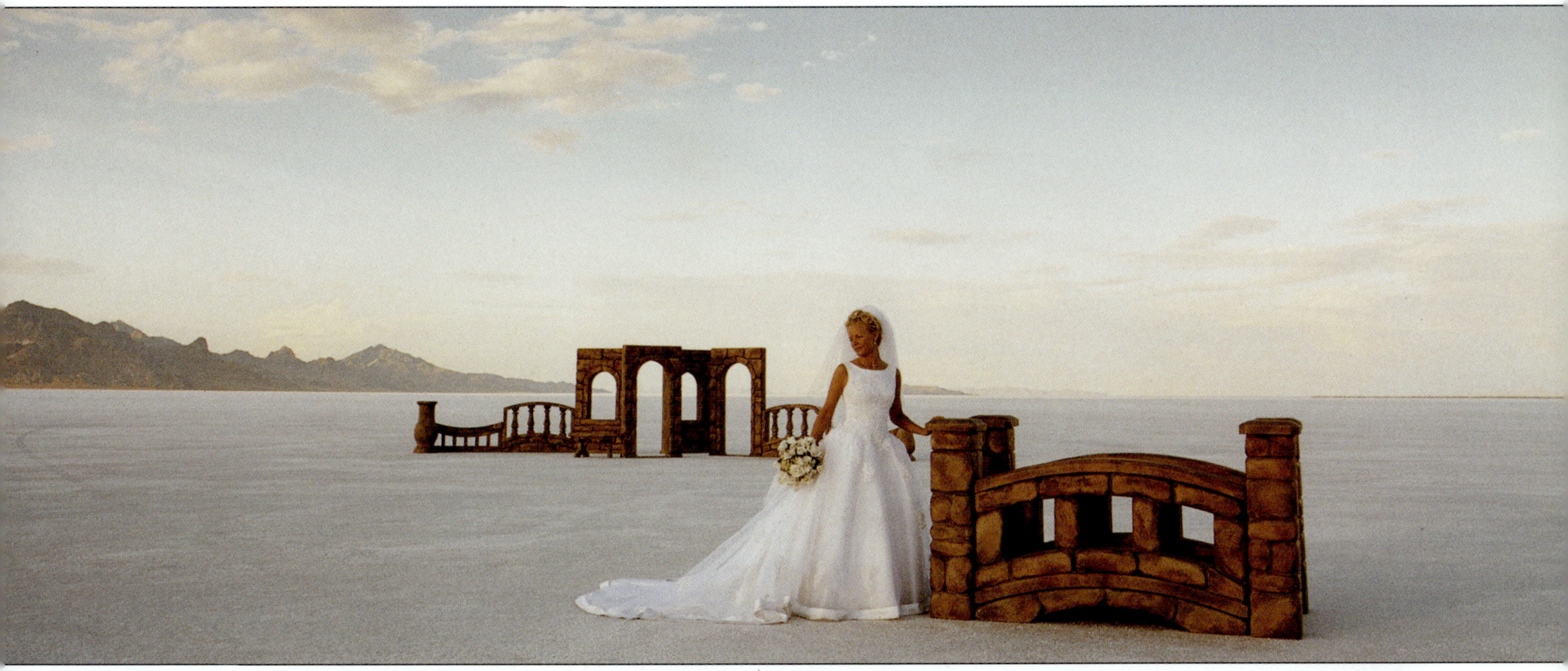

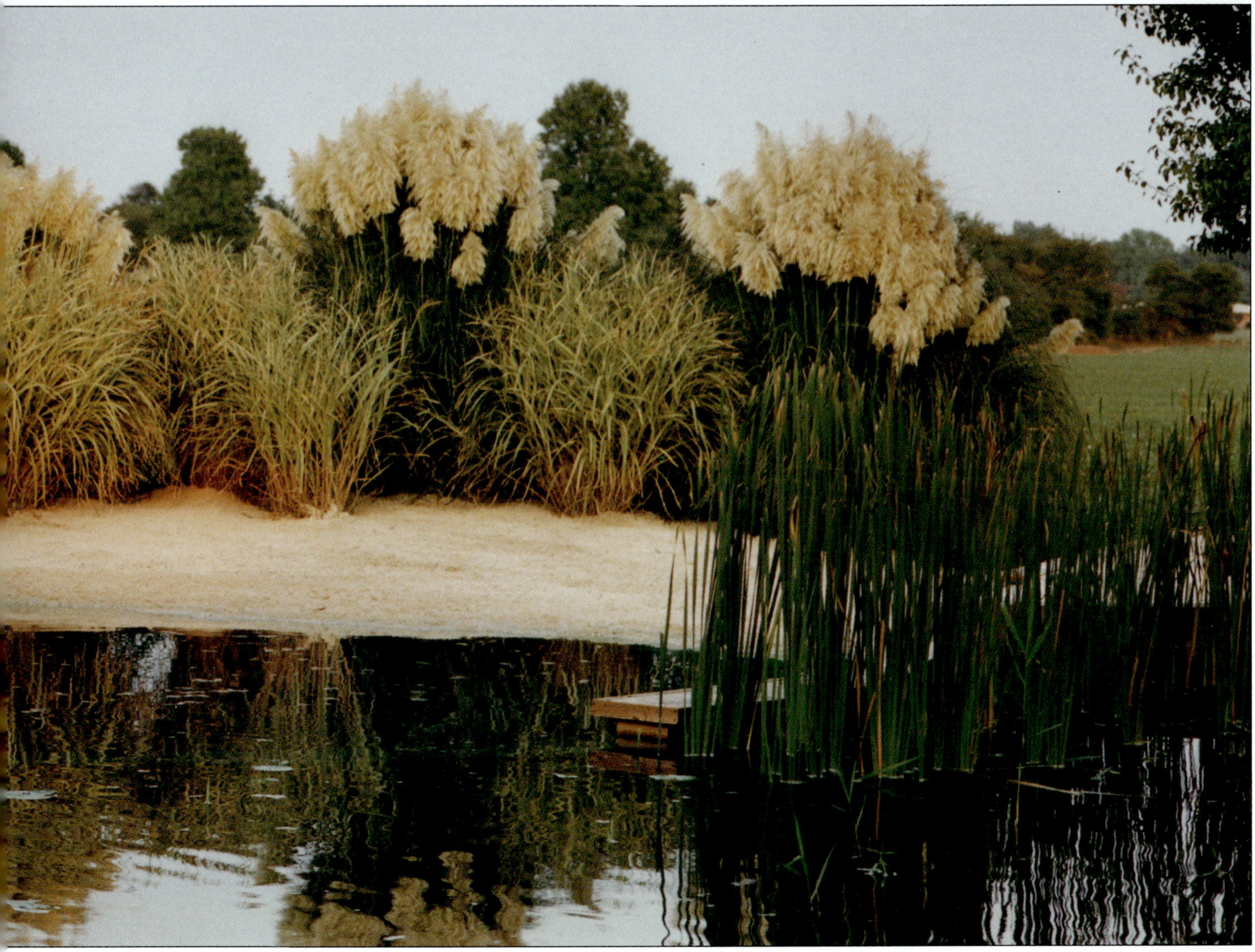

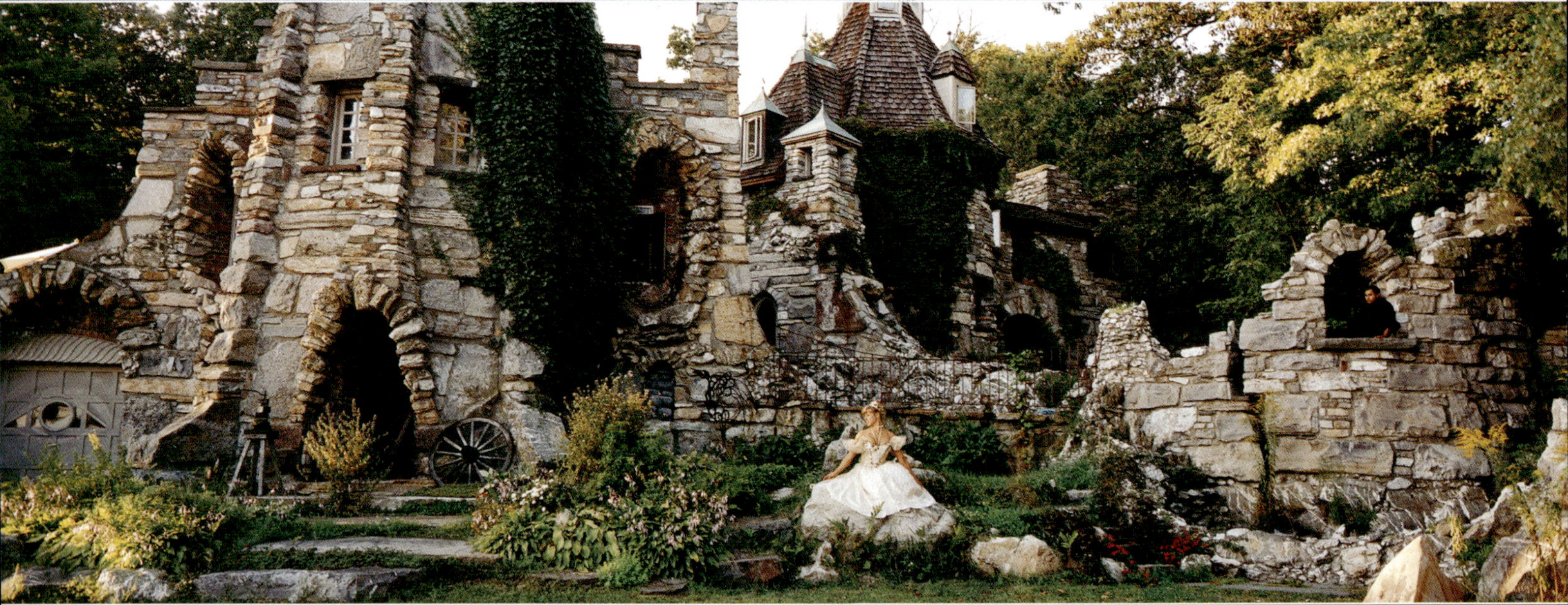

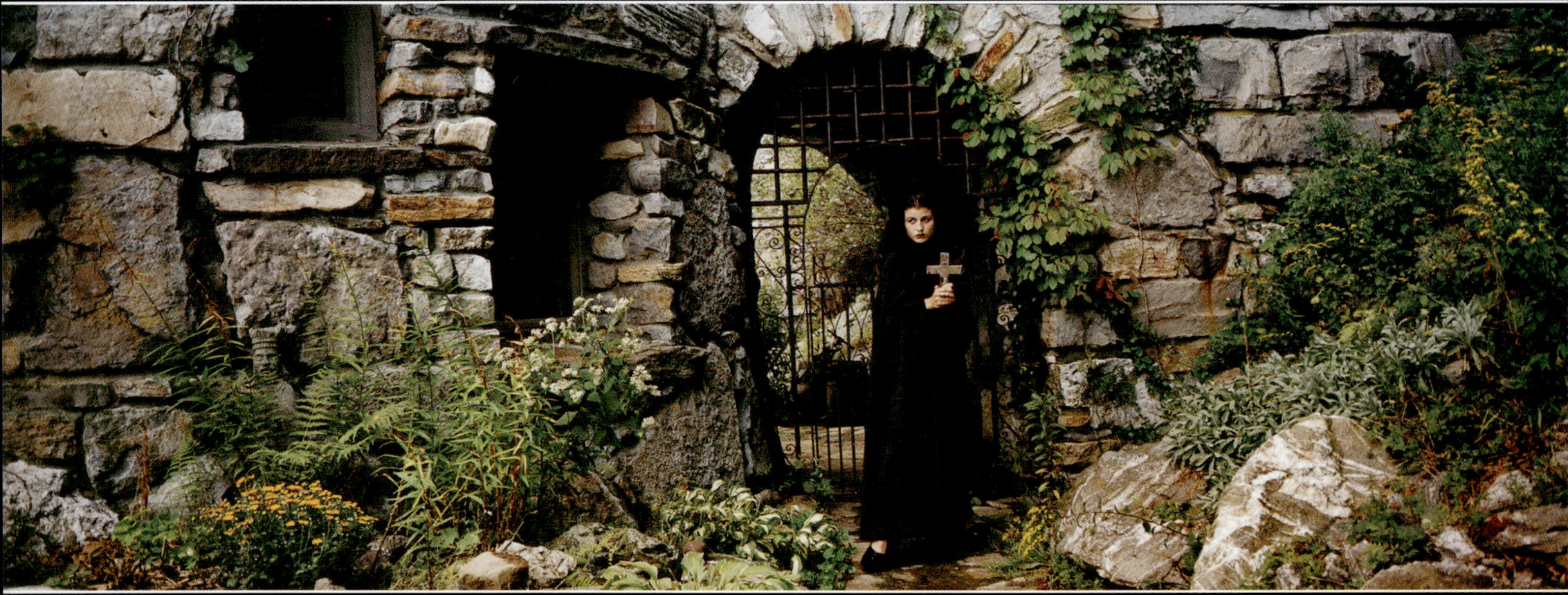

Environmental portraits created on Kodak X-Pan.

Conclusion

Collaborating on this book has been a combination of work and fun. (After all, if a project doesn't involve some fun it gets a bit tedious, right?. We, the authors, sincerely hope that you enjoy the images and text and benefit from our efforts.

There's no easy way around it, mastering a field as complex as portrait photography takes time and effort; just ask Don, who has been plying his craft for more than five decades. By his own admission, he's still learning. Also, be aware that no single person or publication can teach you everything, and not every lesson or technique is applicable or appropriate to every individual photographer's needs.

Glean what you can, apply what works for you, and continue to hone your photographic skills. Above all, enjoy your photography and have fun creating your images. Follow that simple advice and you will be well rewarded.

And never stop "seeing light." It's the key to all great photography. Good luck and good shooting!

Don Blair
Peter Skinner

Biographies

DON BLAIR

Don Blair's career in photography began, at age ten, with the gift of a $3.95 processing kit from his mother. By the time he was in junior high, he had talked his way into a job sweeping up at local a portrait studio/photo lab, where his enthusiasm was quickly rewarded with added responsibilities developing film and, eventually, taking portraits and wedding pictures.

Years later, when the studio owner retired, Blair purchased the studio—and it wasn't long before his reputation began to grow. To this day, his portraits are recognized as some of the best in the industry. Among professionals in the Professional Photographers of America, Camera Craftsmen of America, Intermountain Professional Photographers Association, and Wedding and Portrait Photographers International he is regarded as one of the most respected of all professional portrait photographers.

In addition to the recognition he has received for his classic portraits, Blair is also widely regarded as one of the preeminent instructors of professional photographers. Fifty years ago, Blair began teaching seminars for Kodak, then expanded his scope to begin lecturing to large and small groups across the world. He has also sponsored dozens of up-and-coming photographers who credit much of their success to the man who taught them how to "see light."

At 79, Blair remains active in professional photography and continues to present three or more seminars a month. He also continues to be an active student of photography, embracing the digital revolution and remaining as excited about creating portraits as he was at the start of his legendary career.

PETER SKINNER

After careers in journalism and public relations in New Zealand and Australia, writer/photographer Peter Skinner was invited to participate in a special program at the Brooks Institute of Photography by the institute's president Ernest H. Brooks II. That seven-week course in 1980 led to almost ten years with the institute, during which time Skinner was the director of public relations, workshops, and special projects.

Skinner is a contributing editor to *Rangefinder* and *Photographic* magazines, and his articles have appeared in other photographic publications including *Outdoor Photographer* and the European magazine *Opticon*. From 1991 to 2003 Skinner served as publications editor and communications director for the American Society of Media Photographers, regarded as the leading trade association of its kind in the world. He was the editor and a writer for the 5th and 6th editions of the authoritative *ASMP Professional Business Practices in Photography,* and recently wrote the introduction to *Silver Seas* (Media 27, Inc., 2003), a retrospective of black & white marine images by Ernie Brooks.

Skinner's collaboration with Don Blair on this book is his second project for Amherst Media, his previous being Oscar Lozoya's *The Art of Black & White Portrait Photography.*

Index

OTHER BOOKS FROM

Amherst Media®

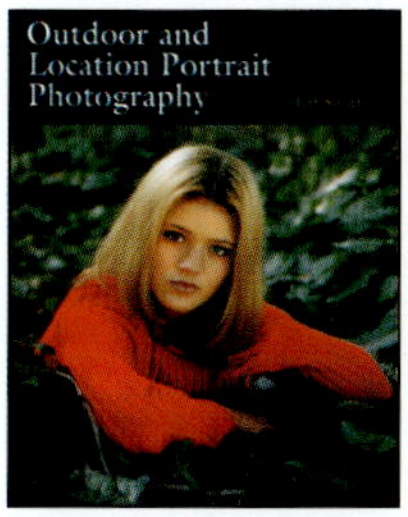

Outdoor and Location Portrait Photography *2nd Ed.*

Jeff Smith

Learn to work with natural light, select locations, and make clients look their best. Packed with step-by-step discussions and illustrations to help you shoot like a pro! $29.95 list, 8½x11, 128p, 80 color photos, index, order no. 1632.

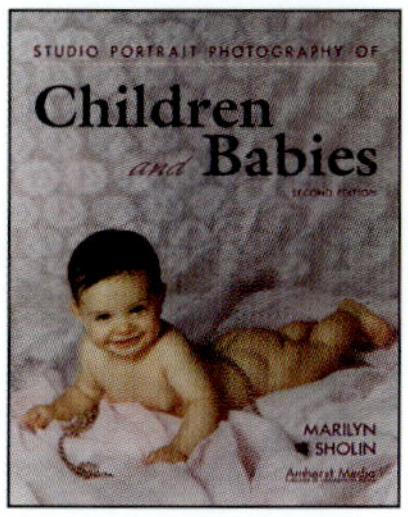

Studio Portrait Photography of Children and Babies, *2nd Ed.*

Marilyn Sholin

Work with the youngest portrait clients to create cherished images. Includes techniques for working with kids at every developmental stage, from infant to preschooler. $29.95 list, 8½x11, 128p, 90 color photos, order no. 1657.

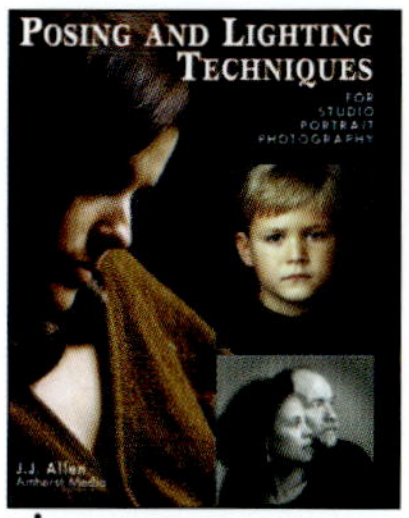

Posing and Lighting Techniques for Studio Photographers

J. J. Allen

Master the skills you need to create beautiful lighting for portraits. Posing techniques for flattering, classic images help turn every portrait into a work of art. $29.95 list, 8½x11, 120p, 125 color photos, order no. 1697.

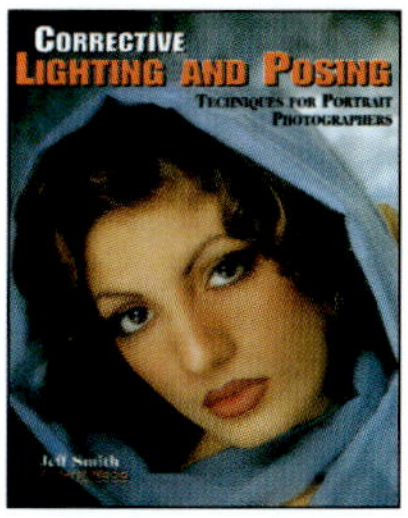

Corrective Lighting and Posing Techniques for Portrait Photographers

Jeff Smith

Learn to make every client look his or her best by using lighting and posing to conceal real or imagined flaws—from baldness, to acne, to figure flaws. $29.95 list, 8½x11, 120p, 150 color photos, order no. 1711.

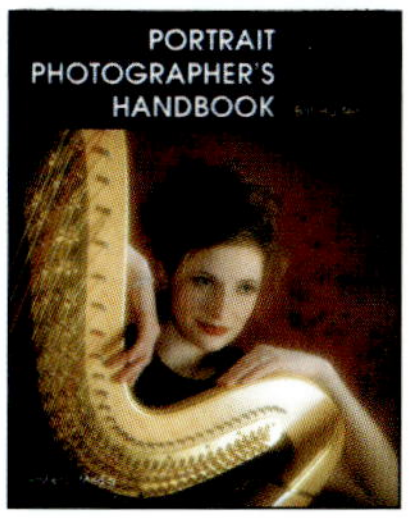

Portrait Photographer's Handbook

Bill Hurter

Bill Hurter has compiled a step-by-step guide to portraiture that easily leads the reader through all phases of portrait photography. This book will be an asset to experienced photographers and beginners alike. $29.95 list, 8½x11, 128p, 100 color photos, order no. 1708.

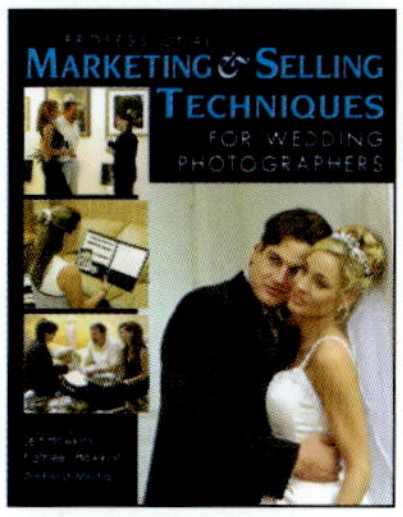

Professional Marketing & Selling Techniques for Wedding Photographers

Jeff Hawkins and Kathleen Hawkins

Learn the business of wedding photography. Includes consultations, direct mail, advertising, internet marketing, and much more. $29.95 list, 8½x11, 128p, 80 color photos, order no. 1712.

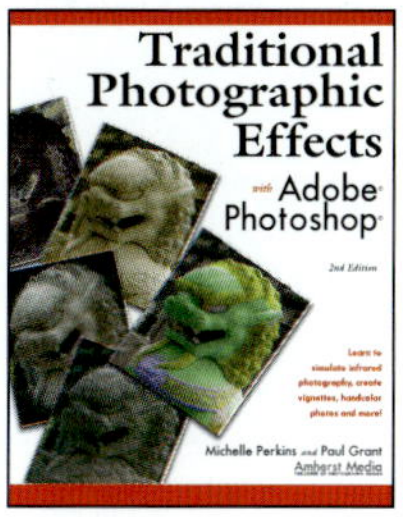

Traditional Photographic Effects with Adobe® Photoshop®, *2nd Ed.*

Michelle Perkins and Paul Grant

Use Photoshop to enhance your photos with handcoloring, vignettes, soft focus, and much more. Every technique contains step-by-step instructions for easy learning. $29.95 list, 8½x11, 128p, 150 color images, order no. 1721.

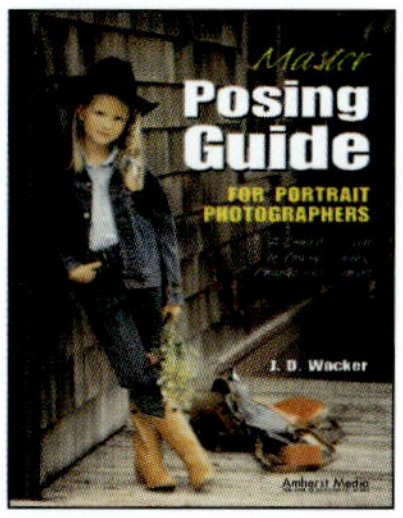

Master Posing Guide for Portrait Photographers

J. D. Wacker

Learn the techniques you need to pose single portrait subjects, couples, and groups for studio or location portraits. Includes techniques for photographing weddings, teams, children, special events and much more. $29.95 list, 8½x11, 128p, 80 photos, order no. 1722.

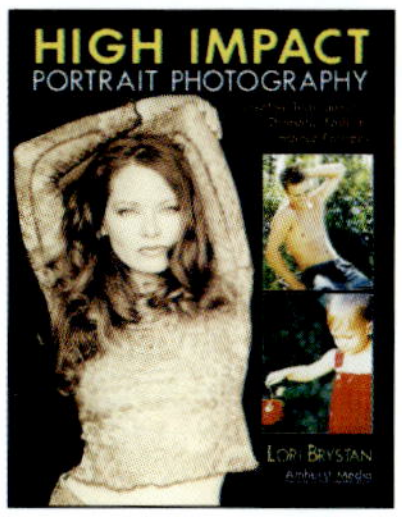

High Impact Portrait Photography

Lori Brystan

Learn how to create the high-end, fashion-inspired portraits your clients will love. Features posing echniques, lighting, alternative processing, and much more. $29.95 list, 8½x11, 128p, 60 color photos, order no. 1725.

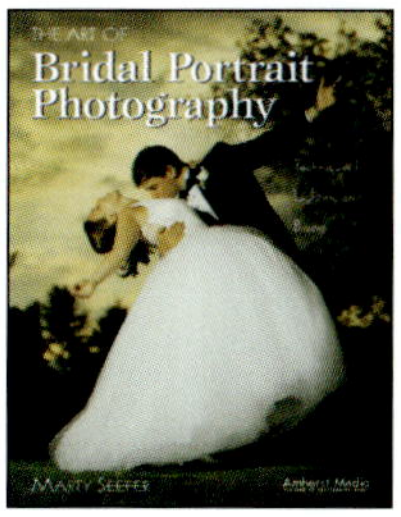

The Art of Bridal Portrait Photography

Marty Seefer

Learn to give every client your best and create timeless images that are sure to become family heirlooms. Seefer takes readers through every step of the bridal shoot, ensuring flawless results. $29.95 list, 8½x11, 128p, 70 color photos, order no. 1730.

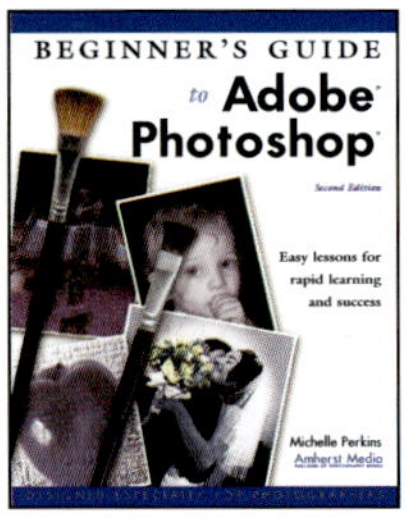

Beginner's Guide to Adobe® Photoshop®, *2nd Ed.*

Michelle Perkins

Learn to effectively make your images look their best, create original artwork, or add unique effects to any image. Topics are presented in short, easy-to-digest sections that will boost confidence and ensure outstanding images. $29.95 list, 8½x11, 128p, 300 color images, order no. 1732.

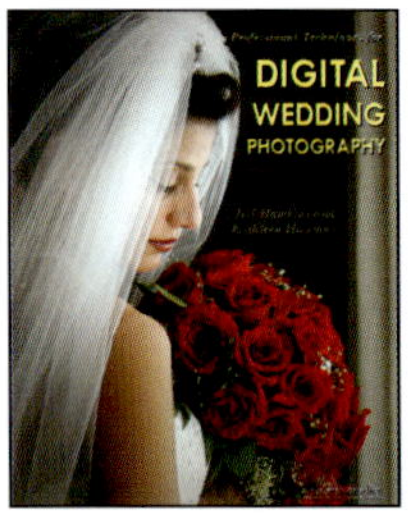

Professional Techniques for Digital Wedding Photography, *2nd Ed.*

Jeff Hawkins and Kathleen Hawkins

From selecting equipment, to marketing, to building a digital workflow, this book teaches how to make digital work for you. $29.95 list, 8½x11, 128p, 85 color images, order no. 1735.

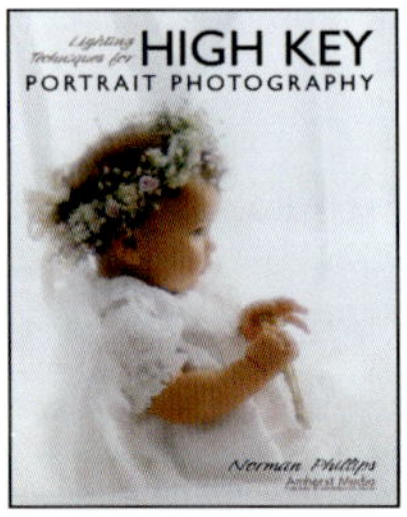

Lighting Techniques for High Key Portrait Photography

Norman Phillips

Learn to meet the challenges of high key portrait photography and produce images your clients will adore. $29.95 list, 8½x11, 128p, 100 color photos, order no. 1736.

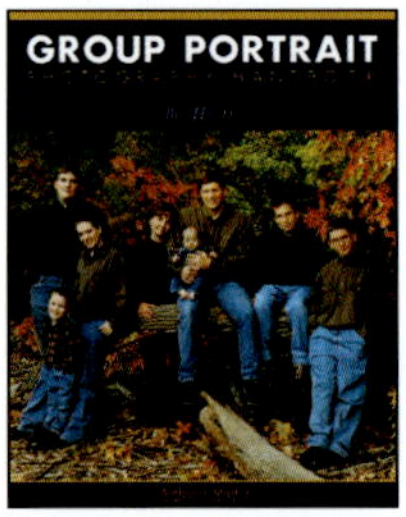

Group Portrait Photographer's Handbook

Bill Hurter

With images by top photographers, this book offers timeless techniques for composing, lighting, and posing group portraits. $29.95 list, 8½x11, 128p, 120 color photos, order no. 1740.

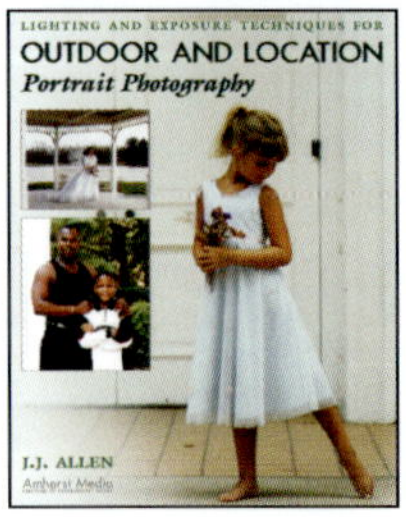

LIGHTING AND EXPOSURE TECHNIQUES FOR

Outdoor and Location Portrait Photography

J. J. Allen

Meet the challenges of changing light and complex settings with techniques that help you achieve great images every time. $29.95 list, 8½x11, 128p, 150 color photos, order no. 1741.

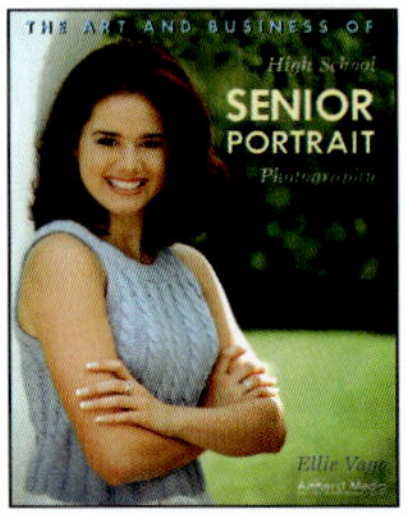

The Art and Business of High School Senior Portrait Photography

Ellie Vayo

Learn the techniques that have made Ellie Vayo's studio one of the most profitable senior portrait businesses in the US. $29.95 list, 8½x11, 128p, 100 color photos, order no. 1743.

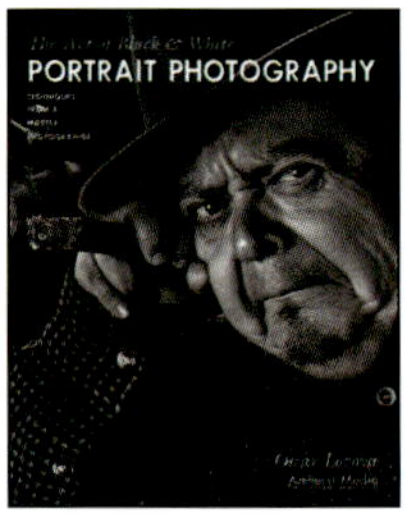

The Art of Black & White Portrait Photography

Oscar Lozoya

Learn how Master Photographer Oscar Lozoya uses unique sets and engaging poses to create black & white portraits that are infused with drama. Includes lighting strategies, special shooting techniques and more. $29.95 list, 8½x11, 128p, 100 duotone photos, order no. 1746.

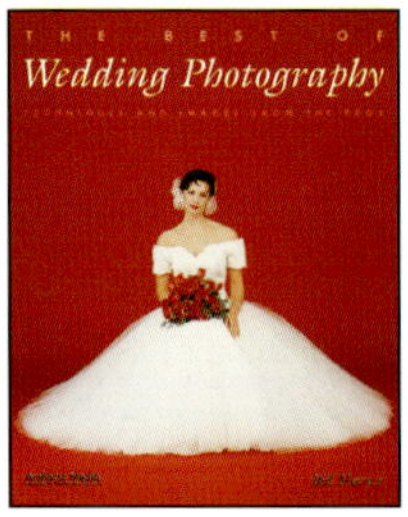

The Best of Wedding Photography

Bill Hurter

Learn how the top wedding photographers in the industry transform special moments into lasting romantic treasures with the posing, lighting, album design, and customer service pointers found in this book. $29.95 list, 8½x11, 128p, 150 color photos, order no. 1747.

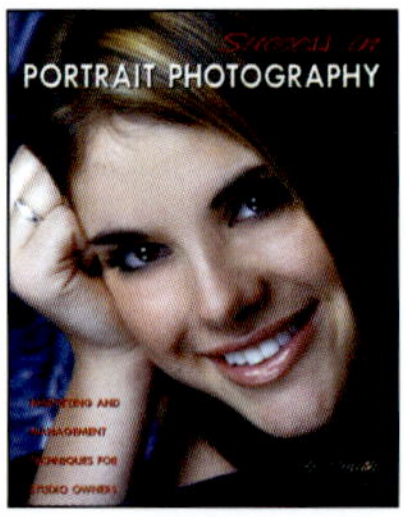

Success in Portrait Photography

Jeff Smith

Many photographers realize too late that camera skills alone do not ensure success. This book will teach photographers how to run savvy marketing campaigns, attract clients, and provide top-notch customer service. $29.95 list, 8½x11, 128p, 100 color photos, order no. 1748.

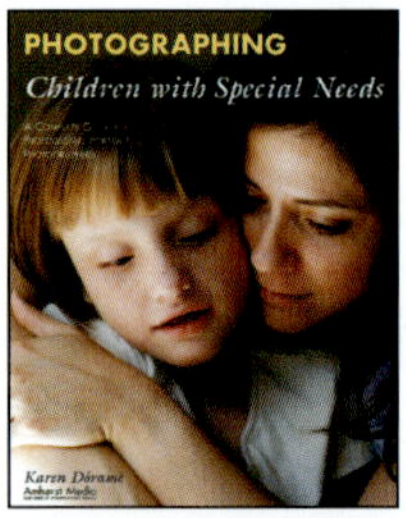

Photographing Children with Special Needs

Karen Dórame

This book explains the symptoms of spina bifida, autism, cerebral palsy, and more, teaching photographers how to safely and effectively capture the unique personalities of these children. $29.95 list, 8½x11, 128p, 100 color photos, order no. 1749.

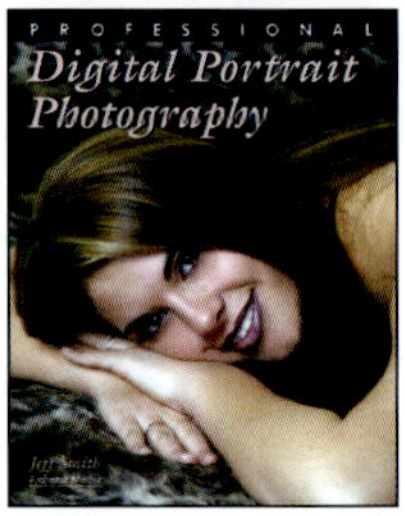

Professional Digital Portrait Photography

Jeff Smith

Because the learning curve is so steep, making the transition to digital can be frustrating. Author Jeff Smith shows readers how to shoot, edit, and retouch their images—while avoiding common pitfalls. $29.95 list, 8½x11, 128p, 100 color photos, order no. 1750.

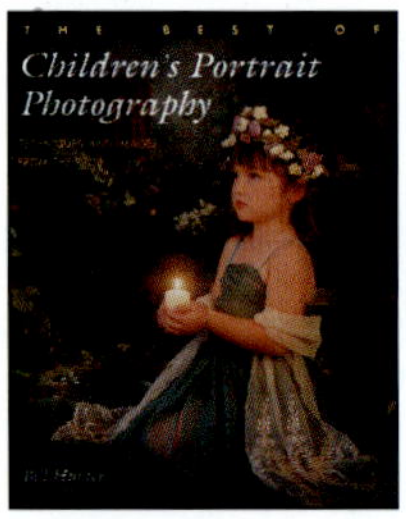

The Best of Children's Portrait Photography

Bill Hurter

Rangefinder editor Bill Hurter draws upon the experience and work of top professional photographers, uncovering the creative and technical skills they use to create their magical portraits. $29.95 list, 8½x11, 128p, 150 color photos, order no. 1752.

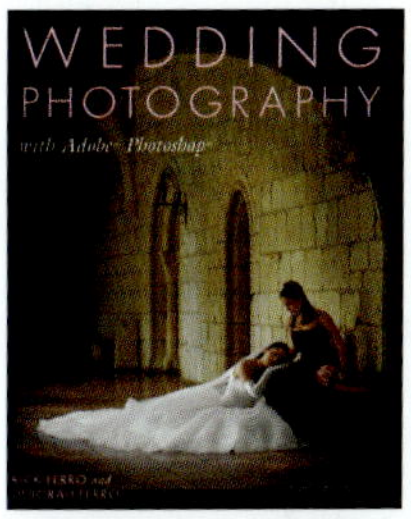

Wedding Photography with Adobe® Photoshop®

Rick Ferro and Deborah Lynn Ferro

Get the skills you need to make your images look their best, add artistic effects, and boost your wedding photography sales with savvy marketing ideas. $29.95 list, 8½x11, 128p, 100 color images, index, order no. 1753.

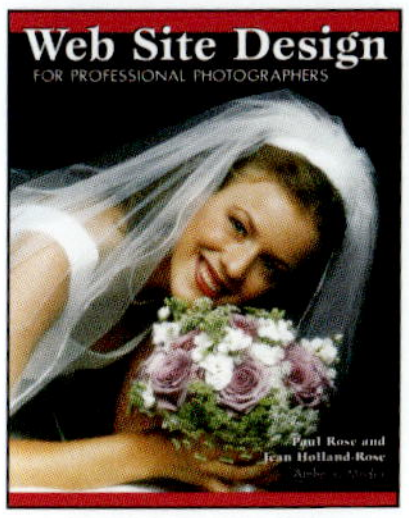

Web Site Design for Professional Photographers

Paul Rose and Jean Holland-Rose

Learn to design, maintain, and update your own photography web site. Designed for photographers, this book shows you how to create a site that will attract clients and boost your sales. $29.95 list, 8½x11, 128p, 100 color images, index, order no. 1756.

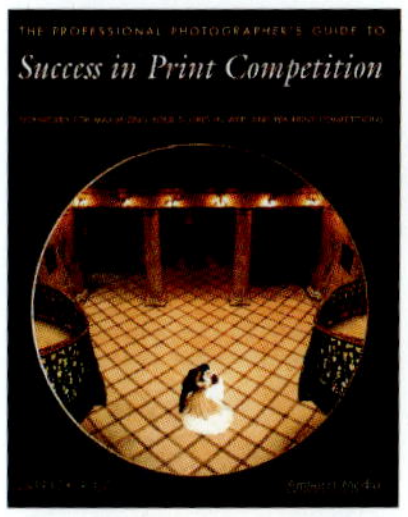

PROFESSIONAL PHOTOGRAPHER'S GUIDE TO

Success in Print Competition

Patrick Rice

Learn from PPA and WPPI judges how you can improve your print presentations and increase your scores. $29.95 list, 8½x11, 128p, 100 color photos, index, order no. 1754.

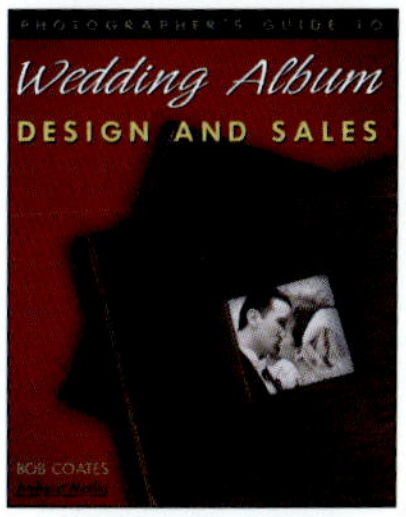

PHOTOGRAPHER'S GUIDE TO

Wedding Album Design and Sales

Bob Coates

Enhance your income and creativity with these techniques from top wedding photographers. $29.95 list, 8½x11, 128p, 150 color photos, index, order no. 1757.

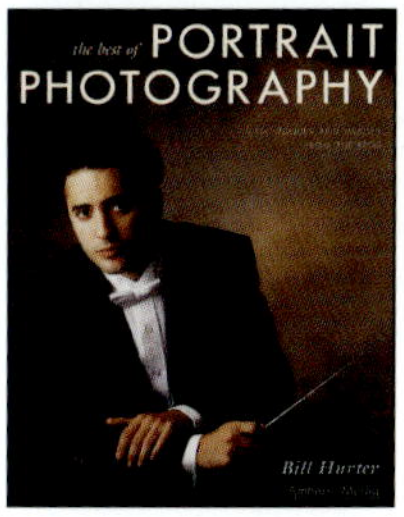

The Best of Portrait Photography

Bill Hurter

View outstanding images from top professionals and learn how they create their masterful images. Includes techniques for classic and contemporary portraits. $29.95 list, 8½x11, 128p, 200 color photos, index, order no. 1760.

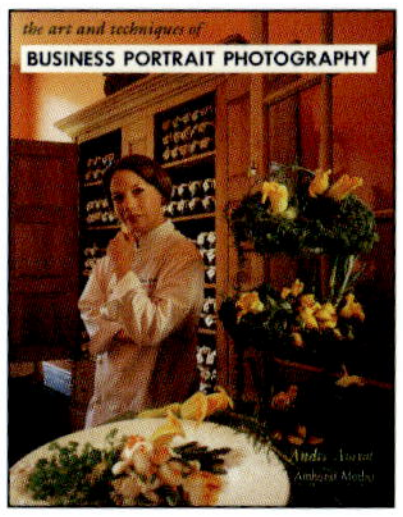

THE ART AND TECHNIQUES OF

Business Portrait Photography

Andre Amyot

Learn the business and creative skills photographers need to compete successfully in this challenging field. $29.95 list, 8½x11, 128p, 100 color photos, index, order no. 1762.

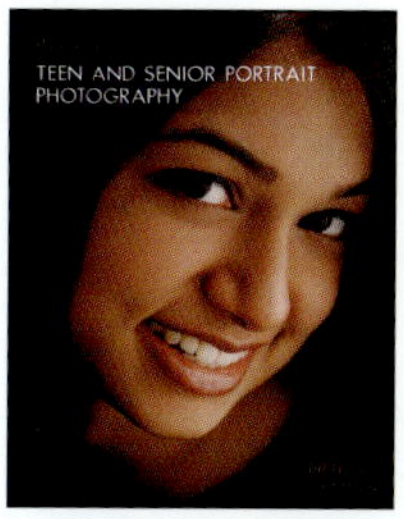

The Best of Teen and Senior Portrait Photography

Bill Hurter

Learn how top professionals create stunning images that capture the personality of their teen and senior subjects. $29.95 list, 8½x11, 128p, 150 color photos, index, order no. 1766.

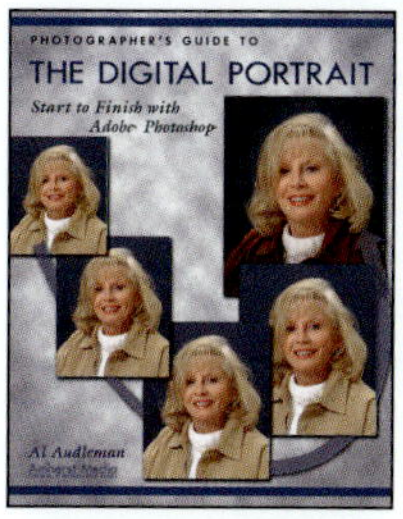

PHOTOGRAPHER'S GUIDE TO

The Digital Portrait

START TO FINISH WITH ADOBE® PHOTOSHOP®

Al Audleman

Follow through step-by-step procedures to learn the process of digitally retouching a professional portrait. $29.95 list, 8½x11, 128p, 120 color images, index, order no. 1771.

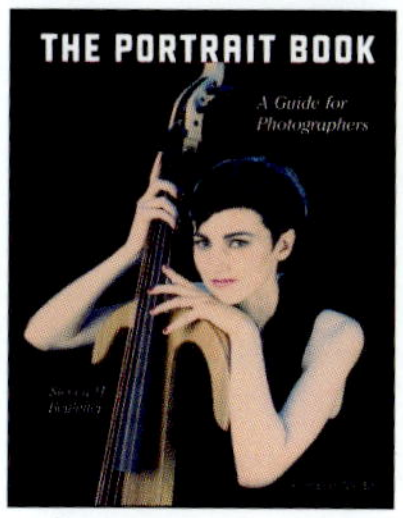

The Portrait Book

A GUIDE FOR PHOTOGRAPHERS

Steven H. Begleiter

A comprehensive textbook for those getting started in professional portrait photography. Covers every aspect from designing an image to executing the shoot. $29.95 list, 8½x11, 128p, 130 color images, index, order no. 1767.

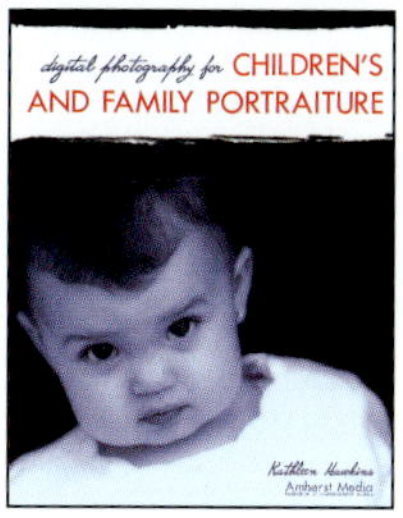

Digital Photography for Children's and Family Portraiture

Kathleen Hawkins

Discover how digital photography can boost your sales, enhance your creativity, and improve your studio's workflow. $29.95 list, 8½x11, 128p, 130 color images, index, order no. 1770.

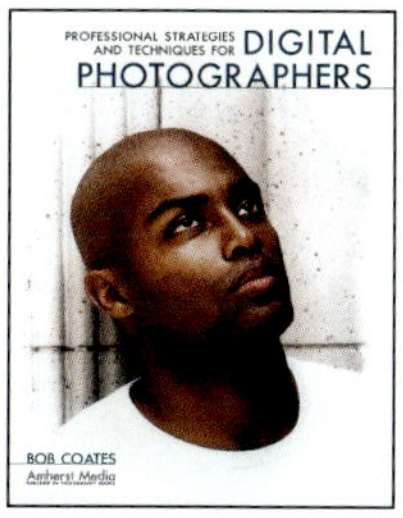

Professional Strategies and Techniques for Digital Photographers

Bob Coates

Learn how professionals—from portrait artists to commercial specialists—enhance their images with digital techniques. $29.95 list, 8½x11, 128p, 130 color photos, index, order no. 1772.

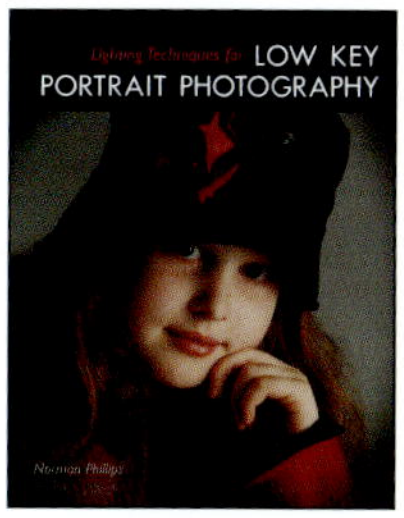

Lighting Techniques for Low Key Portrait Photography

Norman Phillips

Learn to create the dark tones and dramatic lighting that typify this classic portrait style. $29.95 list, 8½x11, 128p, 100 color photos, index, order no. 1773.

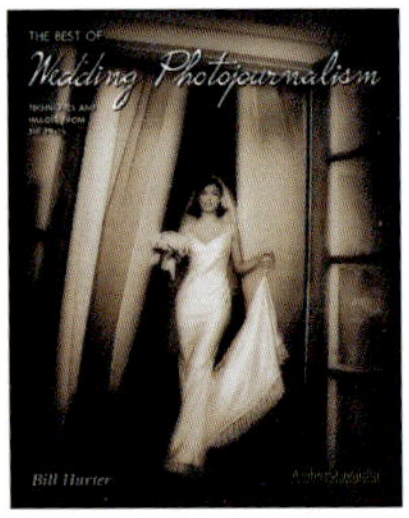

The Best of Wedding Photojournalism

Bill Hurter

Learn how top professionals capture these fleeting moments of laughter, tears, and romance. Features images from over twenty renowned wedding photographers. $29.95 list, 8½x11, 128p, 150 color photos, index, order no. 1774.

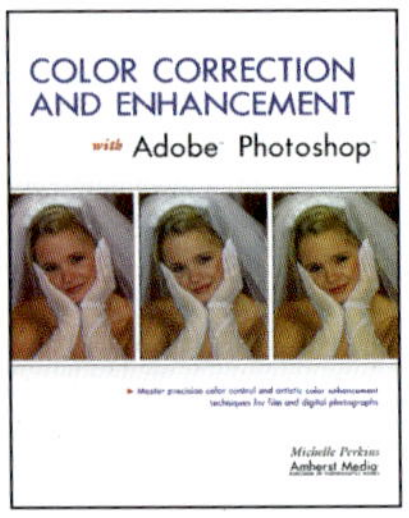

Color Correction and Enhancement with Adobe® Photoshop®

Michelle Perkins

Master precision color correction and artistic color enhancement techniques for scanned and digital photos. $29.95 list, 8½x11, 128p, 300 color images, index, order no. 1776.

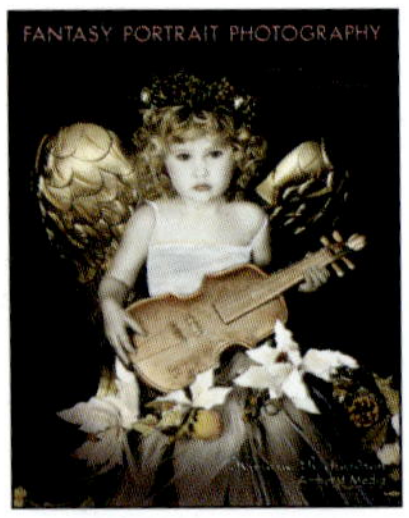

Fantasy Portrait Photography

Kimarie Richardson

Learn how to create stunning portraits with fantasy themes—from fairies and angels, to 1940s glamour shots. Includes portrait ideas for infants through adults. $29.95 list, 8½x11, 128p, 60 color photos index, order no. 1777.

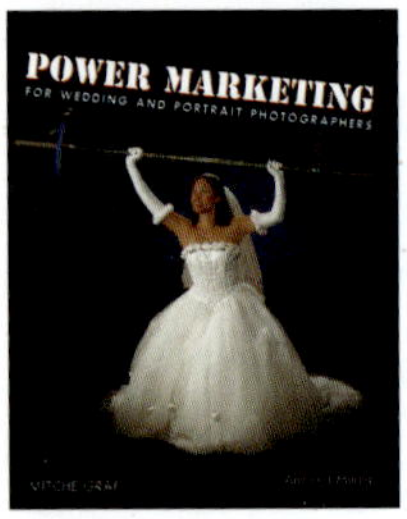

Power Marketing for Wedding and Portrait Photographers

Mitche Graf

Pull out all of the stops to set your business apart and create clients for life with this comprehensive guide to achieving your professional goals. $29.95 list, 8½x11, 128p, 100 color images, index, order no. 1788.

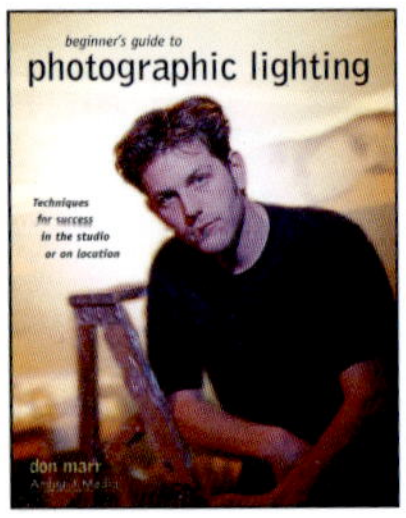

Beginner's Guide to Photographic Lighting

Don Marr

Create high impact photographs of any subject with Marr's simple techniques. From edgy and dynamic to subdued and natural, this book will show you how to get the myriad effects you're after. $29.95 list, 8½x11, 128p, 100 color photos, index, order no. 1785.

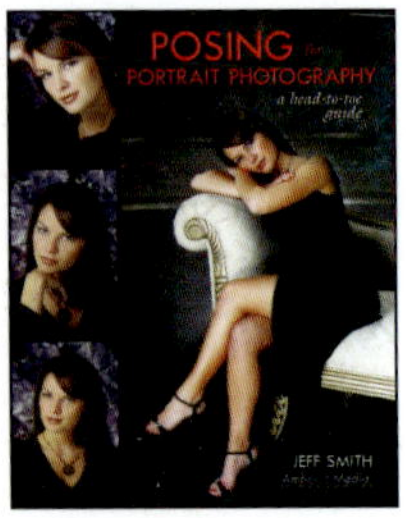

Posing for Portrait Photography

A HEAD-TO-TOE GUIDE

Jeff Smith

Author Jeff Smith teaches sure-fire techniques for fine-tuning every aspect of the pose for the most flattering results. $29.95 list, 8½x11, 128p, 150 color photos, index, order no. 1786.

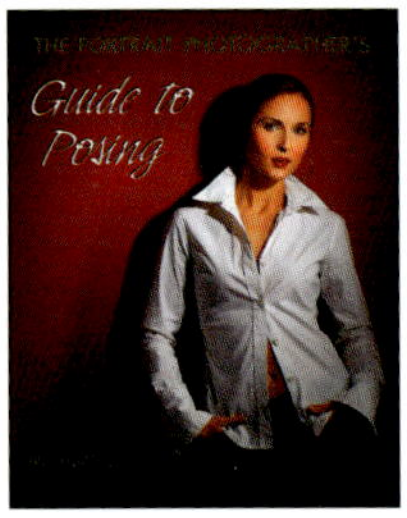

The Portrait Photographer's Guide to Posing

Bill Hurter

Get the posing tips and techniques that have propelled over fifty of the finest portrait photographers in the industry to the top. $29.95 list, 8½x11, 128p, 200 color photos, index, order no. 1779.

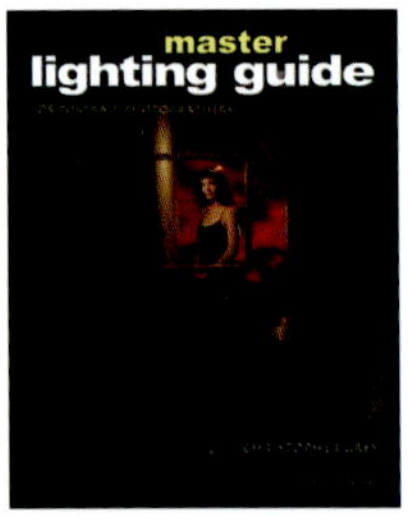

Master Lighting Guide for Portrait Photographers

Christopher Grey

Efficiently light executive and model portraits, high and low key images, and more. Master traditional lighting styles and use creative modi-fications that will maximize your results. $29.95 list, 8½x11, 128p, 300 color photos, index, order no. 1778.

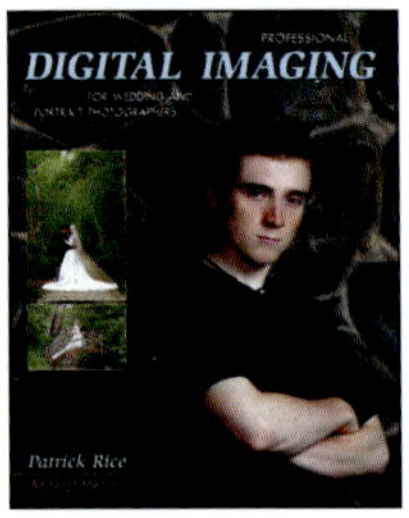

Professional Digital Imaging

FOR WEDDING AND PORTRAIT PHOTOGRAPHERS

Patrick Rice

Build your business and enhance your creativity with the newest technologies, time-honored techniques, and practical strategies for making the digital transition work for you. $29.95 list, 8½x11, 128p, 150 color photos, index, order no. 1777.

MORE PHOTO BOOKS ARE AVAILABLE

Amherst Media®
PO BOX 586
BUFFALO, NY 14226 USA

INDIVIDUALS: If possible, purchase books from an Amherst Media retailer. Contact us for the dealer nearest you, or visit our web site and use our dealer locater. To order direct, visit our web site, or send a check/money order with a note listing the books you want and your shipping address. All major credit cards are also accepted. For domestic and international shipping rates, please visit our web site or contact us at the numbers listed below. New York state residents add 8% sales tax.

DEALERS, DISTRIBUTORS & COLLEGES: Write, call, or fax to place orders. For price information, contact Amherst Media or an Amherst Media sales representative. Net 30 days.

(800)622-3278 or (716)874-4450
FAX: (716)874-4508

All prices, publication dates, and specifications are subject to change without notice. Prices are in U.S. dollars. Payment in U.S. funds only.

WWW.AMHERSTMEDIA.COM

FOR A COMPLETE CATALOG OF BOOKS AND ADDITIONAL INFORMATION